TIME AND PROCESS IN ANCIENT JUDAISM

THE LITTMAN LIBRARY OF
JEWISH CIVILIZATION

The Littman Library of Jewish Civilization is a registered UK charity
Registered charity no. 1000784

TIME AND PROCESS
IN
ANCIENT JUDAISM

◆

SACHA STERN

The Littman Library of Jewish Civilization
in association with Liverpool University Press

The Littman Library of Jewish Civilization
in association with Liverpool University Press
4 Cambridge Street, Liverpool L69 7ZU, UK

www.liverpooluniversitypress.co.uk/littman

Managing Editor: Connie Webber

Distributed in North America by
Oxford University Press Inc., 198 Madison Avenue,
New York, NY 10016, USA

First published 2003
First issued in paperback 2007

Catalogue records for this book are available from the
British Library and the Library of Congress

ISBN 978-1-904113-68-3

Publishing Co-ordinator: Janet Moth
Copy-editing: Leofranc Holford-Strevens
Proof-reading: Philippa Claiden
Index: Sacha Stern
Design: Pete Russell, Faringdon, Oxon.

Printed in Great Britain by
CPI Group (UK) Ltd, Croydon, CR0 4YY

Acknowledgements

THE initial impetus to write about time in ancient Judaism came from Eva Frojmovic's call for papers for a conference on 'Zeman: Jewish Concepts of Time in the Middle Ages', the proceedings of which were published in Jaritz and Moreno-Riaño, *Time and Eternity*. Initially a short article, this work rapidly grew into a book—more rapidly than I really planned or anticipated. Early versions were presented at seminars hosted by Sean Freyne, Martin Goodman, Joseph Tabory, and Jonathan Webber; I am grateful for their assistance and advice. My father Harry Stern assisted me with the Introduction, Uwe Glessmer and Bernard Goldstein with Chapter 3, and Almut Hintze with Chapter 6. Useful advice was also provided by Philip Alexander and Robert Chazan (smaller or more specific contributions are acknowledged inside the text). A draft of the entire script was read by Jonathan Schofer, who made some important remarks, both general and specific. Credit should be given to my anthropological mentors, in particular Jadran Mimica, who taught me to be suspicious of reified abstractions. Finally I am grateful to my wife and family, without whom this book would never have come into existence.

Contents

Note on Transliteration

THE transliteration of Hebrew in this book reflects consideration of content, purpose, and readership. The system adopted therefore reflects a broad approach to transcription, rather than the narrower approaches found in the *Encyclopaedia Judaica* or other systems developed for text-based or linguistic studies. The aim has been to reflect the pronunciation prescribed for modern Hebrew, rather than the spelling or Hebrew word structure, and to do so using conventions that are generally familiar to the English-speaking Jewish reader.

In accordance with this approach, no attempt is made to indicate the distinctions between *alef* and *ayin*, *tet* and *taf*, *kaf* and *kuf*, *sin* and *samekh*, since these are not relevant to pronunciation; likewise, the *dagesh* is not indicated except where it affects pronunciation. Following the principle of using conventions familiar to the majority of readers, however, transcriptions that are well established have been retained even when they are not fully consistent with the transliteration system adopted. Likewise, the distinction between *ḥet* and *khaf* has been retained, *ḥ* for the former and *kh* for the latter; the associated forms are generally familiar to readers, even if the distinction is not actually borne out in pronunciation, and for the same reason the final *heh* is indicated too. As in Hebrew, no capital letters are used, except that an initial capital has been retained in transliterating titles of published works (for example, *Shulḥan arukh*).

Since no distinction is made between *alef* and *ayin*, they are indicated by an apostrophe only in intervocalic positions where a failure to do so could lead an English-speaking reader to pronounce the vowel-cluster as a diphthong—for example in *ha'ibur*—or otherwise mispronounce the word. The *sheva na* is indicated by an *e*—for example *tekufah*, *zeman*; the *yod* is represented by *i* when it occurs as a vowel (*bereshit*), by *y* when it occurs as a consonant (*yerushalmi*), and by *yi* when it occurs as both (*yisra'el*).

Names have sometimes been left in their familiar forms, even when this is inconsistent with the overall system.

INTRODUCTION

Anthropological and Other Perspectives

TIME AND PROCESS: AN OVERVIEW

T HE subject of time has gained popularity in recent years. Although it has always been of interest to Western intellectuals and thinkers, the advent of the year 2000 and of the (so-called) 'millennium' has done much to raise awareness, among the general public, of the dimension of time and its reckoning. The initial impetus of this work was in fact a one-day conference on Jewish concepts of time in the Middle Ages held in that auspicious year, and part of a wider conference on the theme of time in the medieval period.[1]

My involvement in this conference, however, was based on a mistake. I believed that my having written a history of the Jewish calendar (Stern, *Calendar and Community*) gave me the authority to talk about Jewish time. I did not realize, as I was later to discover (and as I argue below in Chapter 3), that the relationship between the Jewish calendar and the concept of time was actually only tenuous. I realized even less that 'Jewish time' might even be, to some extent, an oxymoron (more on this below). My assumption, quite naturally, was that there must have been a distinctive concept of time in ancient Judaism, and that this concept must have been related, among other things, to the Jewish calendar.

I mention this original mistake, the genesis of my work, here to stress that I began my work with the same assumptions as most modern readers. It was only the weight of the evidence that forced me to revise entirely my outlook on the concept of time itself, and on its specific place in ancient Judaism.

Initially I tried to search all ancient Jewish sources for references to the concept of 'time'. I expected to find indications that time was viewed as linear, or cyclical, or both, that the flow of time was experienced as relative or absolute, that time-saving was considered an ethical virtue and time-wasting the opposite, and so forth. To my surprise, nothing in the sources could be found. In early rabbinic sources,

---

[1] The one-day conference, entitled 'Zeman: Jewish Concepts of Time in the Middle Ages', was convened by Eva Frojmovic; it was part of the International Medieval Congress 2000, held at the University of Leeds on 10–13 July 2000, on the theme of 'Time and Eternity' (proceedings were published in Jaritz and Moreno-Riaño, *Time and Eternity*).

for example—on which I initially focused my research—time as an entity in itself is never explicitly mentioned. Although the word *zeman* (usually translated as 'time') is pervasive in early rabbinic literature, it is only used in the specific sense of 'point in time' or '(limited) period of time'. When used as a concept, the word *zeman* only refers to the temporal co-ordination of events, never to the dimension of time as a whole. The dimension of time is also conspicuously absent from passages where its mention would have been most expected: for instance, in accounts of the creation and structure of the universe. This gradually led me to the realization that 'time' as a general concept may have been unknown and alien to early rabbinic Judaism (Chapter 1), and indeed, as I later established, to ancient Judaism as a whole (Chapter 6).

This suggestion, however, appears at first sight surprising, and even invites incredulity. Time is, after all, one of the most fundamental components of reality. How could any sensible person, or indeed any society as a whole, ignore its existence and its reality? How could people account for empirical reality, and particularly the changes and events that occur in the real world, without knowledge of and reference to the dimension of time?

These questions turn out, however, to be fundamentally misconceived. Ethnographers have established that in many (if not most) 'primitive' (or 'pre-modern', or, better still, 'non-modern') societies, the general concept of time is completely unknown. This does not mean that reality is misunderstood. As I shall argue in further detail below, it is perfectly possible to describe reality, including past and future events, without reference to a general, abstract dimension of time: instead, reality can be described in terms of an infinity of concrete, individual processes. In these 'non-modern' societies, the key concept is thus not time but *process*. By 'process' I simply mean a structured or meaningful sequence of events.[2]

This world-view—which, I shall argue, was also that of ancient Judaism—is not only sensible, but also plausible and in some ways commendable. It must be acknowledged, indeed, that in spite of our firm beliefs in the existence of a time-dimension, it is not a tangible or concrete reality. All we experience around us, with our senses, are objects engaged in certain relations which we call 'events'. Sequences of events or 'processes' are the only concrete reality, of which time functions merely as an abstract measurement. Thus, for example, a sequence of many events is a long process, of which the measurement is called a 'long time'. The concept of time as an entity in itself or fundamental structure of reality is only

---

[2] e.g. a sequence of events in causal relationship. Priority of process over time may remind us of Aristotle's famous contention that time is entirely dependent on process or 'motion', so that in a motionless universe, time would not exist. I shall return to Aristotle later in the book (Ch. 5), but would stress at this stage that the 'non-modern' world-view is far more radical than Aristotle's: Aristotle knows the concept of pure time (although he considers it contingent on motion) and is capable of discussing it at great length, whereas 'non-modern' societies manage without this concept completely.

a generalization and synthesis of all the discrete time-measurements of the individual processes which are empirically experienced. In this sense, time as a general category is not a reality but only a reified abstraction. Like all reified abstractions, time may serve a useful conceptual purpose; but it is also to some extent a fallacy. 'Primitive' cultures that ignore this reified abstraction have, in this sense, an advantage over more 'advanced' world-views. For there is a good case to argue that empirical reality is more truthfully described in terms of concrete processes than it is by resorting to the reified, abstracted notion of a universal time-dimension that really does not exist.

In this study, I shall argue that the concept of time as an entity in itself was unknown in ancient Jewish culture, and that reality was experienced only in terms of processes.

This does not mean that ancient Jews conceived of 'process' as a general, conceptual category. Just as there is no word for 'time' in ancient Hebrew or Aramaic (at least in a general, 'pure' sense), I cannot think of any Hebrew or Aramaic word for the concept of 'process'.[3] My argument is not that reality was conceived of in terms of a general, abstract concept such as 'process', but rather that reality was conceived in empirical terms, as consisting of a multitude of discrete and concrete phenomena—activities, motions, changes, and events—occurring simultaneously or in sequence, i.e. processes. Thus although the title of this book, *Time and Process*, may imply two analogous and competing concepts, this is only a shorthand. Time and process are fundamentally different in kind: time is abstract, process is concrete; time is one, process is many; time is reified, process is real.

The evidence for 'ancient Judaism' I shall draw on in this study comes from the wide range of ancient Jewish literary sources that are extant, mainly early rabbinic literature (Chapters 1–4), but also Qumran texts, Apocrypha and Pseudepigrapha, and (though to a lesser extent) Jewish Hellenistic literature (Chapters 5–6). I shall occasionally refer to epigraphic sources, but, as may be expected, relevant epigraphic evidence is more difficult to find. The term 'ancient Judaism' is not intended in this work to imply a single, monolithic, or normative ideology. It is only the sum of all ancient Jewish sources (from the post-exilic period to the end of antiquity), some often very disparate, which in the context of this study happen to converge on the same point: a process-related world-view.

The absence of a concept of time in ancient Judaism is manifest, as mentioned above, in the absence of a word for time (as a whole) in ancient Hebrew and Jewish Aramaic sources. It is also manifest in contexts that we should naturally associate with the concept of a time-dimension: timing, calendar, and chronology. For at first sight, it might seem reasonable to argue that although ancient Jewish sources

---

[3] The modern Hebrew *tahalikh* has no equivalent, to my knowledge, in early rabbinic (or earlier) Hebrew.

are devoid of explicit references to time *per se*, the notion of time is implicit and indeed pervasive in the numerous sources (especially rabbinic) that deal in detail with the practice and methods of time reckoning. However, closer analysis will show that ancient Jewish timing, calendar, and chronology were not predicated on a concept of the time-dimension, but only on the concept of events and processes (see Chapters 2–3).[4] The centrality of timing in rabbinic halakhah (law), or of calendar reckoning in Qumran literature (for example), suggests a high level of interest in astronomical and other processes, but not the underlying, synthetic abstraction which we call 'time' or 'time-dimension'.

The absence of time in ancient Judaism is particularly salient and conspicuous when compared to later Jewish sources from the medieval period. Without going too deeply into the question of periodization, I have restricted 'ancient Judaism' to sources from not later than approximately the seventh century CE, which most would regard as the end of antiquity (at least in the Near East). A significant change occurred some time thereafter in rabbinic perceptions of time, though not before the ninth century. From this later period, and throughout the rest of the Middle Ages, the concept of time in a general, abstract sense is frequently attested in Jewish sources, not only in philosophical writings but also in the more traditional fields of rabbinic ethics and halakhah. Thus, whereas the notion of time is absent from early rabbinic ethics—hence we find there no concept of 'time-saving' or 'time-management', but instead an emphasis on process-related notions such as 'priority' and 'opportunity'—it is almost taken for granted in medieval rabbinic ethics (see Chapter 4). Why Jewish perceptions of time changed so radically from antiquity to the medieval period is an important historical question that I shall address in Chapter 4, and again in the conclusion. But, whether or not this change can be explained, comparison of ancient with medieval Judaism (or alternatively with ancient Greek tradition: see Chapter 5) is in itself instructive, because it renders the absence of a sense of time in ancient Judaism all the more conspicuous.

SCOPE AND METHOD

The importance of processes in ancient Judaism (for example in the context of the calendar and 'timing'—see Chapters 2–3) cannot be overestimated, and should perhaps have been given more emphasis in this study. I have been criticized, perhaps with some justification, for laying excessive emphasis on the negative aspect of my argument: that the notion of time, explicit or implicit, is absent from ancient Judaism. The positive aspect, that processes are central to the ancient Jewish world-view, perhaps requires additional elaboration. Further research is certainly

---

[4] Here I am of course only presenting the main lines of my argument; these questions will be examined in far more detail in the body of the book.

needed into the general status, function, and meaning of processes, in all their variety and diversity, in the cultural context of ancient Judaism. A host of issues have not been raised in this book but clearly deserve in-depth examination: for instance, the process and timing of menstruation (with all its gender-related implications) in tractate *Nidah*. Nevertheless, in writing this book I have chosen to focus on a single issue—the 'absence of time'—because I have felt it essential to correct the time-dominated bias of our modern world-view, and to explain why the notion of time could not be legitimately assumed to be present in, or inferred from, ancient Jewish sources. In doing so, I am laying the grounds for subsequent, more detailed research into temporal or process-related phenomena in ancient Judaism.

Another objection that has been frequently raised against my thesis is that it relies almost entirely on an argument from silence. Although I can demonstrate the centrality of processes in early Jewish thought, even in the context of timing, calendar, and chronology, I cannot positively prove, from the silence of the sources, that the notion of a time-dimension was not tacitly entertained and known. While I accept that my argument is largely from silence, I do not believe that it invalidates in any way the strength of my thesis. The argument from silence can be defended, I believe, on the following three counts:

1. My argument from silence is likely to be rejected if one assumes, *a priori*, that time is an objective, empirical reality. This assumption naturally leads to the next assumption, that knowledge of time must be universal to the whole of mankind. All societies and cultures in the world are aware, indeed, of the existence of the sun and the stars, and the same should equally apply to time. Even if explicit references to time are absent in the sources, it would be reasonable to assume that somehow or other the ancient Jews must have been empirically aware of the time-dimension.

However, as I have stated above (and as will be fully explained below), time is not an empirical reality like the sun or the stars: it is only a reified abstraction. Since time is only a man-made, cultural construct, it need not be shared by all cultures of mankind. Indeed, there is no reason to assume the existence of this concept in any given culture unless there is positive evidence to support it. In this context, my argument from silence is completely valid. If there is no evidence of time in early Jewish sources, there is no need to assume that it existed; the onus is on the other side to prove it.

2. My argument from silence rests on a methodological conviction, which I think many historians would share with me: that one cannot impose a modern idea or concept on any ancient culture without positive evidence to substantiate it. This methodological conviction may be branded by some as minimalist, over-sceptical, and excessively 'British'; but British academics are not alone in holding it. Max Kadushin, for example, gave it a rather dramatic formulation by claiming repeatedly

that the imposition of modern ideas on ancient cultures and ancient sources was tantamount to an act of 'violence' (the post-colonial, and perhaps post-Holocaust, context of this phrase is evident).[5] In the absence of evidence to substantiate a concept of time in ancient Jewish sources, it would certainly not be legitimate to invent one or impose it upon the ancient Jews.[6]

3. Arguments from silence are not automatically invalid. They are only invalid if the silence can be explained in other, extraneous ways. If it could be shown, for instance, that the absence of the concept of time in ancient Jewish sources was due to their literary genre, then it would not prove that the concept of time did not exist. But otherwise, silence must be regarded as culturally significant. The absence of time in ancient Jewish literature is not related to genre; it is conspicuous and calls for an explanation. The only explanation I can plausibly suggest is that it was non-existent in ancient Jewish culture.

A further objection that may be raised against my thesis is its reliance on present-day ethnography and anthropological theory.[7] It may be considered inappropriate to compare ancient Judaism, a relatively 'civilized' (albeit ancient) culture, with the 'primitive'[8] cultures of today's Third World which anthropology has traditionally studied. The absence of a concept of time may be perceived as a typical feature of 'primitiveness' or 'backwardness' which could not be ascribed, in fairness, to ancient Judaism.[9]

Although tainted with some element of prejudice, this objection—often evaded—is serious and deserves proper consideration. One of the conclusions that will emerge from this study is that awareness or ignorance of the concept of time was not necessarily contingent on 'civilization' or 'primitiveness' respectively.

---

[5] Kadushin, *The Rabbinic Mind*.

[6] Prudovsky has recently asked, 'Can we ascribe to past thinkers concepts they had no linguistic means to express?'; see his article of that title. As I shall argue, it is difficult to prove that ancient Jews did not have the linguistic means to express the concept of time: the term *zeman*, if needed, was available and would have been perfectly adequate. But the question may be rephrased as: 'Can we ascribe to past thinkers concepts they *did not* express?' The answer to this question, I think, must be yes, but only if we have a good reason to do so. In the context of time in ancient Judaism, this good reason is lacking. Although the limited amount of literary evidence that is extant cannot be taken to represent the totality of concepts ancient Jews entertained, we cannot legitimately extrapolate beyond the evidence at our disposal (see further Prudovsky, ibid.).

[7] I am not alone, of course, in suggesting this approach. Recent advocates of the use of anthropology in Jewish (and particularly early rabbinic) studies include H. E. Goldberg, *Judaism Viewed*; Eilberg-Schwartz, *Savage in Judaism*; id., *People of the Body*; and Boyarin, *Carnal Israel* (I apologize for the omission of others). Nevertheless, I think it is fair to say that this approach is still very much in its infancy.

[8] The substitution of the more politically correct 'pre-modern' or 'non-modern' (for 'primitive') would do little, in real terms, to allay this type of concern.

[9] Thus Kadushin, *The Rabbinic Mind*, 33–4, argues that anthropological comparisons are inappropriate because, in his view, rabbinic society was 'civilized'. But obviously, the assumption that rabbinic society was 'civilized' is just as problematic as the suggestion that it was 'primitive'.

Although from our modern Western perspective, ignorance of the concept of time may be considered distinctly 'backward' or 'primitive', there is a strong case to argue that this was only an *alternative*, and indeed quite plausible, world-view.

I should perhaps stress, in this context, that ancient Judaism was not completely devoid of abstract concepts, or incapable of any conceptualization. This is not the place to draw up an extensive list of abstract concepts in ancient Judaism, but the most obvious examples include concepts such as *emet* (truth), *ḥesed* (love or kindness), and *din* (justice), and above all, perhaps, the idea of an abstract, image-less God. Although the notion of time is absent in ancient Judaism, the notion of space appears to have some representation; but further research is still needed in this direction.[10] A lucid, and not yet outdated, assessment of conceptualization in early rabbinic thought has already been made by Max Kadushin, and at present it may be sufficient to refer the reader to it.[11] The only generalization I might venture, as a result of this study, is that ancient Judaism did not *reify* its abstract concepts in the same way as in modern (and ancient) Western thought (Chapter 6). But reification is surely not something we should treat as the hallmark of modernity.

Thus, I am making no claim about 'primitiveness' or its opposite in ancient Judaism. I am not using ethnographic material to suggest any particular affinity between ancient Judaism and the present-day societies ethnography describes. All I am suggesting is that they shared a similar view of time and process, not because this view is intrinsically primitive, but simply as an alternative to the modern Western world-view. There may even be a case to argue that in the history of humanity, process-based world-views have always been more common, and that the modern Western concept of time represents, if anything, a more peculiar world-view (this will be argued further in Chapter 6).

ANCIENT JUDAISM AND BEYOND

My anthropological-historical approach has thus led me to the realization that there was nothing specifically 'Jewish' about the ancient Jewish concepts of time

[10] Note that in early rabbinic sources the term *makom* means 'place' rather than 'space'; like the word *zeman*, it designates specific ('punctual') places or areas, rather than the dimension of space as a whole. Nevertheless, passages from rabbinic sources and from the *Sefer yetsirah* which I examine in Ch. 1 suggest an awareness of the concept of space and of its three-dimensional characteristics. The term *makom* is also frequently used in rabbinic sources as a name of God; Urbach, *The Sages*, 66–79 interprets this usage as an expression of God's omnipresence, but this is only based on his assumption that *makom*, in this context, means 'space'.

[11] Kadushin, *The Rabbinic Mind*. The author argues at length that early rabbinic Judaism is not philosophy, because it is not founded on logical inference but rather on everyday experience (see pp. 1–7, 31–2, 47–9, 220–2, 255–6, 278–86, 336–7); nevertheless, the absence of philosophical conceptualization does not preclude the existence, indeed the centrality, of abstract value-concepts in early rabbinic thought (see especially pp. 33–7, 336–7).

and process; I strongly object to recent studies of 'Jewish time' that have posited this as a starting and continuous assumption.[12] The assumption of cultural particularism can sometimes be useful—indeed, there is plenty about ancient Judaism that marks it out, a priori, from other cultures and religions—as long as it is not driven (as in some cases I suspect it is) by ideological or political motivations. There is actually no need to make a virtue of particularism. In the context of this study, at least, the process-based world-view of ancient Judaism is best interpreted as, to some extent, universal.

This becomes all the more evident in Chapter 6, where the argument is extended beyond the limits of ancient Judaism, beginning with the Hebrew Bible. The reader may wonder why I have chosen to go 'backwards' in history, rather than to start from the Bible and then progress to post-exilic Judaism. To a large extent, this choice has been one of scope. The Hebrew Bible is not the intended focus of this work: its focus is only 'ancient Judaism', which strictly means the religion (and, more generally, the culture) of the Jews from the Persian Achaemenid till the later Roman periods. Although the Hebrew biblical books continued to hold a dominant position in Judaism throughout this period, it would be methodologically unsound to assume *ipso facto* that biblical ideas were maintained and carried forth into post-exilic Judaism. The Bible was clearly relevant (indeed central) to Judaism in later antiquity, but only in the specific ways in which ancient Jews read it and chose to interpret it (as evident, for instance, in Qumran or early rabbinic biblical exegesis). For this reason, the Bible itself cannot inform us about ancient Jewish world-views.

My interest in the Hebrew Bible, in Chapter 6, is only to show that a process-related world-view was not restricted or original to the Judaism of later antiquity. Not only is it attested in earlier Hebrew or Israelite sources (the 'Bible'), but it was also characteristic of all the cultures of the ancient Near East (in which I include all the lands from Egypt to Babylonia). Without making any claim about the origins of ancient Judaism—whether entirely derived from the Bible, or influenced by other Near Eastern cultures—I therefore note that its process-related world-view was consistent with a much broader cultural context.

This contrasts remarkably, however, with the concept of time that existed in the same period in ancient Greece (see Chapter 5). Attempts to draw a contrast between 'Jewish' (or 'Hebrew') 'time' and 'Greek time' have often been made in the past, presenting the one as linear and the other as cyclical (respectively); but these have

---

[12] I am thinking in particular of Néher, 'Vision du temps', and S.-A. Goldberg, *La Clepsydre*, the latter at least as far as concerns her analysis of 'Jewish time' until the Emancipation period. In actual fact, most of her work is about Jewish concepts of history and chronology—which I shall argue are really *processes* (Ch. 3)—rather than about the concept of time itself.

long been dismissed as unsubstantiated and flawed.[13] Linearity and cyclicity are both universal to human experience, and therefore unlikely, in any given culture, to be unrepresented or unknown. We all experience linearity through the process of ageing, and cyclicity through recurring phenomena such as the annual seasons. It is impossible to distinguish between Greek and Jewish cultures on the basis of linearity and cyclicity, since both are attested in each culture (as will become evident in the course of this study, at least regarding the Jews, especially in Chapter 3).

The contrast I shall draw between Greek and Jewish culture is actually far more fundamental. The concept of time *per se*, which as mentioned above was absent and unknown throughout the ancient Near East, appears to have been well known in ancient Greece as far back as the sixth century BCE. Time (*chronos*) is treated in classical Greek sources as a category on its own; it is described as a continuum that is constantly 'passing' or 'flowing', and that drives the course of human events and the course of history. This is very close to modern Western views of time, and indeed, the latter clearly have their roots in ancient Greece. But the Greek concept of *chronos* also has parallels in ancient Iran and India. This suggests that the notion of time as such (a peculiar notion, as suggested above) is a specifically Indo-European tradition, which differed, very fundamentally, from the Semitic Near Eastern (and presumably also other) world-views (see Chapter 6).

Ancient Judaism was not immune, however, to the process of Hellenization, and this leads me to conclude this study with reflections on the interface between these two very different world-views. Jewish Hellenistic writers (i.e. those writing in the Greek language), at least some of them, had no trouble assimilating the Greek notion of *chronos* in their works: most distinctive among these are Philo and Josephus (see Chapter 5). But Jewish works in Hebrew and Aramaic, as mentioned above, remain devoid of the concept of time throughout the period of earlier and late antiquity. This should not be interpreted, I shall argue, as deliberate resistance to Hellenization, but rather as indicative of the cultural isolation of the Jews of the ancient Near East.

---

[13] These theories have been convincingly rejected by Barr, *Biblical Words*, 143–50; Momigliano, 'Time in Ancient Historiography', 179–86; Vidal-Naquet, 'Temps des dieux'; Ben Zvi, 'About Time', 18 n. 3; S.-A. Goldberg, *La Clepsydre*; and Rudavsky, *Time Matters*, 2–4; though to a large extent, they have been flogging a dead horse. See also Yerushalmi, *Zakhor*, 107–9 (nn. 4 and 7). The concept of 'cyclical time' raises itself a number of theoretical difficulties, which are often too easily ignored. Anthropologists have pointed out that if time consisted of cycles, events could not recur or be repeated (i.e. a second time): the possibility of recurrence—albeit of an identical event—implies necessarily a *linear* time-line, within which 'first' and 'second' occurrences can be conceived. What is usually meant by 'cyclical time' resembles more, therefore, a spiral: see Gell, *Anthropology of Time*, 30–53, 315 (citing *inter alios* Claude Lévi-Strauss); Hallpike, *Foundations of Primitive Thought*, 343–5.

WHAT, THEN, IS TIME?

Before we begin the first chapter, it is necessary to consider in detail a most basic question, neatly summed up by Augustine already at the end of the fourth century CE:

What, then, is time? There can be no quick or easy answer, for it is no simple matter even to understand what it is, let alone find words to explain it. Yet, in our conversation, no word is more familiarly used or more easily recognized than 'time'. We certainly understand what is meant by the word both when we use it ourselves and when we hear it used by others. What, then, is time? I know well enough what it is, provided that nobody asks me; but if I am asked what it is and try to explain, I am baffled.[14]

Time is so fundamental and familiar to our life experience that we—like Augustine—have difficulty describing or even defining it. But although this notion appears self-evident, it is susceptible to a range of definitions and descriptions, that vary not only from one culture to the next, but also from individual to individual, and even for the same individual, from one situation to the next. This ever-shifting perception of time—itself subject to the vicissitudes of time—accounts to some extent to the difficulties involved in perceiving it.[15]

A traditional distinction is often made between 'linear' and 'cyclical' time; some have added to this a third option, 'alternating' time.[16] Time can be viewed as a continuum, i.e. a single, uninterrupted entity, or else as an unbroken succession of atomistic instants. The flow of time can be perceived as invariable and constant, or as variable and relative. It can be viewed as homogenous, or as qualitatively differentiated into the categories of past, present, and future.[17]

Past, present, and future are self-centric categories that only make sense in relation to the subjective self. In objective terms, indeed, time can only be conceived of as a homogenous (although unidirectional) 'before and after' series. Modern philosophers have been divided as to whether time should be treated as a subjective experience or an objective reality; some would regard these alternatives as mutually incompatible.[18] As a result, theories about time have split into radically

[14] Augustine, *Confessions*, 11. 14. 17 (cited from R. S. Pine-Coffin's translation, pp. 263–4). Many books on time open with this citation, which has consequently become a well-known cliché (see e.g. the opening pages of Barr, *Biblical Words*, and Elias, *Time*).

[15] Munn, 'Cultural Anthropology of Time', notes the impossibility of finding a meta-language that could refer to time without being subject to time itself.

[16] See Gell, *Anthropology of Time*, 30–6. The concepts of linear and cyclical time have been briefly discussed above in the Introduction, and will be discussed further in Ch. 3.

[17] See e.g. G. Bachelard, *L'Intuition de l'instant*; M. Merleau-Ponty, *Phénoménologie de la perception*, 469–95.

[18] On the so-called A-series (the subjective experience of time as past, present, and future) and B-series (the objective notion of time as a before/after series), see e.g. Mellor, *Real Time*; Sorabji, *Time, Creation and the Continuum*; Gell, *Anthropology of Time*.

different groups. Kant, and later the phenomenologists, have argued that time is only a subjective experience of the conscious self—although this idea probably has its roots in Augustine's *Confessions* (on which see Chapter 5). The nature of this subjective experience has been given, in turn, a range of interpretations. According to Kant, time is not something that exists of itself, or an empirical concept derived from experience: it is an *a priori* intuition, a pre-existing structure in our minds that allows us to relate to objects and events.[19] From a very different perspective, the phenomenologist Maurice Merleau-Ponty describes how time is sometimes experienced by the subject as a static landscape through which he is for ever travelling, and sometimes on the contrary, as a dynamic stream that is constantly gushing towards one from the future and then rushing away into the past.[20]

Other philosophers—mainly perhaps in the Anglo-Saxon tradition—have regarded time as a fundamental structure of objective reality. In support of this view, they have invoked the authority of science, especially theoretical physics.[21] Time has thus been described as the fourth dimension of reality, alongside three-dimensional space—a concept derived from the four-dimensional model of the physicist-mathematician Hermann Minkowski. Whether this model, and indeed descriptions of time in modern physics, have been correctly interpreted by these philosophers is a question we shall return to below. However, the concept of time as objectively real and as the 'fourth dimension' of reality is not confined to these philosophers: it is probably shared by most people in the modern world.

Science is perhaps of limited relevance to this study, because we are not in search of what time 'really' is, but rather of how time is conceived in human experience and human culture. It is important to stress that science does not determine how modern man views or experiences time; indeed, it is fair to expect that scientists themselves do not theorize about time in the same way as they experience it in their daily lives. Whatever science has to say about time—and I shall return to this later in this Introduction—does not determine the modern perception of time, because the perception of time is actually a much wider cultural phenomenon that reaches far beyond the strict confines of scientific discourse.

Although the perceptions of time outlined above differ quite considerably, a common denominator that is widely shared by all modern theories—even by the more subjectivist—and probably by most individuals in the modern world, is that *time exists and is real*. This is something over which most modern people are likely to agree. Whether linear or cyclical, continuous or atomistic, homogenous or diverse, time is regarded as an essential component and fundamental structure of the world and/or of our lived experience. Whether the emphasis is placed on 'the world' or on 'lived experience' depends on whether one treats time as objective and

---

[19] See Kant, *Critique of Pure Reason*, 74–91.
[20] See Merleau-Ponty, *Phénoménologie de la perception*, 469–95.   [21] See e.g. Mellor, *Real Time*.

empirical, or as subjective and intuitive. But whether objective or subjective, the reality and existence of time goes generally undisputed. It is generally assumed, moreover, that time constitutes an entity in itself: it exists independently of the rest of reality, being in itself an empty, neutral, and 'pure' extension. Time is usually conceived of as a quantity or 'dimension' (thus susceptible of being measured), but also as a 'flow' that is autonomous, irreversible, and over which we humans have little, if any, control. Finally, since time is a 'thing' on its own, it is treated in modern society as a resource, that can be sometimes scarce and sometimes plentiful; time can be saved, utilized, or wasted, and constitutes for most people a valuable and irreplaceable (because irreversible) commodity.

The assumption that time exists and is real—regardless of its exact nature and finer analytical distinctions—is probably universal to all modern societies; but it is not universal to mankind. As mentioned above, ethnographers have found that in many—if not *all*—'primitive' or non-modern societies, the concept of time as a entity in itself simply does not exist. Reality is explained in terms of events, changes, and processes, but in these world-views, the notion of 'pure time' or an overarching 'time-dimension' is completely absent and unknown. The concepts of time-saving and time-management are, similarly, alien and unknown.

As briefly noted above, this absence of a general concept of time appears at first sight surprising, and even invites incredulity. How could any sensible person or any society account for reality and events without the notion of time, which we assume to be one of reality's most fundamental components? Even if this phenomenon is well attested in non-modern societies, it needs somehow to be explained. In the rest of this Introduction, I shall examine the ethnographic record and evaluate how it can be interpreted. Many anthropologists have doubted that non-modern societies could be completely devoid of any awareness, if only implicit, of 'pure time'; but this is an assumption that I should like to dispute.[22] Our anthropological approach will lead us to reconsider, in general, the nature of 'pure time' and its fundamentally culture-related limitations. It will also provide us with essential tools, as well as an essential context, for ascertaining how—if at all—the concept of time was articulated in the ancient Jewish world-view.

AN ANTHROPOLOGICAL APPROACH

One of the first anthropologists to have noted the absence of time in non-modern societies was Evans-Pritchard. In his study of the Nuer of southern Sudan, he noted, to begin with, the absence of a general word for 'time' in Nuer language: 'the

---

[22] For general anthropological studies of time, see Fabian, *Time and the Other*, Gell, *Anthropology of Time*, and Munn, 'Cultural Anthropology of Time'. A particularly good individual study is Hoskins, *Play of Time*.

Nuer have no expression equivalent to "time" in our language, and they cannot, therefore, as we can, speak of time as though it were something actual, which passes, can be wasted, can be saved, and so forth'.[23] The absence of a word for 'time' is actually quite common in non-modern languages. It has also been noted, for instance, by Bohannan on the Tiv of Nigeria, by Kagame on the Bantu of central and southern Africa, and by Hoskins on the Kodi of Eastern Indonesia.[24] Gell has noted—but without drawing attention to the significance of this point— that the word 'time' is one of the few words which the Muria of central India have had to borrow from English.[25] The absence of a word for time has also been claimed (though not without controversy—see Chapter 6) in the case of biblical Hebrew, and I shall argue that a similar claim can be made with respect to rabbinic Hebrew (Chapter 1). Hallpike suggests that in most non-modern languages, words which ethnographers have previously understood to mean 'time' should really be translated as 'event', 'occasion', or 'period', since it appears that they are never used to designate the concept of time in general.[26]

In the passage just cited, Evans-Pritchard appears to be arguing that the lack of a word for time in Nuer language prevented the Nuer from expressing this notion. Lexical determinism, whereby communication and expression is considered to be restricted and determined by the available lexicon, is undoubtedly a flawed hypothesis. Had the Nuer wished to express the notion of pure time, nothing would have prevented them from inventing a word, or redefining an existing word, to signify it. Indeed we do this regularly, whenever social or other change necessitates the creation of a new expression or new term.[27] All the more flawed would be to argue that cognition itself (and hence culture in general) is entirely determined by language and available linguistic resources, so that the deficiency of a word for time prevented the Nuer or others from conceptualizing this notion.

However, Evans-Pritchard's argument did not rest on purely lexical considerations. A much broader study of Nuer time-reckoning led him to the conclusion that the concept of time, in its modern Western form, did not exist in Nuer cognitive thought. Evans-Pritchard showed that instead of time, the Nuer thought in terms of the succession and sequences of mainly human activities. Thus he noted that the division of their year into seasons was not to be regarded too rigidly, since 'they are not so much exact units of time as rather vague conceptualizations of

---

[23] Evans-Pritchard, *The Nuer*, 103.
[24] Bohannan, 'Concepts of Time', 315–16; Kagame, 'Aperception empirique', 114–15 (pointing out the Bantu emphasis, instead, on the concept of 'event'); Hoskins, *Play of Time*, 58–9.
[25] Gell, *Anthropology of Time*, 89.
[26] Hallpike, *Foundations of Primitive Thought*, 345–6. On Kodi words for time, for example, see Hoskins, *Play of Time*, 58–9.
[27] See e.g. the remarks of Gell, *Anthropology of Time*, 126–31.

changes in oecological relations and social activities which pass imperceptibly from one state to another'.[28] And he went on to write:

Except for the commonest of the terms for divisions of the day they are little used in comparison with expressions which describe routine diurnal activities. The daily timepiece is the cattle clock, the round of pastoral tasks, and the time of day and the passage of time through a day are to a Nuer primarily the succession of these tasks and their relations to one another.[29]

The Nuer concept was therefore summed up as follows:

I do not think that they ever experience the same feeling of fighting against time or having to coordinate activities with an abstract passage of time, because their points of reference are mainly the activities themselves . . . Events follow a logical order, but they are not controlled by an abstract system, there being no autonomous points of reference to which activities have to conform with precision. Nuer are fortunate.[30] . . . We may conclude that the Nuer system of time-reckoning within the annual cycle and parts of the cycle is a series of conceptualizations of natural changes, and that the selection of points of reference is determined by the significance which these natural changes have for human activities.[31]

Similar observations have since been made regarding other cultures.[32] With reference to the Kabyle of Algeria, Bourdieu writes:

Inwardly felt, as the very moment of life rather than as a constraining limit, time cannot be dissociated from the experience of activity and of the space in which that activity takes place. Duration and space are described by reference to the performance of a concrete task; e.g. the unit of duration is the time one needs to do a job, to work a piece of land with a pair of oxen. Equally, space is evaluated in terms of duration, or better, by reference to the activity occupying a definite lapse of time, for example, a day at the plough or a day's walk. The common denominator and foundation of the equivalences is nothing other than the experience of activity.[33]

Or to cite another example:

Kaguru time concepts are concerned simply with the succession of events and their duration and the relation of these successions of events with the present; and this is not

---

[28] Evans-Pritchard, *The Nuer*, 98.   [29] Ibid. 101–2.

[30] It is left to the reader to decide whether this aside—inappropriate by present-day ethnographic standards—is intended to be serious, sarcastic, or covertly patronizing. For a generous interpretation, see Hoskins, *Play of Time*, 220.   [31] Evans-Pritchard, *The Nuer*, 103–4.

[32] On the Tiv of Nigeria, see Bohannan, 'Concepts of Time', 316–22. On the Kodi of Eastern Indonesia, see Hoskins, *Play of Time*, 77–8 (see further below, n. 42): the Kodi do not use an absolute time-scale, but a plurality of temporal scales that consist in fact of sequences and relative positions of events.   [33] Bourdieu, 'Attitude of the Algerian Peasant', 60.

evidence of an abstract awareness of time as a dimension in relation to which several processes can be co-ordinated.[34]

Generalizing from ethnographic studies of this kind—to which can be added further, more anecdotal reports[35]—Hallpike concludes that in 'primitive' society, 'time is spatialized and bound up with particular processes, particular concrete sequences of events in the natural and social worlds'.[36] This statement comprises, in actual fact, two separate claims: (1) that time is spatialized, and (2) that time is not clearly distinguished from process. It is obvious, however, that space and process are different notions and by no means interchangeable. As defined above in the introduction, a process is a structured or meaningful sequence of concrete events; whereas space—which I shall not investigate here in detail—is much closer to an abstraction, with reference to which concrete events and objects can be measured and described (in this respect, space functions rather similarly to time). In the context of non-modern societies, the suggestion (1) that time is 'spatialized' is problematic, because just like time, space is not necessarily universal to all cultures. For example, in spite of some inconsistency in his exposition, Bourdieu suggests quite clearly (in the citation above) that space is subject to the same treatment as time in the Kabyle world-view: both space and time are described and evaluated by reference to concrete activities. The notion that time is spatialized, which Hallpike reiterates further on, assumes the existence of a concept of space which is not necessarily evident in non-modern cultures. Moreover, the ethnographic materials considered by Hallpike and/or cited above do not warrant the inference that time is spatialized.[37]

Hallpike's second proposition (2), on the other hand, is completely plausible. The dominant term in non-modern world-views is not space or spatialization, but clearly process. In the last resort this seems to be the conclusion that Hallpike himself favours. To quote:

[34] Hallpike, *Foundations of Primitive Thought*, 346.

[35] See Hall, *The Silent Language*, 35–6: a modernized Sioux reports that his people have no concept of time, no word for it.

[36] Hallpike, *Foundations of Primitive Thought*, 346. Hallpike's evolutionist notion of the 'primitive' is open to serious criticism, which need not detain us here; see on this Gell, *Anthropology of Time*, 97–117, and Mimica, *Intimations of Infinity*.

[37] Hallpike, *Foundations of Primitive Thought*, 347. If spatialization of time is anywhere to be sought, the modern scientific (or rather popular, pseudo-scientific; see further below) concept of time as a 'dimension', akin to the three dimensions of space (hence the notion of time as a space-like 'fourth dimension'), comes much closer to it. The spatialization of time has become so well ingrained in our culture that an anthropologist like Gell (*Anthropology of Time*) can go as far as describing cultural perceptions of time as 'images' and 'maps' (hence the subtitle of his book: *Cultural Constructions of Temporal Maps and Images*)—a spatial, cartographic metaphor which Gell derives explicitly from the concept of the fourth dimension, and which he fails to appreciate may be culture-dependent and specific to the modern Western world-view. On the spatialization of time in modern science and its broader conceptual implications, see Christensen, 'The Theory of Space-Like Time'.

it is evident that these qualitative sequences are peculiar to each community, so that it becomes impossible to co-ordinate duration, simultaneity, and succession from place to place, while the flow of time will appear to proceed at different rates depending on the nature of the activities, thus making different sequences of events incommensurable.[38]

... primitive time is not uniform, continuous, or homogeneous, being indissociated from spatial concepts, action, and the structure of social relations.[39]

There is indeed a strong case to argue, along Hallpike's lines, that time in non-modern societies is concrete, embedded, and process-linked. It is not, as we perceive it, an entity that flows on its own independently from the rest of reality: it is rather an intrinsic part of environmental change and human activity. Indeed, the very concept of time becomes thereby redundant and unnecessary: the only concepts that are used to describe and interpret the universe are change, activity, events, and process.

Many anthropologists have cast doubt, however, on the suggestion that non-modern societies could be completely devoid of any awareness, if only implicit, of the general category of time. Ethnographic accounts of the absence of this category are sometimes so consistent with each other that one may legitimately wonder whether they are not simply perpetuating an ethnographic tradition that had been initiated originally by Evans-Pritchard on the Nuer.[40] But a more important objection arises from the (often unspoken) assumption that the notion of 'pure time' must be universal, in some form or other, to mankind.[41] This assumption is explicitly defended by Gell, who claims that even in cultures that apparently ignore the notion of time and only refer, instead, to process and to change, the concept of a

[38] Hallpike, *Foundations of Primitive Thought*, 347 (see also pp. 355–6). On this incommensurability, Bohannan, 'Concepts of Time', 323 writes further: 'For Tiv, time is divided by natural and social events into different sorts of periods, but since the events often belong to different logical series, there is little attempt to correlate the different sorts of divisions of time. Tiv make no attempt to correlate moons with markets or either with agricultural activities, or seasons. If one asks how many "moons" there are in a year, the answer varies between ten and eighteen; if one asks the number of markets in a moon, the answer varies between three and eight; if the number of days in a moon, between ten and fifty' (cited by Hallpike, p. 352). As Bohannan goes on to explain, this is largely a matter of choice: in the context of their social life, there is no reason for the Tiv ever to make such correlations. See also, in much more detail, Hoskins, *Play of Time*, 77–8 (and *passim*).

[39] Hallpike, *Foundations of Primitive Thought*, 349.

[40] Evans-Pritchard is frequently quoted by ethnographers in this context, even if the society under study is not that of the Nuer: see e.g. Bohannan, 'Concepts of Time'.

[41] Whether the perception of time is universal or culturally relative has been the subject of much debate among social anthropologists: for discussion and bibliography, see Gell, *Anthropology of Time*; Munn, 'Cultural Anthropology of Time'; and Hoskins, *Play of Time*, 77. The debate, however, has generally centred on the specific features of time perception and representation (e.g. how time is reckoned, how the past is remembered), ignoring the more fundamental question which I am raising here (and which Gell, *Anthropology of Time*, also examines in detail), of whether the category of time itself is universal to all cultures.

time–dimension remains, if only implicitly, a fundamental logical underpinning of their world–view.[42]

Gell's universalistic approach is predicated on the assumption that time is an objective component of the physical world, and hence that no sensible human being could fail, empirically, to acknowledge it. The assumption behind this pseudo-empirical argument, largely informed by the work of the philosopher D. H. Mellor (*Real Time*), needs to be critically assessed. Is time an objective reality? Indeed, is it real at all? In the pages that follow, I wish to argue that time is not 'real' but only a theoretical abstraction; modern society uses this abstraction to describe the world, but it is perfectly possible and valid for the world to be described without it, as consisting only of objects, events, and processes. Since there is nothing illogical or nonsensical about denying the existence of a time-continuum or time-dimension, there is no *a priori* need to assume—as Gell does, but without any good evidence—that all non-modern cultures accept 'deep down' its existence.[43] Sufficient anthropological evidence supports the view, indeed, that in many, if not most, non-modern cultures, empirical reality is adequately described in terms of process, without their having to resort to the abstracted notion of 'pure' time or a universal time–dimension.[44]

---

[42] Gell, *Anthropology of Time*. The same assumption is evident elsewhere in statements such as: 'Time is implicit in Tiv thought and speech, but it is not a category of it' (Bohannan, 'Concepts of Time', 328, quoted with approval by Hallpike, *Foundations of Primitive Thought*, 362), or '[Time is] a perceptual experience with certain universal features' (Hoskins, *Play of Time*, 77).

[43] Furthermore, it seems to me that what matters most in the study of any given culture is not the 'deep', implicit underpinnings of its cognition systems—which nobody expresses and which can never be verified—but rather its conscious and explicit perceptions and representations: in our context, whether the category of time is explicitly recognized, articulated, and used in the context of real-life experience. Gell's universalistic position, confined to a deep implicit level, is therefore somewhat irrelevant. No anthropologist can escape the fact that, at a conscious level, non-modern cultures often (or even generally) have no concept of time *per se*, and account instead for the world around them in terms of process, events, and activity. Gell's critique, *Anthropology of Time*, 263–305, of Bourdieu's *Outline of a Theory of Practice*, whose approach to culture is dominated by the study of explicit representations and 'practice', is therefore unconvincing.

[44] This conclusion resists challenge from Hoskins, who, after noting the absence of a word for time (in a general sense) in Kodi language, states: 'This is not to say that time is not a category of Kodi experience, or not something that can be the subject of reflection and speculation. Rather, this fact only underscores the fact that in English we collapse a number of separate concepts to make our own category of "time", whereas in many other cultures these notions may be kept more rigorously separate. This separation does not give these cultures a sense of "timelessness"; instead it allows them to distinguish aspects of time more carefully than we do ourselves' (*Play of Time*, 58–9). Hoskins is unwittingly imposing our modern, general category of 'time' upon a culture that lacks it, by claiming that this category *implicitly* exists in this culture, although divided into sub-categories ('aspects of time'; she also writes: 'time is concretized in notions of the day, month, and seasons', ibid.). The latter, however, can only be treated as sub-categories or 'aspects' of time if one assumes the existence of a general category, 'time', to subsume them. But if one accepts the absence of such a general category in Kodi culture, these phenomena cannot legitimately be called 'aspects of time'; they can only represent, at most, a range of interconnected processes. The centrality of processes in Kodi culture is evident

TIME: A REIFIED ABSTRACTION

The absence of a concept of time in non-modern world-views is not as strange or as foolish as might appear at first sight. A phenomenological analysis of the modern concept of time reveals, as we shall see, that the notion of time *per se* is culturally determined, and therefore not necessarily universally true. This has not been sufficiently acknowledged by philosophers (even phenomenologists), but it has been well articulated by the social historian Norbert Elias, as well as by some psychologists who will be cited below. Similar conclusions obtain from a completely different perspective, that of theoretical physics. In the next section I shall outline how modern physics has demonstrated that the notion of 'pure' time, of time as an empty extension, or of time as a dimension of the universe, is really only illusory. Thus, phenomenology and science usefully converge (in this case at least!), and provide the framework for understanding how so many human societies and cultures can exist and function without any notion of a general category called 'time'.

The dimension of time which we usually take for granted in our modern world-view is not a tangible or concrete reality; it is not perceptible to the senses. Much the same can be said, indeed, about the notion of 'pure', empty space, although this is outside our present scope. All we experience around us are concrete objects, engaged in certain relations which we call 'events'; events, in turn, are structured in sequences which we call 'processes'. Time is only an *abstract* measurement of processes: it is, primarily, a way of expressing how long a process is. The modern concept of time as a general category, an autonomous flow, an empty extension, or a structure and dimension of the universe, is only a generalization and synthesis of all the discrete time-measurements that can be made of the individual processes which we empirically experience. Time itself, however, is not an empirical experience, nor a palpable reality: it is only a generalized abstraction. Inasmuch as we tend to treat it, in modern culture, as existing and real (see above), time often becomes a *reified* abstraction.

Similar conclusions have been reached by scholars from a variety of disciplines. A psychologist, for instance, argues that events are perceived by the human mind not in terms of time and space, but only in terms of the reciprocal concepts of persistence and change. On time and space, he argues:

Time and space are concepts, abstracted from the percepts of events and surfaces. They are not perceived, and they are not prerequisite to perceiving. They do not give meaning

---

throughout Hoskins's work, even though she persists in subordinating them to the modern category of time or 'temporality' (the word 'time' even appearing in the book's title). To cite just one example, what Hoskins calls the 'value of time' (which is invested by the Kodi in certain objects of antiquity: ibid. 202–20, 367) is really, on her own evidence, the value of past *events* (thus a value which is not time-derived, but process-derived).

to percepts and they are not imposed by the mind on the deliverance of sense. Time and space are intellectual achievements, not perceptual categories . . . the idea of empty time, like the idea of empty space, brings with it insoluble problems for ecology and psychology. This implies that events are what 'fill' time, as if it were a continuum into which events can be put. But this metaphor is surely wrong for the psychology of event perception. Time is not a receptacle for events, just as space is not a receptacle for objects.[45]

A more systematic analysis of time has been made by Norbert Elias, who argues that this concept is a relatively recent invention of modern society. According to Elias, time is not a universal *a priori* of human experience, nor the conception of a flow that exists objectively. Time is a man-made idea: it is only a conceptual generalization and synthesis of all observable events and sequences.[46] The concept of time as a universal dimension is a 'social symbol', 'a symbolic expression of the experience that everything which exists is part of an incessant sequence of events.'[47] More specifically, time refers to a property that all events or sequences of events have in common; it enables, therefore, the comparison of the duration and speed of perceptible processes which otherwise, because of their differences, would not be possible directly to compare.[48]

Time, indeed, is not an independent or tangible reality. It is not perceptible to the senses, nor can it be observed or measured. It is not really 'time' that clocks or other devices measure, but only concrete things such as the length of a working day, or of a lunar eclipse, or a sprinter's speed in the 100 metres. Clocks themselves are only sequences of physical events, that are used as standard reference for the measurement of other events. They are only associated with time because it is the concept of time that enables them to be used in this manner: the concept of time enables the comparison between the movement of clocks and other events to be achieved.[49]

Elias argues that it is the universalistic nature of the concept of time, as well as the standardization of modern clocks through which this concept is articulated, that has misled people into treating time as an independent entity, as something that objectively flows. This common reification, however, should not be a reason to denigrate the concept of time or reject its validity. Far from it: Elias considers the concept of time as a social institution of considerable importance, because it enables individuals in society to achieve a high degree of orientation in their social and natural environment.[50] The formation of the social symbol of time has resulted from the development of increasingly populous, complex, and diverse societies,

---

[45] Gibson, 'Events are Perceivable', 299.

[46] Elias, *Time*, 8, 40. Elias says that he prefers to avoid the term 'abstraction', because of his uncertainty as to what time would be abstracted from (ibid. 174 and 201 n. 1). To me it is clear, however, that the notion of time is abstracted from concrete events and processes. Note that Elias himself uses the term, perhaps unwittingly, in other parts of the same essay.   [47] Ibid. 36.

[48] Ibid. 73, 104.   [49] Ibid. 1–2, 46–7, 107, 120–1.   [50] Ibid. 2, 10, 13, 38, and 84.

where the need for high-level synthesis has become essential for the effective co-ordination of human activities and non-human natural events. This need has become especially pronounced, Elias argues, in 'large urbanized state societies . . . where the specialization of social functions is far advanced, where the chain of interdependencies binding the performers of these functions to each other are long and highly diversified'.[51]

But although Elias accepts the concept of time as the necessary outcome of an advanced stage of social development, he warns against the modern fallacy of its reification or, as he calls it, 'fetishization'.[52] This modern fallacy is partly the result of the misleadingly substantive form of the term 'time',[53] but more fundamentally, it is the result of a common confusion between symbol and reality when the symbol has attained 'a very high degree of adequacy to reality'. This generates the misleading feeling that time is an entity on its own or that time is passing, whereas in reality, it is the sequence of life or world events to which the feeling of passing applies.[54]

TIME IN MODERN PHYSICS

Elias also blames scientists, probably unfairly, for promoting the reification of time in the modern perception of reality. According to Elias, this began when Galileo represented the intervals between regularly repeated events with mathematical equations; time was thus mathematized, and came to be treated as something measurable.[55] Reification of time may have been further promoted by Newton, who famously asserted that 'absolute, true, and mathematical time, of itself and from its own nature, flows equally without relation to anything external'—a traditional formulation of time as an autonomous flow and pure extension.[56]

Elias is clearly unaware that Newtonian absolute time was radically revised in Einstein's special theory of relativity, published in 1905. The implications of this theory were so important to modern physics that they deserve attention here. According to the special theory of relativity, which was experimentally confirmed

---

[51] Elias, *Time*, 121–2. Although this suggestion is not implausible, I shall argue (below, Ch. 5) that the concept of time is of much greater antiquity than Elias recognized, and thus not necessarily related to modern societies or modernity.

[52] Ibid. 74, 104. Elias does not clearly distinguish between 'reification' and 'fetishization'.

[53] Ibid. 42–3.   [54] Ibid. 23.

[55] Ibid. 106–7. Elias is wrong, however, to assume that Galileo's mathematical representations entailed any kind of reification (Harry Stern, pers. comm.).

[56] Cited in Gibson, 'Events are Perceivable', 299. See Hawking, *Brief History*, 18; Davies, *Space and Time*, 2, 11–19. In making this statement, Newton (whom Elias does not refer to) was merely reiterating the conception of time that prevailed in Western culture. But the extent to which he actually subscribed to this conception remains somewhat uncertain: for in his mechanics, the notion of time did not feature at all, as a flow or as an entity (which would have had physical effects); in his mechanics, only time *intervals* are absolute. I am grateful to Harry Stern for clarifying this point.

many times over during the course of the twentieth century, time-intervals are not absolute and with fixed values (as according to Newtonian physics), but relative and dependent on the position and speed of the observer. The closer one approaches the speed of light (which it is impossible to exceed), the more time intervals are 'dilated'—and hence, for example, clocks tick more slowly.[57] The general theory of relativity, published by Einstein in 1915, established further that time intervals are also dilated in strong gravitational fields (this theory has also been experimentally well proven).[58] Consequently, the time interval between two events will be measured differently according to the perspective of the observer.

The implications of these discoveries—which, to emphasize, account for empirical reality (and are thus not just speculative theory)—are far-reaching and beyond our scope. What concerns us most in this context is that the theory of relativity has contributed to the breakdown of traditional, reified notions of time and space. Once it was shown that time intervals are not absolute, but dependent on the situation and reference frame of the observer, it made no sense to treat time as an absolute, autonomously flowing entity.[59] The only firm reality is objects (to be more precise, particles and electromagnetic radiation such as light) and their manifestation in events. Time and space, by contrast, are not real extensions but only conceptual, mathematical devices that are used to situate events and measure the intervals between them.[60] Since time is only an abstract concept, it is defined in modern physics as a standard, but arbitrary, sequence of apparently regular repeated events—e.g. the 'ticks' of an atomic clock—with reference to which other events and intervals can be meaningfully related and measured.[61] The notion of time remains thus essential to modern physics, but only in this event-based definition.[62] The traditional notion that time is a dimension of the universe or a flowing entity,

---

[57] Hawking, *Brief History*, 20–3; Davies, *Space and Time*, 32–55. It is important to stress that this not a distortion of the mechanism of the clock: the same dilation of time intervals applies, indeed, to all the processes within this frame of reference (e.g. the process of ageing, in the 'twin paradox': if one twin stays on earth and the other travels into space at a speed close to the speed of light, when the latter returns to earth he is much younger than his brother). This phenomenon, moreover, is not a mere psychological impression, but an empirical reality that has been experimentally confirmed.

[58] Hawking, *Brief History*, 29–33; Davies, *Space and Time*, 105–7.

[59] The relativity of time also has the result of demolishing absolutist notions of simultaneity (the concept of 'now') and the before-after sequence, since, depending on the perspective of the observer, two events can sometimes occur in reverse order (provided they have can no effect on one another, nor on the observer, without surpassing the speed of light): Davies, *Space and Time*, 35, 220–2; Feynman et al., *Feynman Lectures*, section 17: 3; Landau and Lifshitz, *Classical Theory*, 8–9.

[60] Thus an event is normally defined in terms of the space-time co-ordinates in which it occurs: see Landau and Lifshitz, *Classical Theory*, 4; Davies, *Space and Time*, 53; Hawking, *Brief History*, 23–4.

[61] Feynman, *Feynman Lectures*, sections 5: 1–5. In section 5: 2 he neatly concludes: 'We can just say that we base our *definition* of time on the repetition of some apparently periodic event' (his emphasis).

[62] For example, the 'arrow of time' is a metaphor commonly used by modern physicists, but not to describe the irreversibility of pure time. The commonly perceived irreversibility of time is not a

by contrast, is firmly excluded: 'There is no underlying continuum on whose time everything is built; since, in other words, the idea of the time continuum only arises by a process of abstraction from higher levels of processes, then no sort of time has any privileged claim on reality.'[63]

Remarkably, popular perceptions of time in the modern world have hardly been affected by these major scientific discoveries. Minkowski's model of a four-dimensional space–time (1908), which was only intended as a fictitious, geometrical representation of the mathematical equations of special relativity,[64] has been regularly taken out of its context and function and misinterpreted as a reification of space and time, indeed as a spatialization of time as the 'fourth dimension'. The reified concept of time as a fourth dimension has become so well ingrained in popular imagination that for the last hundred years science-fiction authors have been able to write about 'time machines' as if the time-dimension were a highway along which it might be possible, one day, to travel.[65] In brief, for reasons that deserve further investigation, popular imagination has clung to this very day to traditional views of absolute time,[66] and has consistently misinterpreted modern physics so as to fit this paradigm.[67] This is reflected not only in popular literature, but also in the works of philosophers and—as noted above—social anthropologists.[68]

---

property of time itself: what is irreversible is not time, but large-scale processes, which according to the principle known as 'entropy' have an overwhelming probability of progressing towards increasing disorder, thus giving the universe its irreversible direction. 'Time', in this metaphor, should only be understood in its narrow, event-based definition (see Hawking, *Brief History*, 143–53; Davies, *Space and Time*, 58–9).

[63] Clarke, 'Process', 67. See also Davies, *Space and Time*, 3: 'the elementary conscious experience of time—the flow or motion of the present moment—is absent from the physicist's description of the objective world'; and ibid. 56–7, 59–60, 220–2.

[64] See Landau and Lifshitz, *Classical Theory*, 4–9; Davies, *Space and Time*, 51–2.

[65] The considerable paradoxes arising from the notion of time travel (e.g. how one can travel back to the past without affecting it, and hence without affecting one's own present existence), which science fiction has usually exploited and taken in its stride, are likely to result from the fallacy of time as a quasi-spatial dimension. Relativity does allow the possibility of travel into the future, but not back into the past (Davies, *Space and Time*, 39–40).

[66] This is partly because the Newtonian absoluteness of time intervals is not challenged within the range of normal, human experience, but only at speeds approaching the speed of light or in very strong gravitational fields. See Landau and Lifshitz, *Classical Theory*, 4; Feynman, *Feynman Lectures*, sections 16: 1–2.

[67] The theory of relativity is commonly misinterpreted by non-physicists because of a tendency to interpret references to 'time' in its traditional meaning as an entity. Elias, for example, believes that Einstein reified time (and indeed 'gave new substance to the myth of reified time') by maintaining that under certain circumstances time could contract and expand (Elias, *Time*, 44; see also 84–9, 115–18). Einstein, however, was only referring to the contraction and expansion of specific time intervals from the perspective of specific frames of reference. Elias seems unaware that Einstein's theories, in fact, contributed towards the breakdown of time as a reified entity.

[68] See Mellor, *Real Time*, and Gell, *Anthropology of Time*. As the title of his work indicates, Mellor (on whom Gell depends) argues that the flow of time is 'real', citing alleged support from modern physics.

Recognition that time is not a reality, only an abstraction, has yet to become established in modern experience and modern culture.

PROCESS WITHOUT TIME

The convergence of physics with the phenomenological analysis of time which I have outlined above—whereby all that exists are objects and events, and time is only a reified abstraction—is appealing in view of the trust we generally place in the 'truth' of science. It is precisely because of the attraction of scientific truth that modern physics has been commonly misinterpreted, as explained above, so as to justify the perpetuation of beliefs in the existence of 'real time'. Now that it is established that in actual fact, quite independently from phenomenological studies such as Elias's, physics considers time to be a mere abstraction, it is difficult to resist the truth of this conclusion.

However, my interest is not in the 'truth' as much as in the *plausibility* of non-modern, process-based world-views.[69] Physics confirms the plausibility of a description of the universe without pure time or a time-continuum. Although theoretical physicists still use the category of time, in a stricter definition, as an essential mathematical device, it is recognized that this category is not inherent to reality, and hence that it may be possible to view the world without it. Some predict that future, new theories in theoretical physics may abandon the concepts of space and time completely, and indeed, that future society may forget the use of these words or notions[70]—although we are still far removed from that. There is no inherent reason why the concept of time should be assumed universal, or why it should be assumed that non-modern societies that do not express it conceive of it implicitly or, somehow, 'deep down'. Process without time is a plausible and entirely rational world-view.

Indeed, there may be a case to argue that a process-based world-view constitutes a more satisfactory representation of empirical reality. Although, as Elias argues, the concept of time is essential to the co-ordination of complex modern societies as well as an essential mathematical model for theoretical physicists, it carries the risk of being reified into an independent entity, a dimension of reality, a continuum and autonomous 'flow'. Non-modern cultures that ignore the social symbol of time have, in this sense, an advantage over the modern, popular world-view.

A world-view based on process and without the general concept of time gives rise to a radically different description of reality, but without excluding or ignoring any aspect of universal empirical experience. Aspects of empirical reality which

[69] On the question of 'truth' in the context of ethnography, see Jackson, *Paths toward a Clearing*.
[70] Davies, *Space and Time*, 203.

we consider fundamentally time-related, such as the distinction between past, present, and future, are known and recognized in process-based, non-modern cultures, but interpreted without reference to a temporal dimension or time-continuum. Past, present, and future—to stay with this example—need not be perceived as the separate zones of a subjective[71] time-line: they can be perceived instead as descriptions of the *status* of human or natural events. From a process-perspective, indeed, 'past' is only an event (or process, or sum of events) in a state of completion or of termination; 'present' is an event in process; 'future' is an event in a state of being ready, due, or about to occur.[72] Thus the same 'past', 'present', or 'future' events which we should interpret in terms of time or as situated at various points in a time-line can be experienced and interpreted by others purely in terms of whether they are complete, in process, or about to be.

This process-related perception of past, present, and future may be reflected in some cases in the grammatical features of the language in use. The fuzziness of tenses is notorious in biblical Hebrew,[73] but fuzziness or even complete absence of tense is also attested in the verb-systems of other languages in the world.[74] In such languages, verb-forms do not express tense (which would constitute a reference to the temporal notions of past, present, and future), but rather aspect (e.g. perfective or imperfective, which express whether the event is complete, incomplete, continuous, etc.) and modality (e.g. indicative, subjunctive, or imperative, which express whether the statement is a fact, a possibility, a wish, a command, etc.). This does not mean that in such languages, the time of an action or event cannot be and is not expressed through other means (e.g. adverbial or contextual). In this respect, the absence of tense in a verb-system cannot be taken as evidence on its own of a timeless, process-based world-view.[75] Nevertheless, preference for aspect and modality in the verb-system of a language is likely to be significant: it may suggest that aspect of event and modality of statement are *conceptually* more important, to the language-users, than time of event.[76]

[71] On the subjectivity of the categories of past, present, and future, see above.

[72] I am grateful to Shirley Ardener for her remarks on this.

[73] See e.g. McFall, *Enigma*. Hatav, *Semantics of Aspect and Modality*, argues that biblical Hebrew is completely tenseless.

[74] e.g. ancient and modern Chinese (Larre, 'Aperception', 53), Burmese, and other languages (Comrie, *Tense*, 50–3); see also Gell, *Anthropology of Time*, 127.

[75] As correctly argued by Gell, ibid. 118–31, against Hallpike, *Foundations of Primitive Thought*, 364 (citing Prince, *Science Concepts*, 72); see also Barr, *Biblical Words*, 136–7.

[76] This hypothesis, and indeed the more general theory that language structures and concepts of reality are interrelated and interdependent, was put forward in a rather extreme form by Benjamin Lee Whorf (Carrol, *Language, Thought, and Reality*; but see Lee, *Whorf Theory Complex*). For a more measured approach, see Lucy, *Language Diversity and Thought*. Other possibilities, however, must also be considered: in some cases it may be that preference for aspect and modality reflects not their conceptual, but rather their *functional* importance to the language-users.

This hypothesis still needs to be tested and confirmed; indeed, a consistent correlation is yet to be established between tenseless languages and process-based world-views.[77] But clearly, in the context of a non-modern, process-based world-view, the absence of tense in the verb-system should come as no surprise. For it is far more significant, in a process-based world-view, to describe an event as 'perfect' or complete (for example) than to locate it along the segment of some abstract, artificial time-line called 'past'. There is actually no real need to integrate abstract time-related structures, such as tense, within the grammar of the language, because process-related structures are perfectly adequate expressions of concrete, empirical experience. The fuzziness or absence of a tense system in many languages may thus serve to confirm that the concept of a temporal dimension is not necessary for a cogent experience and interpretation of lived reality.

In the field of Jewish studies, passions are usually aroused when religious or political issues are at stake. This study concerns neither religion as such nor politics; yet it has aroused much passion in seminars where earlier drafts of this work have been presented. I think that the reason why some respondents invested so much passion in attempting to 'prove' the existence of a concept of time in ancient Judaism (with various degrees of success, but this is not the point at present) is that they felt, perhaps only implicitly, that my argument was a threat to the core of their own world-view. I concede that this work is radical, but it is by no means iconoclastic, aggressive, or extreme. In the course of studying ancient (or other) cultures, we must be prepared to emancipate ourselves from our prior assumptions and reconsider some of our most fundamental world-views.

---

[77] This correlation can be attested at least in the context of the Hebrew Bible and of ancient and medieval Chinese culture: see Ch. 6.

ONE

Time—or its Absence—in
Early Rabbinic Culture

A S in many non-modern cultures, the concept of time as a general category is
absent from early rabbinic culture. A survey of the entire corpus of early rabbinic sources, which include the Mishnah, Tosefta, Palestinian and Babylonian
Talmuds, and all the halakhic and early aggadic *midrashim* (dating from the third to
seventh centuries CE), confirms that the category of time is never explicitly
referred to, let alone commented upon or discussed. The purpose of this chapter is
to substantiate this claim. In this chapter, as in Chapters 2–4, I shall focus almost
entirely on early rabbinic literature. Other ancient Jewish sources will be considered in Chapters 5–6.

THE WORD *ZEMAN*

The most common, and indeed almost exclusive, word for aspects of time in early
rabbinic Hebrew and Aramaic is *zeman* (זמן). Although, from the later Middle
Ages until today, this term has been regularly used for the modern concept of time
as a general category, in early rabbinic sources it is never used in this general sense.
As we shall see, *zeman* in early rabbinic sources means either specific points in time
or finite periods of time, but never expresses the dimension of time as a whole.

The origins of the term *zeman* are relatively late. The Bible uses other words for
time or aspects of time: in particular, *et* (עת) which usually means a point in time,
the 'right time', sometimes a 'period of time') and *mo'ed* (מועד) which means, more
specifically, 'appointed time').[1] The same vocabulary is retained at Qumran,[2] but
with the important addition of *kets*, which in biblical Hebrew only means 'end', but

---

[1] On *et* and *mo'ed*, see Barr, *Biblical Words*, 122–3; and, much more extensively, Brin, *Concept of
Time*. Other words include *pa'am* (expressing repetitive occasion, equivalent to German *Mal* and
French *fois*), *yom* (which does not always mean 'day' in the strict sense, and indeed is occasionally
translated in the Septuagint as *chronos*, 'time': see also Eynikel and Hauspie, 'Καιρός and Χρόνος', 383;
I am grateful to James Aitken for referring me to this important article), and *olam* (expressing remote
time or everlastingness). On the latter, and on the concept of time in the Bible in general, see below,
Ch. 6.   [2] See Brin, *Concept of Time*, 264–76.

in Qumran literature is frequently confused with *et* and *mo'ed* and bears the more general sense of '[point in] time' or 'period'.[3]

The term *zeman* first appears in the later books of the Bible:[4] in Hebrew in Nehemiah (2: 6), Esther (9: 27, 31), and Ecclesiastes (3: 1), and in Aramaic in Ezra (5: 3) and Daniel (2: 9, 2: 21, 3: 7–8, 4: 33, 6: 11, 6: 14, 7: 12, 7: 22, 7: 25). There it always means 'appointed or specific point in time', except in Daniel (2: 16), where it means 'specific period of time'. Its verbal cognate, mostly in the *pual* form,[5] is also confined to the later books of the Bible: in Ezra (10: 14) and Nehemiah (13: 31) it serves as an epithet to the word *et* (the earlier biblical term meaning 'point in time'), hence the phrase *itim mezumanim* (Ezra 10: 14) which translates as 'appointed times'. This verbal usage reinforces the punctual connotation of the noun *zeman* in late biblical Hebrew: it does not designate the general concept of time, but only a specific or appointed moment in it.

The term *zeman* is not attested at Qumran, but in mishnaic (or tannaitic) Hebrew, it becomes the most common term for aspects of time, while the biblical term *et* is largely phased out.[6] The term *zeman* primarily retains, in mishnaic Hebrew, its late biblical meaning of 'appointed or set points in time'. We find, for

---

[3] Talmon, '*Qets*'; Barr, *Biblical Words*, 124–5; Brin, *Concept of Time*, 219–21 and *passim*. The Qumran usage of *kets* in the sense of '[point in] time' may be already attested in *Ben Sira* 43: 6 (see below, Ch. 6), and there is evidence that the Septuagint interprets the biblical *kets*, in some cases, as meaning 'time' (Eynikel and Hauspie, '*Καιρός* and *Χρόνος*', 382–3). The same use of *kets* is very rarely attested in rabbinic literature, and only in the plural in a more particular sense (*aḥat lekitsin*, 'once in a while', in JT *AZ* 4: 12 (44*b*); and in the parallel BT *AZ* 61*b*, *lekitsin*, 'at fixed times'). But note that *Genesis Rabbah* 89: 1 (p. 1086 ed. Theodor and Albeck) interprets the biblical word *kets* ('end') as meaning *zeman* ('time'), and see also *Targum Ps.-Jonathan* on Gen. 49: 1, where *kets* apparently means 'time'. The term *kets* in this sense is more frequently attested later in *piyut* (liturgical poetry): see e.g. R. Eleazar Hakalir's *Kerovot leparashat shekalim* (*Ma'atik pelusim*), which reads: פרשה זאת להגות בקץ זה, 'to recite this passage at this time'; or his *Kerovot leparashat haḥodesh* (*Avi kol ḥozeh*), which reads *kets moladeto*, 'the time of its [the moon's] conjunction' (see Wieder, 'The Term קץ', with further examples and discussion).

[4] For the etymological origins of this term, see Mankowski, *Akkadian Loanwords*, 54–5. It appears to have originated from the Akkadian or Ugaritic *simānu/šimānu*, meaning 'proper time', 'occasion', or 'season' (on which see Black et al., *Dictionary of Akkadian*, 323, 373, and below, Ch. 6). From there it seems to have passed into Persian, and then from Persian into Aramaic and Hebrew (as attested in later books of the Bible). Almut Hintze informs me, however, that the term **jamana* is not attested in Old Persian and therefore only conjectural; a direct derivation from Akkadian into Aramaic and/or Hebrew should therefore not be excluded. On these various etymologies see Koehler and Baumgartner, *Hebrew and Aramaic Lexicon*, i. 273; Cohen, *Dictionnaire des racines sémitiques*, 749–50.

[5] *Mezuman*; but see the *kere* and *ketiv* of Dan. 2: 9.

[6] Barr, *Biblical Words*, 124–5. Note how the biblical *et* (in Eccles. 3: 1) is rendered as *zeman* in *Ecclesiastes Rabbah* ad loc. The word *et* does appear, however, in Mishnah *Orl.* 1: 2, Mishnah *Tam.* 1: 4, Tosefta *Pes.* 2: 11 (p. 159), *Mekhilta derabi yishma'el*, 'Shirah' 10 (p. 151 ed. Horovitz and Rabin), etc.; the plural *itim* appears in Mishnah *Tam.* 1: 2, Tosefta *Toh.* 4: 2 (p. 663), BT *Shab.* 31*a*, BT *RH* 28*a*, etc. The word *et* is also attested in the early rabbinic phrase *me'et le'et*, on which see below, Ch. 2. On *kets* in rabbinic sources, see above, n. 3. In Syriac also, the cognate *zabna* is the most common term (Barr, *Biblical Words*, 130–1).

instance, the liturgical phrase *mekadesh yisra'el vehazemanim* (Tosefta *Berakhot* 3: 13 (p. 7)), where *zemanim* means the 'appointed times' or festivals, or the phrase *higia zeman*, 'the time [set for a wedding] has come' (Mishnah *Ketubot* 5: 2). The meaning of *zeman* as '*appointed* time' is reinforced by the common use in mishnaic Hebrew of its verbal cognate, now frequently in *pi'el* form (*zimen*), in the sense of 'to appoint' or 'to designate'. This suggests that the semantic field of *zeman* may be centred on the notion of appointment or designation, rather than on the notion of time.

By extension, however, *zeman* comes to mean in mishnaic Hebrew any 'point in time' (even if not appointed or set): for instance, the time when the month has begun (Tosefta *Arakhin* 1: 8 (543)), or similarly a 'date' (typically, the date that is entered in legal documents: Mishnah *Yevamot* 3: 2). *Zeman* has also the more specific meaning of 'right time' or 'proper time', as in the phrase *ba haḥodesh bizemano* ('the month began at its right time', i.e. after 29 days: Mishnah *Shekalim* 4: 5), or in a halakhic sense, the times when various rituals must be fulfilled: hence the phrases *zeman hamikra*, 'the time for reading [the *Shema*]' (Mishnah *Berakhot* 2: 1), *hapesaḥ bizemano vehaḥatat bekhol zeman*, 'the Passover sacrifice at its proper time and the sin-offering at any time' (Mishnah *Zevaḥim* 1: 1), *hazeman posel*, 'the time [when a sacrifice is offered] may invalidate [it]' (Tosefta *Pesaḥim* 3: 2 (p. 161)). It is in a similar sense that the phrase *mitsvat aseh shehazeman geramah* (Mishnah *Kidushin* 1: 7) should be understood: it does not mean a 'time-bound' or (more literally) 'time-caused' positive commandment, as the phrase is commonly translated, but rather a commandment that becomes binding by the onset of its proper, designated time.[7]

Besides its usage for punctual moments of time, which constitutes only a minor extension of the late biblical usage, the word *zeman* is also used in mishnaic Hebrew to express duration. However, *zeman* in this sense never designates the endless 'flow' or continuum of time, as it does in later medieval and modern sources; it only means a 'time interval', or a 'finite, discontinuous period of time'.[8] Thus it is used for the length of a wardenship (Mishnah *Bava metsia* 3: 7), the period within which a debt must be paid (Mishnah *Bava kama* 8: 6), or a shaky wall pulled down (Mishnah *Bava metsia* 10: 4), or one's first-born cattle kept (Mishnah *Bekhorot* 4: 1). The same sense is implicit in the expression *meḥusar zeman* (literally 'lacking time'), which is applied to sacrifices that have been offered too early, before a required period of time has elapsed (Mishnah *Zevaḥim* 14: 3). By exten-

---

[7] Rovner, 'Rhetorical Strategy', 200–1 nn. 48–9, on *mitsvat aseh shehazeman geramah*. The same meaning applies to the phrase גרם הזמן in *Mekhilta derabi yishma'el*, 'Pisḥa' 8 (p. 28 ed. Horovitz and Rabin).

[8] *Zeman* in this sense can be characterized as 'long' (*merubeh*: Mishnah *Ker*. 3: 9) or 'short' (*muat*: both in Tosefta *BM* 8: 33 (p. 391); in BT *San*. 108*b* the adjectives used are *gadol* and *katan*).

sion, *zeman* can also be used in the sense of a person's 'age' (Mishnah *Nidah* 5: 6) or of a 'season': *zemanah shel reviah*, 'the season of rain': Tosefta *Ta'anit* 1: 2 (p. 214); also in Aramaic, *zimeneh de'aviva*, 'the season of spring': Tosefta *Sanhedrin* 2: 6 (p. 417).

The term *zeman* can also be used in expressions where the reference to either 'point in time' or 'period' is ambiguous. The common phrase *hazeman hazeh* (literally 'this time') can either mean 'now' in a punctual sense, as in the liturgical phrase, *vehigianu lazeman hazeh*, 'And He has enabled us to reach this time/ season': Tosefta *Berakhot* 5: 22 (p. 12), or 'now' in the sense of 'nowadays', i.e. this period (Mishnah *Ma'aser sheni* 5: 7). Most common is the use of *zeman* in adverbial expressions such as *bizeman she-*, 'whenever' (Mishnah *Berakhot* 7: 5), *kol zeman she-*, 'as long as' (Mishnah *Shevi'it* 10: 4) or 'whenever' (Mishnah *Pe'ah* 7: 2), or *le'ahar zeman* ('after a while': Mishnah *Gitin* 8: 8), all pervasive in mishnaic Hebrew, and where the term *zeman* functions sometimes ambiguously either as point in time or as finite period.

Thus it is evident that the main mishnaic Hebrew term for aspects of time, *zeman*, is restricted in meaning to 'points in time' and 'finite periods'. The meaning of *zeman* is similarly restricted in talmudic and midrashic literature.[9]

The term *zeman* is not devoid, for that matter, of any conceptual meaning. Its multiple use, which has been outlined above, suggests undoubtedly an overarching concept or category which we should naturally call 'time'. This concept, however, does not correspond to 'time' in its modern, popular sense: *zeman* is not a self-standing or 'pure' entity, a universal dimension, a flow, or a continuum. The concept of *zeman*, embracing only points in time and finite periods, is that of the 'time of things', or to be more precise, the 'time of events': *zeman* is the measurement of the occurrence and length of processes, natural events, and human activities (social, economic, and ritual). It is only in this specific sense that *zeman* can occasionally serve as a general concept, as in the phrases *hazeman posel* ('time invalidates': Tosefta *Pesahim* 3: 2 (p. 161)) and *mitsvat aseh shehazeman geramah*, 'time-dependent commandment' (Mishnah *Kidushin* 1: 7), which have been discussed already above. The concept of measurement and timing of processes does not imply or necessitate, however, a concept of the universal time-dimension.[10]

---

[9] There is no point in listing references here, as they can be easily compiled from the concordances or electronic CD-ROMs. All I would note is one additional usage of *zeman* (but purely in a punctual sense) in the Aramaic of the Jerusalem Talmud and of Targum Onkelos (on Gen. 2: 24, Num. 24: 1): *had zeman* ('once'), *zeman horan* ('another time'), *zeman tinyanut* ('a second time'), and *zimenin* ('sometimes'; also common in the Babylonian Talmud). The absence of these phrases in tannaitic literature may be due to linguistic difference (between Hebrew and Aramaic) or to historical change (tannaitic literature being generally earlier). However, the meaning of *zeman* in these phrases is much the same as in mishnaic Hebrew.

[10] As has been suggested in the Introduction, and will be argued in further detail in Ch. 2.

It is important to clarify that the absence of word for 'time in general' in early rabbinic literature does not necessarily *prove* that this modern concept of time did not exist. Firstly, as with any argument from silence, it may be objected that the term *zeman* was really used in this modern sense in early rabbinic Hebrew, but that this usage only happens not to be attested in the extant sources. Secondly, as I have argued in the Introduction (with reference to Evans-Pritchard's Nuer), the absence of a general word for 'time' should not have prevented the rabbis or others from conceptualizing this notion, or from giving it some form of verbal or other expression.[11] In other words, the fact that *zeman* is never used in a general sense (but only in a punctual sense, or for periods of limited duration), and that words for 'time' in a general sense are absent in early rabbinic literature, is no more than an argument from silence.

Silence, however, can be quite significant; and in this case I would suggest it is. The concept of time (in a general sense) is so fundamental to our modern perception of reality that if the rabbis had shared it, one would expect them to have referred to it, just as we do quite frequently in our daily speech. Its absence in early rabbinic discourse—and possibly even in the early rabbinic lexicon—calls for an explanation. Whoever rejects the argument from silence and claims that the modern concept of 'time in general' existed in early rabbinic culture has the onus of explaining why this concept is never expressed in its language and never referred to in the vastness of its literature.

THE ABSENCE OF TIME

It might be argued that the absence of the concept of 'time in general' from early rabbinic literature is only a matter of genre. If this concept is only of interest to philosophers and physicists, then since, as is well known, early rabbinic sources are devoid of philosophical discourse or scientific speculation, we should not expect the concept of time to be ever mentioned or discussed.[12]

This argument, however, is built on a false premiss, because it is perfectly possible for people who are neither philosophers nor scientists to discuss and make statements about the nature of time. In all strata of modern society, time is a widely shared concept and an integral part of daily speech. We all often comment, in most cases quite casually, about the passing of time (e.g. that it passes slowly or quickly),

---

[11] A point made in Barr, *Biblical Words*, 94–5, 100–2, with reference to the Bible. The 'lexical argument', which infers theological ideas from a merely lexical analysis, is firmly rejected by Barr, ibid. 110–12, 135–58.

[12] For a similar argument with reference to the Bible, see Momigliano, 'Time in Ancient Historiography', and my remarks thereon in Ch. 6.

or about its financial costs and benefits. Even if statements like 'time flies' or 'time is money' lack the sophistication of philosophical discourse, they are still statements about the nature of time which rabbinic sources, without being philosophical or scientific, could reasonably have made.

In the next few pages, I wish to show that the absence of this concept from early rabbinic literature cannot be treated as fortuitous, or due to incidental factors such as genre. Its absence in passages where it would have been quite reasonable to expect it confirms that the concept itself was alien to early rabbinic culture.

To begin with biblical exegesis, a number of biblical verses lend themselves particularly well to comments about the notion of time, and these comments are made in fact by rabbinic exegetes in the medieval period; but they are not anticipated in early rabbinic literature. Psalm 90: 4 states that 'a thousand years are like one fleeting day in your [God's] eyes', which might have suggested a relativistic perception of the flow of time. Ecclesiastes 3: 1–8 states that everything has its appointed time; verse 15 adds that 'what has been already is, and what is to be has already been'—a suggestive comment about the relationship between past, present, and future. Yet although these verses are frequently cited in early rabbinic literature, they are never used for the purpose of commenting on the concept of time or on its nature.[13] Other verses that might have been relevant to the concept of time, such as Job 9: 25–6 ('my days are swifter than a runner, they flee away'), are never cited at all.

An explicit reference to the dimension of time might also have been expected in the context of the recitation of the *Shema* ('Hear O Israel, the Lord our God the Lord is One', Deuteronomy 6: 4), a central piece of daily liturgy which the Mishnah refers to as the 'acceptance of the yoke of the kingdom of heaven' (Mishnah *Berakhot* 2: 2). Mishnaic law stipulates that the *Shema* must be recited with the *intention* of accepting this divine yoke. But according to an amoraic tradition cited in both Talmuds, it is sufficient, for this purpose, to have the intention of 'making him (i.e. God) king above, below, and in the four directions'—no more is required.[14] The *spatial* dimensions of God's kingdom are thus spelt out, but

---

[13] These verses are only used in early rabbinic literature for artificial exegetical purposes: e.g. Ps. 90: 4 serves as evidence that 'one day' in some other verse can really mean a millennium (e.g. *Genesis Rabbah* 8: 2 (p. 57 ed. Theodor and Albeck); BT *San.* 97a; also in early Christian sources, see 2 Pet. 3: 8). The notion of a flow of time is actually not explicit in these verses; Ps. 90: 4 only refers to the succession of years, which is really a process (more on this in Ch. 3). Abraham ibn Ezra (12th c.) interprets Eccles. 3: 15 as a vivid depiction of the flow of time, but, as we shall see in Ch. 4, the perception of time in medieval rabbinic sources is very different from that of early rabbinic literature.

[14] The text exists in a number of versions: JT *Ber.* 2: 1 (4a) reads: כדי שתמליכהו בשמים וארץ ובארבע רוחות העולם ('to make him king in heaven and earth and the four directions of the world'), and a similar version is found in BT *Ber.* 13b (Munich MS). But the Florence MS of BT *Ber.* reads: כיון דאמליכתא למעלה ולמטה ולארבע רוחות השמים ('since you made him king above and below and to the four directions of heaven'), with a similar version in the printed editions.

remarkably, no reference is made to his eternity or *temporal* dimension.[15] Considering the importance of the *Shema*, recited twice daily and the most fundamental affirmation of God's unity and existence, the omission of the notion of eternity must be treated as significant.

In general terms, the (spatial) omnipresence of God is given far more attention in early rabbinic sources than his (temporal) eternity. His omnipresence is suggested in statements that God fills the whole world,[16] God is everywhere,[17] and his Presence (*shekhinah*) is all over the world.[18] That God is the location of the world, and not the world his location, provides an explanation for one of God's names in rabbinic literature, *hamakom* ('The Place').[19] But the notion of God's eternity is far less commonly and less clearly expressed.[20] Liturgical phrases such as 'he was, he is, and he will be' or 'God was king, God is king, God will be king for ever', frequent in later medieval literature, hardly appear in early rabbinic

[15] For a similar expression of the six spatial dimensions of God's extension, see *Leviticus Rabbah* 28: 5 (p. 659 ed. Margaliot) and parallel in BT *Men.* 62a. A temporal dimension was added to the intention required for the *Shema* recitation, but only in the 13th c. by R. Jonah Gerondi in his *Sefer hayirah*, 31 (appended to id., *Sha'arei teshuvah*, 289). R. Jonah cites the passage from BT *Ber.* but adds to it the clause that God 'was, is, and will be' (היה הוה ויהיה).

[16] *Mekhilta derabi yishma'el*, 'Beshalah', *petiḥta* (p. 82 ed. Horovitz and Rabin), citing Isa. 6: 3 as proof-text; *Leviticus Rabbah* 4: 8 (p. 96 ed. Margaliot), citing Jer. 23: 24 as proof-text; BT *Ber.* 10a.

[17] *Mekhilta derabi yishma'el*, 'Pisha' 8, 10 (i. 67, 79 ed. Lauterbach; pp. 29, 35 ed. Horovitz and Rabin). The text varies tremendously from one recension to the next: some texts read בכל מקום רשותי ('my dominion is everywhere'), others read בכל מקום אני ('I am everywhere'); other texts, however, do not necessarily imply omnipresence (e.g. בכל מקום שהוא רשותי); see text and apparatus in both editions.

[18] BT *San.* 39a.

[19] הקב"ה מקומו של עולם, ואין העולם מקומו: *Genesis Rabbah* 68: 9 (pp. 777–8 ed. Theodor and Albeck). On the early rabbinic notion of God's omnipresence—which may be the underlying meaning of the name *hamakom*—see Urbach, *The Sages*, 66–79.

[20] God's eternity is suggested in a number of biblical sources: for example, Exod. 15: 18 (ה' ימלך לעולם ועד, 'the Lord will reign for ever'), Deut. 32: 40 (חי אנכי לעולם, 'I shall live for ever'), and Ps. 10: 16 (ה' מלך עולם ועד, 'the Lord is king for ever'); the extent to which the key term *le'olam*, commonly translated 'for ever', should be considered temporal is discussed in detail in Ch. 6. Rabbinic sources, however, do not take up this biblical theme or even refer to it in their exegesis of these verses: see e.g. *Mekhilta derabi yishma'el*, 'Shirah' 10 (p. 150 ed. Horovitz and Rabin), and BT *Eruv.* 54a. Only a few references to God's eternity can be found in early rabbinic literature, with the specific phrase חי וקים לעולם לעולמי עולמים ('alive and established for ever and ever'): *Mekhilta derabi yishma'el*, 'Bahodesh' 6 (p. 224 ed. Horovitz and Rabin), BT *Ber.* 28b, 32a (with reference to God's name), *Midrash tanhuma* (Buber), 'Shelah', appendix 2 (p. 39a), and *Midrash zuta*, 'Eikhah' A 21 (55) (p. 31a ed. Buber). For these references I am grateful to Hyam Maccoby, who points out, however, that in some of these passages the same phrase is applied to 'the generations' (presumably of mankind: *Mekhilta* ibid.) or to the eternal life forfeited by Adam (*Midrash tanhuma* ibid.); the same phrase is applied elsewhere, again, to the eternal life of Elijah (*Leviticus Rabbah* 27: 4). It could be argued, therefore, that this phrase does not cover eternity in the past, and has the meaning of 'immortality' or 'everlastingness in the future' rather than of eternity in a general sense. The concept of eternity is certainly more ambiguous in these sources than that of spatial omnipresence in the sources above mentioned. It is no surprise that Urbach makes no reference, in his monumental work on early rabbinic thought (*The Sages*), to the notion of God's eternity.

sources.[21] The absence of the notion of eternity in the context of the *Shema* recitation and elsewhere suggests, perhaps, rabbinic indifference towards the temporal
dimension.

An entirely different source, where explicit references to the temporal dimension are even more likely to have been expected, is the *Sefer yetsirah*, the 'Book of
Creation'. The identification of this late antique work as 'rabbinic' is moot; it is
certainly marginal to early rabbinic literature.[22] This, however, does not matter
much to my argument, since I shall anyway extend it, in due course, to non-
rabbinic sources and ancient Judaism in the widest sense (see Chapter 6). In the
Sefer yetsirah, which presents an esoteric description of the creation and structure
of the universe, time does not figure as one of the universe's dimensions. For
example, the seven double letters of the Hebrew alphabet are said to correspond
to the six directions (up, down, and the four cardinal points) and the centre; a
complete set of spatial directions is thus listed in this passage, but not the direction
or dimension of time.[23] Elsewhere (5: 1), similarly, the twelve simple letters of the
Hebrew alphabet are said to correspond to the twelve directions (equivalent to the
twelve edges of a cube), but there is no reference to the temporal dimension. In
another passage (1: 14), the ten *sefirot* of *belimah* (whatever this means) are identified as the four elements (the spirit or breath of God, air, water, and fire) and the six
directions (up, down, and the four cardinal points);[24] again, this elementary and
schematic description of the universe does not include the dimension of time.

The absence of the dimension of time, indeed of the very word 'time', in the whole
of *Sefer yetsirah* contrasts with the spatial directions that are repeatedly and emphatic-
ally spelt out. Whether these directions should be interpreted as 'spatial' in an
abstract and general sense, rather than, more concretely, as the three-dimensional
characteristics of specific objects and bodies, is a question of equal importance
that needs to be fully considered. There is at least a case for arguing that the concept of space as an infinite, empty extension is as absent from the *Sefer yetsirah* as

[21] The earliest attestation of the phrase היה הוה ויהיה ('he was, he is, and he will be') may be in the
anonymous but early *piyut*, 'Ha'oḥez beyad midat hamishpat', from the Additional Service of Rosh
Hashanah (but some versions read היה ויהי or היה ויהיה: see Zulay, *Yannai*, 336); it is then attested in
the anonymous medieval liturgical poem *Adon olam* (see also above, n. 15). The phrase ה' מלך,
ה' מלך, ה' ימלך לעולם ועד ('God was king, God is king, God will be king for ever') is first attested in
liturgy attributed to R. Eleazar Hakalir (7th c.?) in the *Kerovot* of the first day of Rosh Hashanah, and
in a passage of the *Heikhalot* (Schäfer, *Synopse zur Hekhalot-Literatur*, 62–3, paragraph 126). It then
appears in tractate *Soferim* 14: 4 (p. 267 ed. Higger), which is considered to be a slightly later work (8th
c.?—see Stemberger, *Introduction to the Talmud and Midrash*, 227–8).

[22] For a convenient summary of the debates surrounding the *Sefer yetsirah*, see Dan, '*Unique
Cherub*', 39–42; also Wasserstrom, 'Sefer Yeṣira'; Stemberger, *Introduction to the Talmud and Midrash*,
343–5. For a more detailed study, see Liebes, *Sefer yetsirah*.

[23] *Sefer yetsirah* 4: 3. All references are to the Warsaw edition (1884).

[24] The text reads: אלו עשר ספירות בלימה: רוח אלהים חיים, רוח מרוח, מים ממים, אש ממים, רום
ותחת, מזרח ומערב, צפון ודרום; see similarly 1: 13.

is the concept of time. Nevertheless, the concept of three-dimensionality is evident in its explicit references to the six directions, whereas equivalent temporal notions are conspicuously absent from these passages. For a work that is entirely concerned with the structure of the universe and its creation, this omission must surely be regarded as significant.

It has often been argued that the *Sefer yetsirah* is replete with implicit references to the space-time continuum. Whether time is implicit in this source, or in other parts of early rabbinic literature, is a question that I shall turn to in the next section. All that has been established so far—on the basis of early rabbinic biblical exegesis, the intention prescribed for the recitation of the *Shema*, and the structure of the universe depicted in *Sefer yetsirah*—is that *explicit* references to the concept of time are absent in rabbinic literature, even in passages where this concept would have been most naturally expected. Even if time is implicit in some sources—which, in the last resort, I shall show is incorrect—the lack of explicit statements about time is itself confirmation, in my view, that the concept of 'time in general' was fundamentally alien to early rabbinic culture.

IMPLICIT AWARENESS? THE TIME–CONTINUUM

The possibility of an implicit awareness of 'time in general' in early rabbinic literature deserves, nevertheless, a fair and thorough investigation. Timing, time-reckoning, calendars, chronology, and other important features of early rabbinic culture would appear, at first sight, to assume a notion of (and ideas about) the time-dimension; these will be examined in detail in the next two chapters. In the rest of this chapter, I shall assess whether implicit references can be found, in early rabbinic literature, to some of the most fundamental aspects of our modern concept of time: the time–continuum, and the passage (or flow) of time.

My argument in this and the next chapters will be, in a nutshell, that in all these contexts early rabbinic sources do not assume a notion of time, but only in fact a notion of *process* (more precisely, a notion of *many* processes). The distinction between process and time (the former, a concrete reality, the latter, a reified abstraction) has been explained in some detail in the previous chapter, and constitutes, in a sense, the whole argument of this book. Close analysis of the source-material and its cultural context will reveal that in apparently temporal contexts such as timing and time-reckoning, early rabbinic literature only assumes the existence of a range of activities, events, and processes, without ever resorting to the abstract synthesis of the time-dimension.

Let us first return to the *Sefer yetsirah*—since we have just been dealing with it. A number of its passages have been construed by medieval and modern scholars as implicitly referring to the dimension or continuum of time, as a basic structure of the created universe. For instance, *Sefer yetsirah* (1: 5) identifies the ten *sefirot* of *belimah* with the following five pairs of opposites: beginning–end, good–bad, up–down, east–west, and north–south.[25] The last three pairs are spatial, while the first, beginning–end, has often been interpreted as a reference to the dimension of time.[26]

This interpretation, however, is unwarranted on a number of counts. Firstly, 'beginning' and 'end' are not directions (like up–down, east–west, and north–south) but limits; limits are incompatible with the notion of an infinite time-continuum. This interpretation necessarily assumes—but without any good evidence—that the dimension of time is finite. Secondly, the terms used in this passage for 'beginning' and 'end', *reshit* and *aḥarit*, are always used in Hebrew in the sense of 'beginning (or end) of something'; the usage of *reshit* and *aḥarit* in the absolute, as 'beginning' and 'end' *per se*, is completely unattested.[27] As the beginning (or end) of specific things, *reshit* and *aḥarit* refer primarily to the limits of individual *processes*. 'Beginning' and 'end' of processes are not necessarily temporal notions, and certainly do not imply or necessitate the existence of a time-continuum (as I have argued in the Introduction). There is no good reason to interpret this passage as a reference to the concept of time. *Reshit* and *aḥarit* may simply represent, in a schematic or generic way, the individual processes that are constituents of the created universe; alternatively, perhaps more likely, these terms represent the limits of the universe as a whole, its beginning (creation) and its end (destruction). But there is no justification for reading into this passage an abstract or reified notion of the time-dimension— particularly as this notion is not explicit elsewhere in the *Sefer yetsirah*.

A similar analysis applies to the term *shanah* ('year'), which appears in what is often called the second part of *Sefer yetsirah*. A systematic correlation is drawn there between year, world, and person (*shanah, olam, nefesh*): the 'year', with its twelve months and the seven days of the week, corresponds to the 'world', with its twelve zodiacal constellations and the seven planets, as well as to various parts or organs of the 'person'; all these, in turn, are correlated with the different letters of the Hebrew alphabet.[28] The notion of 'year' (*shanah*) has widely been taken as a metaphorical reference to time.[29] Liebes defends this interpretation on the basis

---

[25] Each of these terms is preceded with the word *omek*, hence 'depth of beginning, depth of end, etc.'.

[26] See Gruenwald, 'Some Critical Notes', 495; Dan, *'Unique Cherub'*, 44; Liebes, *Sefer yetsirah*, 23–4 (comparing it with Einstein's concept of the fourth dimension!).

[27] The only possible exception, which troubled Jewish medieval commentators, is Gen. 1: 1; but *Bereshit* presumably means there 'at the beginning (of the Creation)'. See further Ch. 6.

[28] *Sefer yetsirah* 3: 3–8, 4: 4–12, 5: 2, 6: 1–2.

[29] e.g. Dan, *'Unique Cherub'*, 43; Liebes, *Sefer yetsirah*, 18–21, 145, 192, 207, 243. See also S. C. Goldman, 'Beginnings and Endings', 64, 68, ascribing to the *Sefer yetsirah* the notion that time is a 'dynamic principle of nature, ordering the Sphere of Being', and 'the *locus* of dynamism'. This interpretation reflects the views of R. Judah Halevi (12th c.) in his *Sefer kuzari* (4: 25), which Goldman cites, but finds no support in the text of the *Sefer yetsirah* itself. R. Judah Halevi may be the first to have interpreted *shanah* there as meaning 'time'.

of a lengthy passage of *Sefer yetsirah* (4: 4–12), where *shanah* does not refer to
the annual period of twelve months (as it does in *Sefer yetsirah* 5: 2), but only to the
seven-day week: for this passage states repeatedly that there are 'seven days in
the year (*shanah*)', which actually means, seven days in the week. Liebes infers that
the term *shanah* must have a wider meaning than 'year', since sometimes it can also
mean 'week'. Since the only common denominator, in his view, between 'year' and
'week' is time, it must follow that *shanah* means 'time' in general.[30]

Liebes overlooks yet another use of the term *shanah* in the *Sefer yetsirah*: its subdivision, in 3: 4-8, into the three seasons called 'hot', 'cold', and 'temperate'.[31]
These are clearly not units of time, but only climatic seasons. The common
denominator between these seasons and the units of week and year cannot be the
abstract notion of 'time'. It is more appropriate, in fact, to suggest 'process' as the
common denominator between them. As will become clearer in Chapters 2–3,
years, months, weeks, and days are not really units of pure time, but only calendrical categories that represent the duration or length of either astronomical and
seasonal processes (years, months, days), or socially sanctioned cycles of human
activity (weeks). Years, weeks, and the three seasons all have in common that they
are well-known, standard processes that are cyclically recurring. This may explain
why elsewhere (6: 1–2), *shanah* is said to be governed by a cycle (*galgal*). There is
thus no reason to invest the term *shanah* with the concept of 'pure time'—for
which, to emphasize, there is no explicit evidence throughout the *Sefer yetsirah*.
The concept of 'year' or *shanah* seems only to refer to standard cyclical processes,
with reference to which human activities can be correlated, synchronized, or
measured.

Many have been tempted to interpret the triad 'year–world–person' as a symbolic representation of the interrelated dimensions of time ('year'), space ('world'),
and man or the subjective self ('person'),[32] all three subsumed by a transcendent
linguistic scheme (the alphabet). However, this is an inappropriate imposition of
modern categories on an ancient source. There is no indication that 'person'
(*nefesh*) represents subjectivity, the 'self', or man in general. 'Person' refers only to
the physical human being, with all his or her parts and organs, which as a microcosm are structurally analogous to the parts of the wider universe. 'World' (*olam*),
likewise, does not represent the general dimensions of space: it refers specifically to

---

[30] Liebes, *Sefer yetsirah*, 270 n. 15. Liebes suggests further that the *Sefer yetsirah* may have been
influenced by the Greek usage of the term *chronos* ('time') in the sense of 'year', which is attested in the
Hellenistic period. This suggestion is interesting, not least because this usage of *chronos* is found in a
Jewish source, *Testament of Judah* 7: 10. But whether this would have influenced the *reverse* usage of
shanah in the sense of 'time' is questionable.

[31] In Hebrew רויה, קור, חום. My translation of רויה as 'temperate' follows Liebes, *Sefer yetsirah*,
270 n. 19; but for an alternative translation, see ibid. 239.

[32] See ibid. 18–21, 145: 'year, world, and person' mean 'time, space, and man'.

the constellations and planets of the sky—spatial objects, perhaps, but certainly not the concept of space itself. The correspondence between these heavenly objects and human body parts does not represent the interface between man (or the subjective self) and the dimensions of space, but rather, the cosmic harmony that is assumed to exist between the different parts of the heavenly macrocosm and human microcosm. A similar interpretation applies to 'year' (*shanah*). This term and its constituents (twelve months, seven days, and three seasons) are not components of the abstract notion of time: as stated above, they are only process-related categories. 'World', 'year', and 'person' do not represent abstract concepts even symbolically: they are only the principal elements of the concrete universe, which correspond to each other, in each of their parts, in harmony.

Implicit references to the time-continuum have often been read into other talmudic and midrashic passages that similarly deal with the structure of the world and its creation. There again, I would argue, they are totally inconclusive. Mishnah *Ḥagigah* 2: 1 discusses whether it is permitted to investigate the 'work of Creation' (*ma'aseh bereshit*), and concludes that whoever reflects on the following four questions would be 'better not to have been born': מה למעלה, מה למטה, מה לפנים ומה לאחור . These four questions appear to relate to the outer confines of the universe, but their exact translation is ambiguous. They could be translated either in spatial terms as 'what is above, what is below, what is in front, and is behind', or in both spatial and temporal terms, as 'what is above, what is below, what is before and what is after'.[33] But according to the parallel text in the Tosefta, it is clearly the latter, spatial and temporal meaning that is intended, as it reads: מה למעלה, מה למטה, ומה היה, ומה עתיד להיות—'what is above, what is below, what has been, and what is to be'.[34]

At first sight, therefore, the phrase as a whole may be interpreted as an implicit reference to the space-time continuum. Yet 'what has been and was is to be' cannot be treated as meaning the *continuous* past and *continuous* future, and thus the totality of the time-continuum: for it would be absurd to suggest that the Tosefta prohibits studying the past in general. Indeed, the Tosefta itself explains in the same passage that it is only forbidden to ponder on what existed before the creation

---

[33] Danby, *Mishnah*, 213, opts for the latter: 'What is above? What is beneath? What was before time? And what will be hereafter?'

[34] Tosefta *Ḥag.* 2: 7 (p. 234). In some recensions (the *editio princeps* and MS Vienna) this wording only appears at the end of the passage, and functions clearly as an explanation of the wording of the Mishnah. The temporal interpretation is also assumed in BT *Ḥag.* 16a (see below, n. 36). Nevertheless, the interpretation of the Mishnah remains contentious among medieval commentators. Rashi (on the Mishnah in BT *Ḥag.* 11b) opts for the spatial interpretation, while some Tosafot (interpolated in Rashi's commentary, ibid.) opt for the temporal, and other Tosafot (ibid. s.v. *yakhol*) are undecided. See Lieberman, *Tosefta kifeshutah*, v. 1295–6, with parallels in ancient Near Eastern sources where the phrase is meant in a purely spatial sense. There are considerable recensional variations in this passage of Tosefta, but they do not affect its general interpretation.

of the world; whereas from the creation of Adam onwards, any pondering is permitted. Thus 'what has been' refers specifically to what was before the creation;[35] and by analogy, we may assume that 'what is to be' means after the world will cease to exist. These phrases clearly refer, therefore, to what lies *beyond the limits* of the created universe—beyond the 'beginning' and 'end' of *Sefer yetsirah* 1: 5 (see above)—but not to the continuum of time as a whole.

It is also worth noting that the Babylonian Talmud argues, in this context, that the spatial limits of the universe, the 'extremities of the sky', are identical with its temporal limits, 'when it was created' (both paraphrases of Deuteronomy 4: 32), so that a statement of the former makes a statement of the latter redundant.[36] The meaning of this assumption is that what lies (today) beyond the extremities of the sky is identical with what existed before the world was created. Thus according to the Babylonian Talmud, the temporality of the mishnaic phrase 'what is before and what is after' is not intrinsically important: for the phrase designates something that also exists today, beyond the extremities of the sky. All the Mishnah means to prohibit is the study of what lies *beyond the scope* of our universe; whether this means beyond its space or beyond its time is not important, as indeed the Talmud does not distinguish, in this context, between them.[37]

Further in this passage, the Babylonian Talmud lists the ten things that were created on the first day: heaven and earth, *tohu* and *bohu*, light and darkness, wind and water, the 'measure of day' and the 'measure of night' (*midat yom umidat lailah*).[38] The latter has often been interpreted as meaning the creation of time itself.[39] However, all this passage refers to is the creation of a *measure* of time, or to be more precise, the measure of two *processes*: day and night. It should be noted, furthermore, that this list is only an exegetical derivation from the first verses of Genesis (1: 1–5), which have nothing to say about the dimension of time or its creation, just as, indeed, they have nothing to say about the dimensions of space *per se*.[40]

A similar interpretation applies to *Genesis Rabbah* 3: 7,[41] according to which the 'order of times' (*seder zemanim*) had existed before the Creation: 'Rabbi Judah ben

---

[35]   This interpretation is also explicit in JT *Ḥag.* 2: 1 (77c), and implicit in *Genesis Rabbah* 1: 10 (pp. 8–9 ed. Theodor and Albeck).

[36]   BT *Ḥag.* 12a: השתא דנפקא ליה מ"למקצה השמים ועד קצה השמים", "למן היום אשר ברא אלהים אדם על הארץ" למה לי? The Talmud presumably interprets the mishnaic questions מה לפנים ומה לאחור in a temporal sense (i.e. 'what is before and what is after'), as explicitly later in BT *Ḥag.* 16a.

[37]   There is no need, however, to interpret this passage of the Talmud as indicative of a 'spatialization' of time, or of some conceptual confusion between time and space: for the dimensions of time and space are not the object of any discussion here. All that is discussed are the limits of the knowable universe.   [38]   BT *Ḥag.* 12a; also in *Pirkei derabi eli'ezer* 3.

[39]   Urbach, *The Sages*, 210–11; see also Rudavsky, *Time Matters*, 7.

[40]   *Pace* Sasson, 'Time . . . to Begin', 191–2, on which see discussion below, Ch. 6.

[41]   p. 23 ed. Theodor and Albeck.

Rabbi Simon said: "Let there be evening" is not written here, but "And there was evening" (Genesis 1: 5)—hence we know that an order of times existed before this.' Although this was understood by medieval philosophers as meaning that time pre-existed Creation and was not itself created,[42] all this passage really refers to is the division of day and night, or more specifically, the pre-existence of 'evening'. Day, night, and evening—i.e. the regular succession of light and darkness—are processes which do not necessarily imply the abstract notion of 'time'.

A passage of Targum may imply the notion of a space-time continuum, although on balance, I would also treat this passage as inconclusive. The Targum (*Targum Jonathan*) on Isaiah 6: 3 ('Holy, holy, holy the Lord of Hosts') appears to ascribe omnipresence and eternity to God in a single statement, and thus to predicate, by implication, the notion of a space-time continuum. The three 'holies' are rendered by the Targum as follows:

ומקבלין דין מן דין ואמרין: קדיש בשמי מרומא עילאה בית שכינתיה, קדיש על ארעא עובד גבורתיה, קדיש לעלם ולעלמי עלמיא ה׳ צבאות[43]

And they were crying one to another[44] and saying: holy in the high heavens above, the house of his *shekhinah*, holy on earth, the work of his might, holy for ever and ever and ever the Lord of Hosts.

The text of this passage is problematic, and must be scrutinized before attempting any interpretation. Almost all the manuscripts,[45] and so the *Sidur* of R. Sa'adiah Gaon,[46] read in the last clause: קדיש בעלם עלמיא. The text of the printed editions I have cited above (קדיש לעלם ולעלמי עלמיא) is first attested in a

---

[42] Maimonides, *Guide of the Perplexed*, 2: 30; Hasdai Crescas, *Or adonai*, 1: 2: 11 (proposition 15). The same assumption is made by Urbach, *The Sages*, 210–11.

[43] So according to first printed editions (D. Bomberg, Venice, 1515–17 and 1524–5). I am relying on the critical editions of Sperber, *Bible in Aramaic*, 12–13, and Stenning, *Targum of Isaiah*, 20–1, the latter with English translation. I am grateful to Jonathan Webber for pointing out this passage to me, and to Alberdina Houtman for her assistance with it.

[44] So according to Stenning (*Targum of Isaiah*, 20–1) and Chilton (*Isaiah Targum*, 14), but the word *min* does not readily translate as 'to'. Houtman suggests instead: 'and they were taking from one another' (pers. comm.), but the meaning of this remains unclear. Nevertheless, this translation was favoured by 11th-c. Franco-German commentators (Rashi on Isa. 6: 3, and R. Meir b. Isaac, *Akdamut*, letter *yod*; see also the *kedushah* of the *yotser*, in Hurwitz, *Mahzor vitry*, 65), who interpreted this phrase as meaning that the angels receive a signal from one another so as to chant the three 'holies' in unison.

[45] i.e. all the MSS used by Sperber, *Bible in Aramaic* (for this passage six in all), and all those used by Stenning, *Targum of Isaiah* (with eight additional MSS). The only exception is the manuscript cited by Stenning as 'A Nuremberg ms.', which reads as in the printed editions. This manuscript is the Codex Solger, dated from 1291 CE, which Houtman ('Targum Isaiah') argues was the basis of the first printed editions. It is thus no surprise to find that the reading of the printed editions, otherwise alien to the MS tradition, is attested in this single MS. Note also the unique reading of Paris, Bibliothèque Nationale de France, MS hébreu 75, which seems to conflate the other two: בעלם ולעלמי עלמיא.

[46] Davidson et al., *Sidur rav sa'adiah gaon*, 40; also in Abudarham (see below).

secondary liturgical source of the early twelfth century, the *Mahzor vitry*.[47] It then appears in the early-thirteenth-century commentary on Isaiah by R. David Kimhi (Radak).[48] Aburdarham (fourteenth century) refers to it as the popular liturgical reading, but discards it as erroneous and favours the reading of R. Sa'adiah, which he also attributes to the *seder* of R. Amram.[49] There is a strong likelihood, indeed, that the latter reading is more authentic, since it is the earliest and attested in almost all the manuscripts.[50]

If we accept קדיש בעלם עלמיא as the correct reading, what is the meaning of this phrase? Stenning translates it as 'holy for endless ages', thus ascribing it much the same meaning as the printed version (קדיש לעלם ולעלמי עלמיא).[51] This interpretation is presumably based on Targum Isaiah 65: 18, where the same phrase (בעלם עלמיא, *be'alam alemaya*) appears as a translation of the Hebrew *adei ad* (so according to all manuscripts and editions). Since the Hebrew *adei ad* clearly means 'for ever', it is difficult to invest its targumic rendering with any other interpretation.[52] Thus, inasmuch as *be'alam alemaya* means 'for ever' in Targum Isaiah 65: 18, it may arguably mean the same in Targum Isaiah 6: 3.

However, in Targum literature the term *be'alam* or *be'alema* (i.e. עלם or עלמא with the preposition -ב) does not mean 'for ever', but always 'in the world'.[53] This provides some justification for Abudarham's interpretation of Targum Isaiah 6: 3 (which he reads, as noted above: קדיש בעלם עלמיא) as 'holy in the world of worlds', and as referring to God's omnipresence in the transcendent world of the

---

[47] Hurwitz, *Mahzor vitry*, 74, in the ובא לציון prayer.

[48] Kimhi on Isa. 6: 3, interpreting this clause as a reference to God's eternity.

[49] *Sefer Abudarham* (Warsaw, 1878), p. 34*a*. An anonymous Ashkenazi prayer-book, perhaps from the same period, also favours the latter reading (R. Sa'adiah's) and rejects the former as erroneous: Hershler, *Sidur rabenu shelomoh*, 123.

[50] R. Sa'adiah is from the early 10th c. CE. It is also easy to explain how the erroneous reading לעלם ולעלמי עלמיא could have originated in the liturgy: by assimilation with Targum Onkelos to Exod. 15: 18 (ה' מלכותיה קאים לעלמא ולעלמי עלמיא), which is cited in the same prayer (ובא לציון) in proximity. Note that in the *Mahzor vitry* (ibid.), the version cited as the Targum of Exod. 15: 8 is ה' מלכותה קאים לעלם ולעלמי עלמיא, exactly the same wording as the *Mahzor*'s version of Targum Isa. 6: 3. This erroneous reading would then have been transferred from liturgical works (such as the *Mahzor*) to the Codex Solger, by the end of the 13th c.

[51] Chilton similarly translates 'holy in eternity' (*Isaiah Targum*, 14–15 and n.), but it is unclear which text he is using.

[52] Stenning himself, however, inconsistently translates Targum Isa. 65: 18 as 'in the world of worlds which I create' (*Targum of Isaiah*, 216). Does this suggest that he changed his mind?

[53] See Targum Onkelos Gen. 3: 22, Deut. 32: 12; Targum (1) Esther 3: 1; Targum Eccles. 1: 8–9; but Targum Prov. 10: 25 is possibly ambiguous. The term *be'alma* is very common, always in the sense of 'in the world', in the Targum Neofiti (Kaufman and Sokoloff, *Concordance to Targum Neofiti*, 1098–9). The term *olam* without the preposition *be-* is often found in Targum in the sense of 'world': Targum Onkelos Num. 23: 9; Targum 2 Sam. 23: 1, 5, and 7; Targum Ezek. 1: 14; Targum Ps. 89: 3, etc. On the ambiguous meaning of *olam* in early rabbinic Hebrew and Aramaic, meaning both 'for ever' and 'world', see Ch. 4. The Hebrew *be'olam* (with the preposition *be-*) is not attested in the Bible.

angels.[54] A similar interpretation is also attested in an undated medieval midrashic work.[55] The translation 'holy in the world of worlds' is certainly plausible in our passage: the verse as a whole, in its targumic rendering, would mean that God is holy in the high heavens, on the earth, and in the 'world of worlds', possibly some transcendent realm. All three 'holies' would thus be spatial, as is indeed the continuation of the Hebrew verse: 'his glory fills the whole earth'.[56]

But even if we accept Stenning's translation, or (for argument's sake) the textual reading of the printed editions, the term le'alam (לעלם) in the sense of 'for ever' would not imply the notion of a time-continuum. The meaning of this term will be discussed in detail in Chapter 6, where it will be shown that alam/olam does not express the temporal notion of 'eternity', but rather the event-related notion of 'permanence' (e.g. God is permanently holy). Thus on any interpretation, this Targum passage cannot be taken to imply the existence of a space-time continuum.

Space and time are often mentioned together in rabbinic sources, but only as co-ordinates of events, not as self-standing 'dimensions' or continua. Thus when the Mishnah states, in the context of the invalidation of sacrifices, 'if the thought of time [zeman] precedes thought of place [makom]' (Mishnah Zevaḥim 2: 5), it means time and place in a purely punctual sense (hence the translation 'place' rather than 'space'). The same applies to the questions asked during the interrogation of witnesses: 'In which sabbatical cycle? In which year? In which month? In which [day] of the month? In which day [of the week]? At what hour [sha'ah]? In which place [makom]?' (Mishnah Sanhedrin 5: 1). And again, in an ethical teaching: 'Despise no man, and dismiss no thing, for there is not a man that has not his hour [sha'ah], and there is not a thing that has not its place [makom]' (Avot 4: 3).[57] Time and place, in all these passages, function only as the punctual co-ordinates of processes or events, without any indication of belonging themselves to the continuous dimensions of 'pure' space and time. The juxtaposition of space and time in a single passage does not imply our concept of the space-time continuum.

IMPLICIT REFERENCES? THE PASSAGE OF TIME

The experience of the passage (or 'flow') of time is fundamental to our modern world-view. This experience is largely subjective and subject-dependent, and can

---

[54] Sefer Abudarham, loc. cit.

[55] J. D. Eisenstein, Otsar Midrashim (New York, 1956; orig. pub. 1915), 306 (s.v. מעין חכמה): וזה פירושו: קדוש בכל עולמים.

[56] Houtman favours this interpretation, and argues further that a similar interpretation should be applied to Targum Isa. 65: 18, where בעלם עלמיא is likely to refer to the 'world-to-come', thus: 'They will rejoice in the world-to-come which I create' (pers. comm.).

[57] The term 'hour' (sha'ah) could be translated here as 'time', but only in the punctual sense of 'right time'.

thus lead to the perception that the flow of time is relative. The passage of time is also associated with the experience of age and of one's 'past'. Each of these themes will be examined, in turn, in this final section. An attempt will be made to find references to these themes in early rabbinic sources; it will be shown, however, that even implicitly these themes cannot be found.

The Babylonian Talmud asks why Deuteronomy 4: 26 threatens 'speedy' punishment for the sin of idolatry, whereas this punishment, the destruction of the First Temple, was actually delayed by 852 years. It answers that 'speedy [*meherah*] for the Lord of the universe is 852 [years]' (BT *Gitin* 88a–b, BT *Sanhedrin* 38a). At first sight, this may suggest the relativity of the flow of time: what appears to us a long period is, to God, only very short.

However, this passage is not referring to time, but rather to *speed*. Speed is primarily an attribute of movement, i.e. activity and process, but not of the passage of time. The period of 852 years need not be interpreted as a 'chunk' of time: it can be cogently interpreted in this passage as a process, a 'chunk' of *history*. The Talmud means that the cycles of seasons, historical processes, and human events that constituted this 852-year period occurred speedily from God's perspective—presumably, because of their relative triviality. This passage is clearly expressing a notion of relativity, but not the relativity of time *per se*.

The relativity of time is also implicit, at first sight, in a midrashic comment on a list of biblical verses where the phrase 'many days' is used. The Midrash states: 'Were they really "many days"? (No), but because they were days of affliction, Scripture calls them "many"'.[58] This seems to suggest that when a person is afflicted, time appears, subjectively, to be flowing more slowly; this passage would thus constitute an implicit reflection on the passage of time and its relativity.[59]

However, the notion of time is not exactly the subject of this passage. All it suggests is that affliction generates the feeling that a greater *number of days* have passed. This does not mean that time flows more slowly, but only that one loses count of how many days have gone by. Thus, this passage makes perfect sense in process-related terms, without any conception of a continuous flow of time *per se*.

The passage of time is often associated with the experience of age. Age is usually measured, in the ancient as well as in the modern world, by the number of years of

[58] *Leviticus Rabbah* 19: 5 (pp. 429–30 ed. Margaliot). The verses, in order of appearance in this passage, are 2 Chron. 15: 3, 1 Kgs. 18: 1, Exod. 2: 23, Esther 1: 4, and Lev. 15: 25. See also parallels in *Esther Rabbah* 2: 2, *Tanhuma*, 'Metsora' 6, *Tanhuma* (Buber), 'Metsora' 14 (p. 266). A similar idea, in reverse, is implied in the biblical text itself in Gen. 29: 20: because Jacob loved Rachel, the days spent working for her appeared to be few. Early rabbinic literature, unfortunately, does not appear to comment on this verse (see Kasher, *Torah shelemah*, p. 1169, no. 63, cited from R. Tuviah b. Eliezer (12th c.), *Midrash lekah tov*, on Exod. 2: 23).

[59] So is the interpretation of Kasher, 'Concept of Time'. This rather uncritical article aims to show how the early rabbis anticipated modern views of time.

a person's life. This would suggest that age is time-related, and represents in fact the amount of time a person has lived. The concept of age in early rabbinic literature may thus have something to reveal, if only implicitly, about the experience of time and its passage.[60]

On further investigation, however, it becomes evident that the concept of time *per se* is not essential to the experience of age. Even in modern society, age is often experienced as the extent to which a person has physiologically, psychologically, and socially matured; it is thus a process, rather than an abstract measure of time. The number of a person's years, by which age is traditionally measured, does not indicate the amount of time that has passed since birth, as much as the degree to which the person has 'aged' or become 'older'.[61]

This finds expression in a statement attributed to R. Eleazar b. Azariah, which is cited in the Mishnah and hence in the Passover Haggadah: 'I am like 70 years old' (*harei ani keven shivim shanah*).[62] The qualifying 'like' (*ke-*) probably means that this number was only approximate, as R. Eleazar b. Azariah was himself unsure about his age. Beyond childhood, indeed, age was largely irrelevant in ancient Jewish life,[63] as well as in the ancient world as a whole; this is why knowledge of the age of adults was usually imprecise.[64] However, the Babylonian Talmud understood this statement to mean that R. Eleazar b. Azariah was not really anything near the age of 70—he was actually 18—but that his recent appointment as 'head of the academy', together with a timely, miraculous growth of white hair, had made him feel *as though* he were 70.[65] That he was actually as young as 18 may be dismissed as talmudic exaggeration. But where I think we may trust the Talmud is in the suggestion that a statement of one's age (e.g. '70') does not necessarily represent the actual number of years lived, but rather the extent to which one has aged, in terms of physical appearance as well as in terms of social

---

[60] There is no biblical or rabbinic Hebrew word for 'age'. The word *gil*, later used in the sense of 'age', appears once in the Bible (in Dan. 1: 10) and a few times in rabbinic literature (*Ruth Rabbah* 2: 8 (on Ruth 1: 3), BT *Yev.* 120a, BT *Ned.* 39b, BT *BM* 30b) but only in the sense of 'generation' or (better) 'peer-group'.   [61] See Elias, *Time*, 69.

[62] Mishnah *Ber.* 1: 5; the same expression is attributed to R. Joshua in *Mekhilta*, 'Bo' 16 (p. 59 ed. Horovitz and Rabin). These are among the rare instances in rabbinic literature where someone states his own age. For instances in the Bible, see below, n. 64.

[63] The concept of age is halakhically important in rabbinic literature, but not much beyond the age of 20: see e.g. BT *Ket.* 39a (the age of puberty and adulthood) and BT *Kid.* 29b–30a (the age of marriage). *Avot* 5: 21, however, presents a typology of ages ranging from 5 to 100.

[64] Age-rounding is a common phenomenon in ancient funerary inscriptions, among Jews as well as non-Jews, and is likely, as in this passage, to reflect ignorance of one's precise age: see van der Horst, *Ancient Jewish Epitaphs*, 73–84. For age-rounding in the Bible (in direct speech), see Gen. 17: 17, 47: 9, Deut. 31: 2, 2 Sam. 19: 36; for another example of age-rounding in rabbinic sources, see *Genesis Rabbah* 38: 13 (p. 362 ed. Theodor and Albeck), expanded in *Song of Songs Rabbah* 2: 16 (on 2: 5).

[65] BT *Ber.* 28a; the parallel in JT *Ber.* 4: 1 (7d), according to which he was only 16, does not refer to Mishnah *Ber.* 1: 5. In various recensions of this tradition, his actual age varies between 16, 17, and 18.

standing.[66] This is because age is not the experience of the passage of time, but rather of a process.

The passage of time, finally, is also often associated with the experience of the 'past'. It is often assumed that conceptions of the past have something to reveal, if only implicitly, about time and the experience of its flow. However, as I have argued in the Introduction, the notion of 'past' is not necessarily temporal: in non-modern societies, it is commonly interpreted as a process or an aspect, in the sense of 'that which is finished and/or complete'. This conception of the past is also apparent in early rabbinic culture. Words for 'past' and 'future' exist in early rab-binic Hebrew (though not as grammatical categories, but only in a historical sense): most prominently, *avar* and *atid*.[67] But the usage and meaning of these terms sug-gests that they are process-linked rather than temporal. In a phrase like 'one gives thanks for the past (*leshe'avar*) and prays for the future (*le'atid lavo*)',[68] the term *leshe'avar* literally means 'that which has passed' (cf. the English term 'past'), and *le'atid lavo*, often used elsewhere for the distant, eschatological future, literally means here 'that which is ready to come'.[69] Other recensions of this mishnaic phrase, attested in its citation in the Babylonian Talmud (*Berakhot* 54a), include *le'atid* (on its own), 'that which is ready', and *mah she'atid liheyot*, 'that which is ready to be'.[70] The meaning of these expressions is hardly temporal: they only refer to the aspect of something that is 'yet to be'. The same applies to another early rab-binic term for the future, *hanolad*, literally 'that which will be (or: is to be) born'.[71] 'Past' and 'future' are thus not positions along an abstract, subjective time-line, but rather concrete processes and events that are either complete or 'ready' to be.

The process-related nature of past, present, and future in early rabbinic culture is reflected, to some extent, in its verbal system. Fuzziness of tense is notorious in biblical Hebrew (on which see Chapter 6), but it is also attested, albeit to a lesser extent, in early rabbinic Hebrew. In early rabbinic Hebrew, the perfect is generally used for the past, but the active participle is used *both* for the present and the

---

[66] This is the interpretation suggested by Maimonides in his commentary on the Mishnah.

[67] *Avar* and *atid*. I have not been able to identify a term for 'present'. The term *hoveh*, which is used in modern Hebrew for 'present', means 'reality' or 'the normal situation' in early rabbinic Hebrew (as in Mishnah *BK* 5: 7), but not the general, temporal concept of 'present'.

[68] Mishnah *Ber.* 9: 4: *noten hoda'ah leshe'avar, vetso'ek le'atid lavo*. For another example, see Mishnah *Ketubot* 9: 6.

[69] I am ignoring in these translations the preposition *le-*, which means 'for'. Although the term *atid* has come to mean just 'future' in modern Hebrew, in the early rabbinic period it had not lost its origi-nal, biblical meaning of 'ready' (attested in Esther 3: 14, 8: 13). The Jerusalem Talmud assumes that *atid* means 'ready', which is why it exclaims, in relation to a tannaitic interpretation of the biblical term עתי ('timely', Lev. 16: 21): 'is *atid* not the same thing as *mezuman* [appointed]?' (JT *Yoma* 6: 3, 43c).

[70] The former in the Soncino and Venice editions of the Babylonian Talmud, the latter (על מה שעתיד להיות) in the Munich MS: Sacks, *Mishnah zera'im*, 86 (Hebrew pagination).

[71] e.g. *Avot* 2: 9. The future tense ('will be born') is probably a more appropriate translation of *hanolad* than the present tense ('is born').

future; the imperfect is primarily used as a modal subjunctive, sometimes, but not necessarily, in the future. These usages, it should be noted, are not always entirely consistent.[72] In addition, some periphrastic constructions such as *atid l-* or *sofo l-* (+ infinitive) can be used to express the future, but the semantic meaning of these phrases is, again, significant: *atid l-* means 'he/it is ready to', and *sofo l-* means 'his/its end is to' (i.e. he/it is destined to). Thus in semantic terms, these phrases express process and aspect rather than time or tense.[73]

Past and future in the form of history and eschatology are of no small importance to the early rabbinic world-view[74]—even if there are no specific words 'history' or 'eschatology' in the early rabbinic lexicon. History and eschatology, however, are events and processes, not segments of pure time. The concept of past and future as segments of a subjective time-line is only a modern abstraction, derived from the general abstraction of time, that has little place in early rabbinic culture.[75] Rabbinic literature is only concerned with processes, from which the notion of time, even implicit, cannot be cogently inferred.

---

[72] Note that in BT *Ber.* 52*b*, Babylonian *amora'im* entertain the possibility of using the active participle (בורא) for the future as well as for the past.

[73] For *atid* in a subjunctive sense, see Targum Onkelos Genesis 4: 10. Other periphrastic constructions specific to mishnaic Hebrew include היה + participle. See Sharvit, 'Tenses'; Kutscher, *History of the Hebrew Language*, 131–2; Sáenz-Badillo, *History of the Hebrew Language*, 193–5; Pérez Fernández, *Introductory Grammar*, 107–43; Azor, *Syntax*, 1–27. These works supersede Segal, *Grammar of Mishnaic Hebrew*, 150–65, who simplistically assumed that perfect was used for the past, imperfect for the future, and participle for the present. I am grateful to Lewis Glinert and Shimon Sharvit for their assistance.

[74] See e.g. Yerushalmi, *Zakhor*, ch. 1.

[75] The significance of early rabbinic history, chronology, and eschatology will be studied in more detail in Ch. 3.

TWO

Timing and Time-Reckoning

TIMING IN RITUAL HALAKHAH

THE thesis outlined in the previous chapter, that early rabbinic culture did not conceive of time as a category or entity in itself, appears to run counter to the importance accorded in ritual halakhah (law) to timing, time-reckoning, and hence, one would assume, to time itself. At first sight, it would seem that there is no timing without time, and hence, that rabbinic timing should reveal an underlying concept of the time-dimension.

On closer examination, however, it will turn out that early rabbinic sources conceive of timing only with reference to concrete processes, such as natural phenomena and human activity. Timing can thus be defined as the *co-ordination* of activities and events; this definition is functional and cogent without any notion of 'pure' time or of the dimension of time. I shall argue, therefore, that even at an implicit level it is difficult, and indeed inappropriate, to infer ideas about 'time' from this source-material.

The proper timing of rituals is a central theme of mishnaic and subsequent rabbinic law, arguably to the point of an obsession.[1] It is important to dwell on this observation, because even if it can be shown, as I shall, that timing has little to do with the 'dimension of time', it will remain a fact of inherent significance that timing was central to early rabbinic society and culture. The timing of human activities—in this case, mainly ritual—would have been essential for the functional as well as the conceptual structuration of social interaction and social life. The early rabbinic practice of timing thus deserves to be studied as a social process or procedure, even if it will prove irrelevant to the concept of time itself.

Timing is so important to the Mishnah that it begins, perhaps programmatically, with this very theme: at what times in the evening and in the morning should the *Shema* be recited (Mishnah *Berakhot* 1: 1–2).[2] The same concern occurs again and

---

[1] Concern with proper timing is not particular to rabbinic Judaism, but rabbinic sources are considerably more informative than any other ancient Jewish source. This is why this chapter focuses entirely on early rabbinic literature. Among Qumran sources, see CD 10: 15–16 (the Damascus Document), where the commencement of the sabbath is defined according to the position of the sun's disc.　　　　　　　　　　　　　　　　　　　　　　　　　[2] On the *Shema*, see above, Ch. 1.

again, throughout the tractates of the Mishnah. Timing regulates the performance of prayer, the observance of the sabbath and festivals, and last but not least, the complex procedures of sacrifice. If a sacrifice is offered before its proper time, it can have the status of *meḥusar zeman* (literally, 'lacking time': Mishnah *Zevaḥim* 14: 3); if it is performed with an intention not to abide by its time limits, it has the status of *ḥuts lizemano* (literally, 'outside its time': Mishnah *Zevaḥim* 2: 3); generally, the wrong timing can render sacrifices invalid (Tosefta *Pesaḥim* 3: 7 (p. 161)).

As has been shown in the last chapter, the term *zeman* is not used in these passages in the sense of 'time' in general, but only in the sense of specific points in time or periods. Nevertheless, it may be appropriate to ask whether timing in mishnaic halakhah does not imply an underlying notion of 'time in general', albeit embedded in a concrete context of ritual activity. The question is whether an independent, self-standing notion of time can be abstracted and inferred out this context.

Although much attention is given to timing in halakhah, the times that are provided in the Mishnah and elsewhere are generally expressed in terms of processes, such as human activity and (more commonly) natural phenomena. A typical example can be found at the very beginning of the Mishnah. The question of when the *Shema* should be recited in the evening is answered as follows: 'From when the priests enter to eat their heave-offering, until the end of the first watch—so R. Eliezer. But the sages say: until midnight. R. Gamliel says: until the rise of dawn' (Mishnah *Berakhot* 1: 1). The timings in this passage are not abstract or absolute time-measurements. The priests eating their heave-offering is only a human activity, in co-ordination with which the *Shema* must be recited. The end of the first watch is not precisely defined, but is likely to depend on how, in practice, night watchers divide their duties.[3] Midnight (*ḥatsot*) is not an abstract clock time (as in its modern sense), but the mid-point between the natural phenomena of nightfall and the rise of dawn (or alternatively, between sunset and sunrise). Times are thus not measurements within the time-dimension: they are quite simply events.

This suggests a very different concept of timing from ours. We tend to understand timing as the ordering of activities within the abstract scale of time. In our perspective, the scale of time functions as a universal measuring device, that may be likened to a tape measure or a ruler; timing consists in positioning activities and events at various points along this linear ruler. Early rabbinic timing, by contrast, ostensibly ignores the dimension or scale of time, and is based entirely on standard events or processes such as day-rise and nightfall. Timing consists entirely in establishing a relationship, such as precedence or simultaneity, between various halakhic activities and these standard events. As a result, the meaning of timing can be simply reduced to 'synchronization' or 'co-ordination': in this case, co-ordination of the recitation of the *Shema* with other human activities (the priests eating their

---

[3] Tosefta *Ber.* 1: 3 (p. 1) records a dispute as to whether there are three or four watches in one night.

heave-offering, the changing of the night watchers) or natural phenomena (midnight, the rise of dawn). Timing as co-ordination is completely process-linked; it does not require or even presuppose any implicit notion of an abstract time-dimension.[4]

Non-halakhic sources also suggest that timing and time reckoning were commonly linked to natural phenomena. An *ad hoc* method of wall-scratching appears in a number of *midrashim*: when Moses told Pharaoh that the plague of hail would begin at the same time the next day, he made a scratch in the wall and said: 'when the sun reaches this point, hail will descend'. Similarly, when God promised Sarah a child exactly one year later, he made a scratch in the wall and said: 'when the sun reaches this point, you will give birth'.[5] What is distinctive about most rabbinic sources, however, is their use of *standard* events or processes, such as dawn and night, midday and midnight, and a range of others (such as the 'call of the rooster' in Mishnah *Yoma* 1: 8, Tosefta *Pesaḥim* 10: 9–11 (p. 173), etc.), that are pervasive in halakhah and form a systemic basis of all halakhic timing.

The only unit of timing that is occasionally used in early rabbinic sources and not directly process-linked is that of the 'hour', *sha'ah*.[6] This time-measurement already appears, in fact, in the continuation of the Mishnah passage above-quoted, on the recitation of the *Shema* in the morning (Mishnah *Berakhot* 1: 2). Alongside the process-linked times of 'sunrise' and 'when one can tell the difference between white and blue', the Mishnah mentions the 'third hour' (*shalosh sha'ot*, literally 'three hours') as the latest time for the morning the *Shema*.[7] At first sight, this concept of 'hour' could be interpreted as an abstract, quantitative measurement of pure time. The timing of the morning the *Shema* would thus not be defined by synchronization with some other activity or event, but only by reference to an

---

[4] I prefer 'co-ordination' to 'synchronization', because the latter refers implicitly to a notion of 'time', which might be a little misleading. In addition, 'synchronization' may imply simultaneity, whereas I wish to refer to both simultaneity and sequence.

[5] *Exodus Rabbah* 12: 2 (Moses and Pharaoh), and *Midrash tanḥuma* (Buber), 'Vayera' 36 (p. 54a) (God and Sarah). See also *Genesis Rabbah* 33: 7 (p. 313 Theodor and Albeck).

[6] On this rabbinic usage of the term *sha'ah*, which otherwise (and usually in rabbinic sources, e.g. BT *Ber.* 5: 1, Mishnah *Toh.* 8: 3) means a short or indefinite period of time, see Barr, *Biblical Words*, 106–8. The word *sha'ah* is unattested in the Hebrew Bible; it only occurs in Aramaic passages of Daniel, chs. 3–5, in the sense of a short, indefinite period. Barr (ibid.) surmises that the usage of *sha'ah* in the sense of 'hour' must be quite ancient, since similar terms are used in ancient Babylonian sources (in particular, Babylonian astronomical sources), and *some* word for 'hour' must have been used when measuring time with the sundials or other solar devices referred to in 2 Kgs. 20: 9–11 and Isa. 38: 8; but this is pure speculation. The division of the day into twelve (or any other number of) parts is not attested in any form in the Bible, and therefore cannot be assumed. Further meanings of *sha'ah* in early rabbinic literature are 'right time', as in *Avot* 4: 3 (see above Ch. 1 n. 57), and 'opportunity', on which see below, Ch. 4.

[7] 'Three hours' means the end of the third hour of daylight, approximately 9 a.m. The fact that hours are calculated on the basis of daylight suggests in itself a process-linked element, which I shall presently consider.

abstract, measurable time-line. But whether the hour division implies a notion of abstract or 'pure' time requires further analysis.

THE HOUR DIVISION

It must first be emphasized that the concept of hours is uncommon in early rabbinic halakhah and literature. In most cases, as outlined above, halakhic timings are defined in relation to human activities or natural phenomena.[8] This may reflect the difficulty, in the context of the ancient world, for ordinary people to work out precisely the hour of the day. Although the precise onset of some natural phenomena was difficult for them to ascertain (e.g. dawn and dusk),[9] hours were far more problematic.[10] The Mishnah rules that witnesses could not be expected to know whether an incident occurred in the second or the third hour (Mishnah *Sanhedrin* 5: 3).[11] Subdivisions of the hour were even more difficult to ascertain: although they are mentioned in a few sources, their use was clearly only theoretical, because nobody was able to measure them in practice.[12]

Ignorance of the hour of the day would have been due, in large part, to limited access to clocks or time-measuring devices. Significantly, time-measuring devices are very rarely mentioned in early rabbinic literature. There are lone references to

---

[8] Times are rarely given in hours in the Mishnah: see Mishnah *Ber.* 1: 2, 4: 1, Mishnah *Pes.* 1: 4, 5: 1, Mishnah *San.* 5: 3 (not in a ritual context), Mishnah *Edu.* 6: 1, Mishnah *Neg.* 2: 2; see also Mishnah *Ket.* 10: 6. In halakhic *midrashim* such as the *Mekhilta*, the term *ḥatsot* ('midday') is often replaced with *shesh sha'ot* ('six hours'): Friedman, 'Baraitot', 167. It is unclear whether this reflects a historical development or change, e.g. towards more abstract forms of time-reckoning.

[9] On the Temple officials' difficulty of establishing the time of dawn—leading sometimes to embarrassing errors—see Mishnah *Yoma* 3: 1–2; on the impossibility of knowing the precise time of dusk (hence the beginning of the sabbath), see e.g. *Genesis Rabbah* 10: 8 (p. 85 ed. Theodor and Albeck). For similar reasons, the precise time of midnight was considered impossible to ascertain: *Mekhilta* 'Bo' 14 (p. 42 ed. Horovitz and Rabin). According to BT *Ber.* 3*b*, only God knows when exactly it is midnight.

[10] According to *Lamentations Rabbah* 1: 31 (see variant recension in S. Buber's edition (Vilna, 1899), p. 34*a*), R. Yohanan b. Zakkai was able to tell the hours of the day and of the night without any clock, in a dark room and completely cut off from the outside world. This, obviously, was the exception that proved the rule.

[11] See similar idea in BT *Pes.* 94*a*, and the extensive discussion on this topic ibid. 11*b*–12*b*.

[12] This is evident e.g. from BT *Pes.* 11*b*–12*b*, even though the possibility of subdividing the hour is raised in BT *San.* 40*b*. The minute subdivision of the hour into 1 hour = 24 *onot* (עונות) = 24² *itim* (עיתים) = 24³ *rega'im* (רגעים) (Tosefta *Ber.* 1: 3, p. 1; JT *Ber.* 1: 1 (2*d*); *Lamentations Rabbah* 2: 19) was obviously only theoretical and of no practical use whatsoever. See also R. Eleazar Hakalir's *Siluk le-parashat shekalim* (discussed on pp. 78 ff. below), with a different expression of the same subdivision of the hour, and a note that some subdivide the hour even further! For an apparently different division of the hour, see BT *Ber.* 7*a* and Lieberman, *Tosefta kifeshutah*, i. 2. In non-astronomical Graeco-Roman sources, however, the hour appears never to be subdivided into smaller units, clearly because of the difficulty of measuring them in practice (Field, 'European Astronomy', 120).

a stone sundial (*even sha'ot*, literally 'hours-stone'),[13] to an *orologin* (a loan-word from the Greek *hōrologion* for an unspecified 'hour-dial' or 'clock') belonging to a king,[14] and to a *clepsydra* (another Greek loan-word), a water-clock that is used in (presumably Roman) courts to measure the defence's speaking-time.[15] These references are not only very rare, but also suggest that ownership or use of sundials or clocks was restricted to people of high political standing.[16]

It is no surprise, therefore, that precise reckoning of the hour is hardly ever mentioned in early rabbinic sources: there is no account, for instance, of anyone attempting to establish whether the third hour has ended and thus whether the time of the morning the *Shema* has elapsed.[17] In normal situations, ordinary people could only estimate the hour of the day: they would look at the sun's position and make a reasonable guess. The Mishnah passage above mentioned (Mishnah *Sanhedrin* 5: 3) rules that although witnesses could not be expected to distinguish between the second and the third hour, they could be expected to distinguish between the fifth and the seventh, because in the fifth hour (one hour before mid-day) the sun is to the east, whereas in the seventh hour (one hour after midday) the sun is to the west.[18] Everyone knew when it was the fourth hour, we are told else-where, because that was the time of the morning meal (BT *Pesaḥim* 12b).

Yet although in practice hours were only approximately measured, and only with reference to natural phenomena or human activities, the theoretical concept of the hour division may still have implied in itself a concept of 'pure time', i.e. of

[13] The term occurs in Targum 2 Kgs. 9: 13 and the parallel Targum Isa. 38: 8 (*even shaya*, referring to the steps of Ahaz), and in two parallel passages of the Mishnah referring specifically to the sundial's rod or *gnomon* (*masmer shel even shaot*: Mishnah *Kel.* 12: 4–5 = Mishnah *Eduy.* 3: 8). In the *Mekhilta derabi shimon bar yoḥai* (on Exod. 12: 29, p. 28 ed. Epstein and Melamed), finally, God is described as sitting on a stone sundial, an expression of his exact knowledge of the time of midnight (clearly metaphorical, since a sundial is useless for ascertaining the time of midnight). A clearer version of this *midrash* is in Margaliot, *Midrash hagadol*, 207.

[14] JT *RH* 1: 3 (57b) (and parallel in *Pesikta rabati* 15: 18): אורלוגין. This reference serves as a parable for the rabbinic court's monopoly over calendar decisions.

[15] *Genesis Rabbah* 49: 12 (ed. p. 514 Theodor and Albeck): חלף סידרא. This Aramaic transliteration of *clepsydra*, in the medieval MSS, suggests an *interpretatio Judaica* of the word as meaning something like 'switch the order'.

[16] On sundials in the Graeco-Roman world (with a comprehensive catalogue), see Gibbs, *Greek and Roman Sundials*. Sundials from the Near East appear in this work in relatively small proportion, but note two sundials from Jerusalem (p. 308); to these may now be added the Qumran sundial, on which see Albani and Glessmer, 'Instrument de mesures astronomiques', and eid., 'Astronomical Measuring Instrument'. See also Evans, *History and Practice of Ancient Astronomy*, 129–32; id., 'The Material Culture of Greek Astronomy'; and Field, 'European Astronomy', 118–22.

[17] The closest account I have found of precise time-measuring is a reference in *Midrash tanḥuma*, 'Beshalah' 28 (a relatively late source, although see Stemberger, *Introduction to the Talmud and Midrash*, 305–6) to the Amalekites' working out the times of the day for astrological purposes, seemingly on the basis of the position of the sun.

[18] See also BT *Shab.* 35a–b; BT *Pes.* 11b–12b, 94a.

time as a measurable dimension and entity. At first sight, indeed, the division of the day into twenty-four units of equal length is arbitrary, artificial, and divorced from any objective or tangible reality. The arbitrariness of the hour division is particularly pronounced in modern society, where hours are only notional and twelve o'clock, for instance, hardly ever corresponds to the real, astronomical midday (when the sun is at its highest point, or half-way between sunrise and sunset). The discrepancy between our hours and astronomical reality is due to a number of factors, including the widespread use of mechanical clocks that can only always indicate the same, uniform hours (hence the need to invent, in the early modern period, an artificial 'mean time'), daylight saving, and the convenience of using the same times within internationally recognized time zones (even if 'real' times differ considerably from the easternmost to the westernmost points of any given time zone). The result is that the relationship between the hour division and concrete reality has become unclear, but equally unnecessary: for hours are defined entirely by the artificial clock. Since they do not correspond to any sequence of concrete phenomena, hours are naturally interpreted in modern society as measurements of pure time or of the time-dimension.[19]

In the ancient world, however, the hour division was much less abstract and divorced from concrete reality. It is well established that the hours in use in the Graeco-Roman world were generally seasonal. 'Seasonal hours' represent a division of daytime (from sunrise to sunset)[20] into twelve equal sections, which vary in

[19] In actual fact, however, man-made clocks do not measure pure time: they are only sequences of events, e.g. the circular motion of needles around a dial, which are used as standard reference for measuring other processes or sequences (Elias, *Time*, 1–2, cited above in the Introduction). Note Bohannan's observation that although some Tiv of Nigeria have adopted the use of modern clocks, they persist in interpreting the hours as units of measurement of a *process*—the motion of the needles around the dial of the clock—rather than as units of measurement of the abstract time-dimension ('Concepts of Time', 328). Elias, *Time*, 41–2, shows, however, how the development and propagation of man-made timing devices (such as clocks) in the later medieval period led to the gradual disengagement of society from its natural environment, and to the association of timing no longer with natural phenomena such as sunrise and sunset, but only with artificial, man-made concepts such as the time-dimension. Thus the invention of clocks promoted to some extent the development of the modern abstract concept of time. Elias's argument represents a commonly shared opinion (see also Gourévitch, *Catégories de la culture médiévale*, 152–4), but it has been challenged by Landes, *Revolution in Time*, who argues (perhaps not very convincingly) that, on the contrary, the development of an abstract notion of time in the later Middle Ages stimulated the invention of mechanical clocks.

[20] So according to all the ancient literary evidence, and the evidence of sundials from the Hellenistic and Roman periods: Gibbs, *Greek and Roman Sundials*, 4–6. Rabbinic sources, however, consistently assume that the day begins at dawn (i.e. before sunrise) and ends at dusk with the appearance of the stars (i.e. after sunset): see Mishnah *Meg.* 2: 4, JT *Ber.* 1: 1 (2*b*), BT *Shab.* 34*b*, 35*b*, BT *Pes.* 2a, BT *Meg.* 20*b*; and by implication (since the new moon usually becomes visible 20 minutes after sunset) Mishnah *RH* 3: 1, JT *RH* 3: 1 (58*c*), and *Mekhilta* 'Bo' 1 (p. 6 ed. Horovitz and Rabin). On this basis, some medieval commentators concluded that the 12-hour division had to be calculated from dawn to dusk (Tosafot on BT *San.* 41*b*, s.v. *ehad*); but it is not clear that the early rabbinic definition of 'daytime' (i.e. from dawn to dusk) should necessarily have tallied with the 12-hour division. The

length according to the season of the year (because days are longer in summer and shorter in winter) and according to terrestrial latitude. These contrast with the uniform hours that are used today, and that remain constant throughout the year; the latter are called by astronomers 'equinoctial hours', because they are equivalent, in theory at least, to seasonal hours at the equinox (in practice, however, these hours are defined through the artificial means of the clock). Sundials in the ancient world were all designed to indicate seasonal hours; sundials indicating equinoctial hours were only invented in the medieval period.[21] Literary evidence also confirms that seasonal hours were normally used, for daily-life purposes, in the ancient world.[22] Although ill-defined in early rabbinic literature, 'hours' in early rabbinic literature are therefore likely to have been *seasonal*; we must assume so, at least, in the absence of any evidence to the contrary.[23]

passage in JT *Ber.* 1: 1 (2*c*) and *Leviticus Rabbah* 26: 4, stating that at the equinox day and night are of equal length, need not be taken as exact (which could only have meant the day running from sunrise to sunset). See Benish, *Times in Halakha*, i. 112–27.

[21] See Gibbs, *Greek and Roman Sundials*, 4–6, 10; Benish, *Times in Halakha*, i. 77–88. All sundials that have been discovered from the Hellenistic and Roman periods are constructed in such a way that the shadow of the gnomon's *point* indicates the hour; this would only yield seasonal hours (a number of rings must be drawn on the dial for the different seasons of the year: for a good illustration, see also Albani and Grasshoff, 'An Instrument for Determining', 20–2). Medieval and modern sundials are more sophisticated, in that they use the shadow of the gnomon's *edge*; the gnomon must be positioned in parallel to the axis of the earth in order to indicate equinoctial hours.

[22] Preference for seasonal hours explains why schemes were developed in Babylonia, from the earliest times, for converting the hours of water-clocks into seasonal hours (water-clocks could be used at night, but, unlike sundials, their hours were uniform): see Britton and Walker, 'Astronomy and Astrology in Mesopotamia', 46–8 (referring for example to MUL.APIN, a text dating from before the 7th c. BCE). Similarly, Vitruvius (*De Architectura* 9: 8, later 1st c. BCE) describes complex devices for adjusting water-clocks in such a way that they would indicate seasonal hours: the assumption clearly is that in everyday life, seasonal hours were preferred. Equinoctial hours were also used by the ancients but only for the purposes of astronomy—and more precisely, for the purposes of theoretical astronomy, since astronomical observations were often recorded (at least by early Hellenistic astronomers) in seasonal hours (Gibbs, *Greek and Roman Sundials*, 10; Rochberg-Halton, 'Babylonian Seasonal Hours'). See also Toomer, *Ptolemy's Almagest*, 23; Jones, *Astronomical Papyri from Oxyrhynchus*, i. 14, 102–5, with ii. 26–35 (P. Oxy. 4142), a conversion table from the 4th c. CE for converting seasonal hours into equinoctial hours (I am grateful to Bernard Goldstein for this reference); Albani and Glessmer, 'Instrument de mesures astronomiques', and eid., 'Astronomical Measuring Instrument'. The Greeks also divided the *night* into twelve seasonal hours (from sunset to sunrise), but this division is rare in rabbinic literature, where the night is usually divided into three or four watches (see above, n. 3). The terminology used in Greek astronomical sources is ὧραι καιρικαί ('seasonal hours': e.g. Vitruvius, *De Architectura* 9. 7. 7; Ptolemy, *Almagest* 4. 11, 7. 3) and ὧραι ἰσημεριναί ('equinoctial hours').

[23] That there are twelve hours in the day is explicit e.g. in *Genesis Rabbah* 100: 9 (p. 1294 ed. Theodor and Albeck), and BT *San.* 38*b* (less explicitly in its parallels: *Leviticus Rabbah* 29: 1; *Avot derabi natan* (A) 1, p. 3*a*; ibid. (B) 1, p. 4*b*). *Pesikta derav kahana* 16: 5 (p. 271 ed. Mandelbaum) mentions twelve hours in the day and twelve hours in the night, and this is also the assumption of BT *Ber.* 3*a–b*. It is significant that early rabbinic sources do not bother to specify whether their hours are seasonal or equinoctial; this is probably because the former could be taken completely for granted. The

Preference for seasonal hours was not forced upon the ancient world for purely technical reasons (i.e. the design of sundials): it was also a practical convenience. The function of seasonal hours, as opposed to uniform hours, was not to measure the flow of time *per se*, but rather to measure one's distance from natural phenomena such as sunrise, noon, and sunset, around which most of human activity was regulated. In societies where artificial lighting was inadequate and expensive, and where most activities had to be confined to daylight, it was much more useful to know how far one was to sunrise or sunset, than to know an abstract, arbitrary time such as '9 a.m.' or '5 p.m.' What the 'third hour' actually means, in Mishnah *Berakhot* 1: 2, is half-way between sunrise and noon. Thus, the division of the day into seasonal hours was not only regulated by natural phenomena, but also *indicative* of them. Seasonal hours, in the ancient world as well as in rabbinic literature, constituted a measurement of the course of the sun, or rather of the length of daylight; they were not a measurement of 'pure time' or of the time-dimension.

THE MEASUREMENT OF DURATION

Another indication that 'hours' in early rabbinic literature were not intended to measure 'pure time' is the fact that they are never used to measure duration:[24] they only serve to identify specific points in time or parts of the day. For instance, the duration which we refer to as 'twenty-four hours' is called instead, in rabbinic literature, *me'et le'et*, 'from one time to the next'.[25] Periods that are shorter than one day are measured not in hours, but by entirely different means that are very clearly process-linked.

---

question was only first raised and debated in the later medieval period. Maimonides (late 12th c.) argued that early rabbinic hours were seasonal (which he refers to in Judaeo-Arabic as סאעאת זמאניה, later to be translated into Hebrew as *sha'ot zemaniyot*: Blau, *R. Moses b. Maimon: Responsa*, i. 251–5, no. 134; and Maimonides' commentary on Mishnah *Ber.* 1: 2), and most halakhic authorities have taken his view. R. Asher ben Yehiel (the Rosh, early 14th c.) was among the few to argue that early rabbinic hours were uniform and fixed (*Tosafot harosh*, on *Ber.* 3b, s.v. *kivan*). See also, among other sources, Tosafot on BT *Eruv.* 56a, s.v. *ve'ein*, and Benish, *Times in Halakha*, i. 99–111. It may be expected, however, that the few passages in rabbinic literature that refer to hours in an astronomical context mean uniform, equinoctial hours: BT *Eruv.* 56a (which gives the mean length of seasons as 91 days 7½ hours), and BT *Arakh.* 9b (Ravina's reference to the discrepancy of hours accumulated in a lunar calendar that consistently alternates 29- and 30-day months; see Stern, *Calendar and Community*, 202). Equinoctial hours are also implicit in BT *RH* 25a (the length of the lunation), but the authenticity of this passage is dubious (see Stern, *Calendar and Community*, 201–2).

[24] With the exception of the very few astronomical passages in BT *Eruv.* 56a and BT *Arakh.* 9b (see n. 23).

[25] e.g. *Mekhilta* 'Nezikin' 7 (p. 274 ed. Horovitz and Rabin); Mishnah *Nid.* 1: 1–6; Mishnah *Zav.* 2: 3. The phrase may be derived from Ezek. 4: 10–1. Ancient Greek astronomers use the term νυχθήμερον, 'night-day' (Toomer, *Ptolemy's Almagest*, 23).

The most common of these is the *mil*. Although this unit is normally spatial and a measure of length or distance (equivalent to 2,000 cubits), in some contexts it represents the *duration* equivalent to an average person's walk over this distance. This unit of measurement, which may be multiplied or divided into fractions, can be used in a wide range of contexts. It is used to determine not only the duration of walks,[26] but also the period of dusk (between sunset and night),[27] and the duration of, or intervals between, a range of other events and activities.[28] In this respect, the *mil* represents a universal unit of duration.[29]

The concept of *mil* as a unit of both distance and duration may suggest spatialization of time, but this is actually unlikely. Many passages state explicitly that *mil* as a unit of duration is based not just on sheer distance, but also on the activity of *walking*: commonly used phrases are *kedei hilukh (arba'ah) mil* ('as long as a (4)-*mil* walk'),[30] *mahalakh arba'at mil* ('4-*mil* walk'),[31] and *kedei sheyehalekh adam mil* ('as long as a man would walk a *mil*').[32] This confirms that the duration of a *mil* was conceived of in terms of the process or activity of walking, rather than in terms of spatial distance or space.

Process and activity similarly characterize other units of duration which can be found in rabbinic sources: for instance, the unit of 'as long as an immersion and wiping' (*kedei tevilah vesipug*), i.e. the duration equivalent to a person immersing his body in water (for purification) and then wiping it dry. Like the *mil*, this unit can be multiplied (e.g. 'as long as two immersions and wipings'); however, rather than being universal, it is appropriately confined to the context of the laws of purity and impurity.[33] The same applies to the duration of 'as long as one slaughter' (*kedei shehitah*), which is appropriately confined to the context of the laws of animal slaughtering.[34]

---

[26] Mishnah *Yoma* 6: 8: the walk of the scapegoat in the desert (on the Day of Atonement).

[27] The period known as *bein hashemashot*: opinions include half a *mil*, two-thirds of a *mil*, etc.: JT *Ber.* 1: 1 (2*b*–*c*); BT *Shab.* 34*b*–35*a*. With similar reference to the period of dawn: JT *Yoma* 3: 2 (40*b*); *Genesis Rabbah* 50: 10 (p. 525 ed. Theodor and Albeck); BT *Pes.* 93*b*–94*a*.

[28] The duration of digestion: BT *Ber.* 53*b*. The period for dough to become leavened: JT *Pes.* 3: 2 (30*a*); BT *Pes.* 46*a*. The duration of skin-tanning (BT *Ḥul.* 122*b*), and hence how long before the sabbath skins should be given to the tanner: JT *Shab.* 1: 9 (4*b*). How long after eating blood-letting is effective: BT *Shab.* 129*b*. For how long the old moon's crescent was visible: JT *RH* 2: 4 (58*a*). The interval required between going to the lavatory and having sexual relations: BT *Git.* 70*a*; *Kalah* 1: 11.

[29] Variations on the unit of *mil* are the shorter measurements of 100 cubits (BT *Suk.* 26*a*, the length of a short nap) or 4 cubits (JT *Ber.* 3: 5 (6*d*), JT *Meg.* 3: 1 (73*d*), BT *Meg.* 27*b*: the interval required between urinating and praying); see also Tosefta *Zav.* 1: 11 (p. 677).

[30] JT *Pes.* 3: 2 (30*a*), JT *Shab.* 1: 9 (4*b*), BT *Pes.* 46*a*, BT *Suk.* 26*a*. Also BT *Ber.* 53*b* (כדי להלך ד' מילין).   [31] JT *Yoma* 3: 2 (40*b*); see also JT *RH* 2: 4 (58*a*); *Kalah* 1: 11.

[32] JT *Ber.* 1: 1 (2*b*), BT *Shab.* 34*b*, BT *Pes.* 46*a*.

[33] Mishnah *Zav.* 1: 4–5; and Tosefta *Zav.* 1: 9–13 (p. 677), with a detailed definition of this unit of duration. See, however, BT *Shab.* 35*a* (cited below), where immersion is possibly used as a way of measuring the duration of dusk.   [34] Mishnah *Ḥul.* 2: 3.

More common, elsewhere, is the unit of 'as long as eating one *peras*' (*kedei akhilat peras*), i.e. the duration equivalent to a person eating the volume of one *peras* (about 300 cc). This measurement is again confined to its own appropriate context, i.e. eating: thus, it determines the maximum duration allowed for the eating of a smaller volume of food (e.g. *kezayit*, the equivalent volume of one olive) to qualify, halakhically, as an act of eating.[35] It also determines how long a person can stay in a contaminated house before they incur impurity;[36] although, in this context, the person is not actually eating, the unit of eating one *peras* is used because the law in question (contraction of impurity in a contaminated house) is exegetically derived from a verse where eating is mentioned (Leviticus 14: 47).

Another unit of duration that is usually (but not always) confined to its own context is 'as long as one utterance' (*kedei dibur*). This rather short period is defined as the duration equivalent to a disciple greeting his master.[37] An interruption of this length is considered halakhically significant, and marks, for instance, the commencement of a new and separate utterance.[38]

Even shorter is the measurement of *keheref ayin*, which means something like the wink of an eye and is virtually equivalent to an instant.[39] Some equate it with a subdivision of the hour called *rega* ('instant').[40] Like the *mil*, it is not context-bound but a universal measuring unit.

The concepts of *mil*, immersing and wiping, slaughtering, eating one *peras*, the shortest utterance, and the eye wink are in most cases only *notional*, in the sense that nobody would actually walk a *mil*, immerse and wipe, slaughter an animal, eat a *peras*, greet his master, or wink his eye in order to ascertain the length or duration of a simultaneous process.[41] It may be assumed that in practice, these measurement

---

[35] Eating a *kezayit* over a longer period of time would not qualify as an act of eating, because it would be deemed nibbling. See Mishnah *Ker.* 3: 3, Tosefta *Ter.* 7: 3 (p. 37), Tosefta *Pes.* 1: 12 (p. 156), Tosefta *Yoma* 5: 3 (p. 189), Tosefta *Ker.* 2: 2 (p. 563), Tosefta *Mik.* 7: 5, 7: 7 (p. 660), JT *Shab.* 1: 1 (2*b*), BT *Ber.* 37*b*, BT *Pes.* 44*a*, 114*b*, BT *Yoma* 80*b*, BT *Suk.* 42*b*, BT *Naz.* 36*b*–37*a*, BT *AZ* 67*a*, BT *Zev.* 31*b*, 70*a*, BT *Men.* 75*b*, BT *Ḥul.* 35*a*, BT *Ker.* 12*b*–13*b*.

[36] Mishnah *Neg.* 13: 9–10, Tosefta *Neg.* 7: 8–9 (p. 627), *Sifra* 'Metsora' ad Lev. 14: 47. Because no actual eating is involved in this context, Mishnah *Neg.* 13: 9 must specify which type of food is *notionally* assumed to be eaten.

[37] Tosefta *Ned.* 5: 1 (p. 280), JT *Naz.* 4: 1 (53*a*), BT *Naz.* 20*b*, BT *BK* 73*a*–*b* (with a typical text of this greeting), BT *Mak.* 6*a*, BT *Shevu.* 32*a*–*b*.

[38] See n. 37, and Tosefta *Naz.* 3: 2 (p. 286), JT *Dem.* 7: 6 (26*c*), JT *Shevu.* 4: 3 (35*c*), BT *BB* 129*b*, BT *San.* 40*b*, BT *Tem.* 25*b*. In one case, *kedei dibur* applies to a situation involving no utterance: the interval between the death of a person and the tearing of one's clothes as a sign of mourning (JT *Ber.* 2: 1 (4*b*), JT *MK* 3: 7 (83*c*), BT *Ned.* 87*a*).

[39] See e.g. JT *Ber.* 1: 1 (2*b*–*c*), BT *Shab.* 34*b*, *Mekhilta* 'Bo' 14 (pp. 51–2 ed. Horovitz and Rabin).

[40] JT *Ber.* 1: 1 (2*d*).

[41] With only a few exceptions: Mishnah *Yoma* 6: 8, cited below, suggests that someone would actually walk a *mil* in the vicinity of the Temple in order to measure the scapegoat's simultaneous progress in the desert. In this case, the *mil* was used not in its universal sense, but specifically to measure the

units were mentally internalized. But although these units could thus become mental, imagined concepts, their relation to concrete processes and activities (walking, immersing, slaughtering, eating, speaking, winking) remained essential, because the latter would generate and redefine the imagined concepts on a continual basis. The duration of a *mil*, for instance, only made sense if it was constantly related back to the concrete experience of walking. It is clear, indeed, that the notion of *mil* was never entirely obvious, and needed to be constantly redefined. This may explain why the progress of the scapegoat in the desert (on the Day of Atonement) had to be estimated, for those who had remained in the Temple, by 'walking a *mil*, returning a *mil*, and waiting a *mil*' (Mishnah *Yoma* 6: 8). It may also explain why R. Hanina had to comment on R. Nehemiah's measurement of dusk (*bein hashemashot*), which he gave as one half-*mil*, as follows: 'Said R. Hanina: Whoever wants to know the measurement of R. Nehemiah [of one half-*mil*] should leave the top of [Mount] Carmel with sun[set], go down, immerse in the sea, and come out—this is the measurement of R. Nehemiah' (BT *Shabat* 35*a*).[42] Thus, concrete processes or activities remain the foundation of these units of duration.

In some cases, the relationship between the duration unit and the activity it is based on is so close that the duration unit is considered halakhically equivalent to the activity itself. Thus according to Mishnah *Shevuot* 2: 3, the transgression of being in the Temple in a state of impurity is incurred either by prostrating oneself, or by remaining idle for the period of *kedei hishtahava'ah* ('as long as a prostration'): the unit of duration is equivalent to the activity to which it relates.[43] Similarly, in BT *Makot* 21*b*, R. Ashi is attributed the ruling that remaining idle for the period of *kedei lifshot velilbosh* ('as long as taking off and putting on a garment')

scapegoat's *walk*. But in JT *RH* 2: 4 (58*a*), an actual 4-*mil* walk (by R. Hiya) appears to have been used to determine the duration of the visibility of the old moon's crescent (3 *mil* according to the version of *Tanhuma* (Buber), 'Bo' 8, p. 24*a*; on this passage and its various versions, see Ch. 3).

[42] So according to the Babylonian Talmud. It is difficult to imagine how this could all be done within the time of a half-*mil*'s walk. In the Jerusalem Talmud (JT *Ber.* 1: 1 (2*b*)), however, R. Hanina's saying is presented without reference to R. Nehemiah, and not as an explanation of his measurement of a half-*mil*. Moreover, in this version, the context of R. Hanina's saying is clarified: the point of immersing oneself in the sea at this time is to eat the heave-offering in a state of purity immediately at nightfall, after the end of dusk (see Mishnah *Ber.* 1: 1, cited above). Because the laws of heave-offering were not observed in Babylonia, outside the land of Israel, the original significance of R. Hanina's saying would have become irrelevant to the authors of the Babylonian Talmud. The Babylonian Talmud's version appears therefore to have been tampered with, whereas the Palestinian Talmud's version may be more authentic. See further Ginzberg, *Commentary*, i. 24–7. The text of the Babylonian Talmud remains significant, nevertheless, in expressing the uncertainty people may have felt regarding the measurement of a half-*mil*.

[43] BT *Shevu.* 17*a* investigates whether the person remaining idle must be in a situation where he *could* have prostrated himself if he so wished (as opposed to a situation where he could not, e.g. if he was hanging in the air). For a completely different textual version of this passage, see Tosafot ad loc., s.v. *talah*. The status of these two versions requires proper investigation, but I suspect that Tosafot's version is spurious.

is equivalent to actually taking it off and putting it on: consequently, a person wearing a forbidden garment (a mixture of wool and linen) for such a period is considered to have taken it off and put it back on again, and is thus liable for two punishments. The close relationship, in these two cases, between the duration unit and its equivalent activity highlights the process-related nature of duration measurement in early rabbinic culture.

ZEMAN AND CO-ORDINATION

To sum up this chapter, time-reckoning in mishnaic halakhah as well as in daily practice did not depend on a concept of time as an abstract, universal dimension in relation to which all human activity can be measured. As in many other non-modern societies, points in time and duration of time were always measured with reference to concrete, discrete processes. The activity of timing consisted entirely, in fact, in co-ordinating human activities (e.g. ritual) and/or natural processes (e.g. the motion of the sun or the duration of daylight) with one another. Although timing could be regarded as highly important, it did not necessitate a general category of 'pure' time. All rabbinic sources suggest, instead, is that activities and events, in human society and in the wider environment, could be co-ordinated with each other in a variety of normative ways, in relations of either succession (sequence) or simultaneity.[44]

Since timing could thus be reduced to the succession, simultaneity, and generally the co-ordination of processes, it might just be possible—if not slightly perverse—to strike out completely the word 'time' from our translations of early rabbinic literature. Because of its modern connotations, the English word 'time' is indeed often misleading. The term *zeman*, which I translated in the previous chapter as 'point in time' and 'period of time', may be taken to express no more than the notions of simultaneity or co-ordination of processes. This interpretation may find linguistic support, moreover, in the related verb *zimen*: this term, found in mishnaic and later Hebrew, is always used in the sense of 'to appoint', 'to prepare', or 'to designate', without any temporal implication. I propose, therefore, that rather than 'point in time' and 'period of time', which are misleading because of the modern connotations of the word 'time', we translate *zeman* in general terms

---

[44] It may be useful in this context to refer to Elias's distinction between the reified noun 'time' and the verb 'to time': 'The verbal form "to time" makes it more immediately understandable that the reifying character of the substantival form, "time", disguises the instrumental character of the activity of timing. It obscures the fact that the activity of timing, e.g. by looking at one's watch, has the function of relating to each other the positions of events in the successive order of two or more change-continua' (Elias, *Time*, 43). 'In its most elementary form, "timing" means determining whether a change . . . happens before, after, or simultaneously with another' (ibid. 48). Thus, timing only denotes the human activity of 'synchronization' (ibid. 71–4).

as 'event or process with which another event or process is *designated* to coincide or be co-ordinated'. The specific translation of *zeman* would depend on context, but to refer to just one example, the phrase *zeman keriat shema*[45]—usually translated as 'the time for reciting the *Shema*'—could be rendered instead as 'the process designated to coincide with the reciting of the *Shema*'; this process being, in the morning, the onset of dawn 'when one can tell the difference between white and blue'.

But although perhaps more accurate, these translations are too clumsy and cumbersome to be of any real use. The word 'time' remains far more convenient, for the purpose of English translation, than the alternative I am suggesting here. Let us retain, therefore, the word 'time', but with the clear understanding that this word does not imply, in early rabbinic culture, anything temporal: it only means the coincidence and co-ordination of concrete events, activities, and processes.

[45] BT *Ber.* 2*a*, etc. In Mishnah *Ber.* 2: 1 the equivalent phrase is *zeman hamikra*.

THREE

Calendar, Chronology, and History

CALENDAR and chronology are usually understood as systems of time-reckoning. Calendars are structures of medium-size units of time, ranging typically from the day-unit to the year. Chronologies are structures of large-size units of time, such as years, eras, and the whole of history. The question that I shall raise in this chapter is whether calendar and chronology reckon or measure time as such, and thus imply or necessitate the concept of time as a continuum, dimension, or structure of reality. This problem is similar to that of the previous chapter—which dealt with small-size units of time, the day and its subdivisions—but on a larger scale. The study of calendars and chronology will lead us to consider, more in general, the early rabbinic view of history, and specifically whether any particular concept of time can be inferred from early Jewish notions of calendar, chronology, and history.[1]

In this chapter, again, I shall restrict myself to the evidence of early rabbinic literature. The argument will be extended to the whole of ancient Judaism in Chapter 6.

CALENDARS AND TIME-MEASUREMENT

Because of the common assumption that the calendar is a system for measuring time, or, as I once put it, a way of 'making sense' of the dimension of time,[2] attempts have often been made to infer from calendars an underlying notion of the time-dimension. I must plead guilty of having made this mistake myself. These assumptions may hold true, to some extent, in the context of modern culture; but in the context of early rabbinic culture the relationship between calendars and time-measurement must be completely reconsidered.

The calendar should not be perceived, necessarily, as a time-measuring scheme. Its primary purpose, in any society, is to facilitate the co-ordination of events and activities, and to measure the duration of activities and processes. It is only

---

[1] On the early rabbinic view of history, see Herr, 'Conception of History'; Gafni, 'Concepts of Periodization'.   [2] Stern, 'Fictitious Calendars', 104, and *Calendar and Community*, p. v.

perceived as a time-measuring scheme if one has a preconception of time as a self-standing dimension that is susceptible of being measured, and that needs, for whatever reason, to be measured; but even then time-measuring as such remains a marginal function of the calendar. In the context of early rabbinic culture, there is little doubt that the main, if not sole, purpose of the calendar is to co-ordinate and measure the duration of activities, events, and processes: for instance, to determine the dates of festivals, establish the length of contracts and agreements, etc. The calendar is fully purposeful without any underlying notion of the time-dimension.

The structure of the calendar itself, furthermore, is generally not based on 'time' or any notion of the time-dimension. Most calendars are constructed entirely on the basis of the courses of the moon or of the sun, or—as in the rabbinic calendar—on both; in this respect, the calendar is solely process-based. The reason why the moon and sun are employed in the construction of calendars is that their courses are universally knowable, and reasonably regular and predictable. Moreover, the courses of the moon and the sun are directly or indirectly relevant to most people's lives, because they govern the seasons and many other environmental phenomena. The courses of the moon and the sun do not have, however, intrinsic time-measuring properties. They are simply used in calendars as convenient, standard reference scales or 'yardsticks', in relation to which earthly events and activities can be scheduled, measured, and co-ordinated. The calendar can thus be cogently defined as the representation of a standard sequence, itself a predictable process or combination of processes, that is used to schedule, measure, and co-ordinate other, more irregular sequences and sets of processes in human experience and social life.[3]

Since the calendar is not meant for the measurement of time as such, nor is it constructed on the basis of an abstract time-dimension, any attempt to infer an underlying concept of time from a particular calendar becomes completely futile. As we shall see in the following pages, calendar-derived notions of time turn out in reality, in most cases, to be notions about astronomical (lunar or solar) cycles, human activity, and historical events—in other words, process-related notions that have no bearing on time *per se* or on the time-dimension.

The same holds true, as we shall later see in this chapter, for chronology. Despite its etymology, 'chronology' is not the reckoning of pure time: it is better defined as a sequence of historical events than as the representation of an abstract time-line. In early rabbinic sources, at least, chronology appears completely process-related and thus irrelevant to the notion of time or its continuum.

---

[3] See in more detail Elias, *Time*, 10, cited above in the Introduction. This definition is analogous to my definition of *zeman*, which I have proposed above (end of Ch. 2). I have also shown in Ch. 2 that hours were not units of time as such, but a subdivision of the process of daylight (or of the diurnal course of the sun), with reference to which human activity and events could be co-ordinated.

CYCLICAL TIME?

The notion that time is cyclical has often been inferred from the rabbinic (or Jewish) calendar.[4] This has not merely been deduced from the annual or periodical recurrence of festivals, which is common to almost all calendars in the world and thus hardly distinctive or unique. The notion of cyclicity that appears to be particularly Jewish derives from the early rabbinic idea that in some way, historical events periodically recur, in the Jewish calendar, on the same days of the year.

This idea is expressed, for instance, in a passage of the Mishnah that lists five calamities that happened in different historical periods on the same days of the year (the fast days of 17 Tamuz and 9 Av):

Five things happened to our fathers on 17 Tamuz, and five on 9 Av.

On 17 Tamuz the tablets [of the Law] were broken, the daily sacrifice was interrupted, the city[-wall] was breached, Apostomos burnt the Torah, and a statue was placed in the sanctuary.

On 9 Av it was decreed that our fathers would not enter the land [of Israel], the Temple was destroyed—the first and the second time—Betar was captured, and the City [Jerusalem] was ploughed (Mishnah *Ta'anit* 4: 6).

The recurrence of similarly disastrous events—and most distinctly, the destruction of the first and second Temples—on the same day of the year, may be taken as indicative that time is cyclical.

A similar interpretation may be applied to a famous dispute between R. Eliezer and R. Joshua, of which the most systematic presentation is in the Babylonian Talmud. According to R. Eliezer, a number of historical events occurred in the month of Tishrei, or more specifically at the beginning of this month, on the date of Rosh Hashanah (the new year festival); while R. Joshua assigns these events, or at least some of them, to the month of Nisan. The events in question are the creation of the world, the birth and death of all three Patriarchs, the release of Sarah, Rachel, and Hannah from barrenness, Joseph's release from prison in Egypt, the Israelites release from hard labour in Egypt, and the future redemption of Israel.[5] The analogy between these events is evident: they are all critical events in the early history and ultimate eschatology of Israel, with, in most cases, a connotation of redemption and release.

---

[4] On the conflicting claims that have often been made regarding linearity and circularity in the ancient Jewish concept of time, see Introduction above.

[5] BT *RH* 10b–11b; see also JT *RH* 1: 2 (56d). The events assigned by R. Joshua to the month of Nisan are the creation of the world, the birth and the death of all three Patriarchs, and the future redemption of Israel; but he does not dispute the occurrence of the others in Tishrei. R. Eliezer agrees, for his part, that Isaac was born at Passover (in Nisan).

Another relevant passage is a *piyut* (liturgical poem) of R. Eleazar Hakalir (seventh century?), which has found its way into the Passover Haggadah.[6] This text, largely based on earlier rabbinic exegetical traditions, provides a list of all the historical and eschatological events that allegedly occurred, or will occur, on the date of Passover. These events all share in common, with the story of the Exodus itself, the themes of rescue of Israel and (principally) destruction of its enemies: Abraham's rescue of Lot, the visit of the three angels and their announcement of Isaac's birth, the destruction of Sodom, the destruction of Egypt and plague of the firstborn, the fall of Jericho, Gideon's victory over Midian, the destruction of Sennacherib's Assyrian army, the writing on the wall that appeared to Belshazzar, the fast of Esther, the execution of Haman, and the future fall of Rome. It is as if the date of Passover has an intrinsic property that designates it for the destruction of Israel's enemies—whatever their period and place—and the redemption of Israel.

Some sources suggest further that the event of the Exodus from Egypt recurs, in some form, on the date of every Passover. This annual recurrence is implicit in the mishnaic statement that 'in every generation a person must see himself as if he has come out of Egypt' (Mishnah *Pesahim* 10: 5).[7] It seems that the annual observance of Passover would have been supported by the belief that the events commemorated on this date were being somehow re-enacted or were occurring again.

The notion that particular days of the calendar, especially festival and fast days, are designated for the historical or eschatological recurrence of analogous events, finds a general formulation in R. Yose's saying: 'good things are brought to pass on good days, and bad things on bad days'. This saying aims to explain why both the first and second Temples were destroyed on the same date (9 Av), the same day of the week (at the end of the sabbath), the same year of the sabbatical cycle, and at the time of the same priestly course.[8] According to R. Yose, recurrence of events is due to the intrinsic properties of specific dates in the Jewish year. But the original wording of his saying, which I have only paraphrased (a literal translation is difficult to achieve), adds a further dimension to his theory: its key-term is *megalgelin*, 'roll' (hence the more literal translation: 'good things are *rolled* unto good days'), which clearly evokes the notion of circle or cycle—the term *galgal* (circle) will be

---

[6] This *piyut* is *Omets gevurotekha*, part of R. Eleazar Hakalir's *kerovah* for the first day of Passover (in the Ashkenazi ritual, for the second day of Passover), and incorporated at the end of the Passover Haggadah.

[7] The context of this passage indicates that it is specifically at the time of Passover that this experience, every year, occurs. See also Tosefta *Pes.* 10: 9 (p. 173), which may be suggesting this idea more clearly. On this and other possible examples (relating e.g. to the Revelation at Mount Sinai at the time of the annual festival of Shavuot) see Heinemann, *Ways of Aggadah*, 43 and 164; Bregman, 'Past and Present', 46–9.

[8] Tosefta *Ta'an.* 4: 9 (p. 220), and numerous parallels including BT *Ta'an.* 29a and *Seder olam* 30 (see also JT *Ta'an.* 4: 8 (68d)): מגלגלין זכות ליום זכאי וחובה ליום חייב.

encountered again below. The cyclical implication of R. Yose's theory of recurrence is thus almost explicit in his saying.[9]

Recurrence of events on the same dates of the year implies not only that history repeats itself in a cyclical manner, but also that its cyclicity is rigorously structured by the annual Jewish calendar, and generated, indeed, by properties inherent to specific days of the calendar's year. The cyclicity of the annual calendar—which goes well beyond the trivial fact that its dates are annually repeated—may imply, in turn, the notion that time itself is cyclical. The recurrence of historical events could thus be attributed to a fundamental property of time itself.

This interpretation is possible, but only if one assumes the existence of time as an autonomous entity. In the context of early rabbinic literature, however, historical cyclicity is not associated with the concept of time: it is only conceived of as the recurrence of specific processes and events. Thus an early rabbinic adage states explicitly that 'the world [olam] is like a wheel [galgal]'[10]—it is the world that is cyclical, not time per se. The broader context of this adage, bereavement and mourning, suggests an even more restricted meaning: 'the world is like a wheel' does not refer to the physical circularity of the earth or of the firmament, but rather to the cyclicity of world events, and even more specifically, to the cycle of life and death.[11] Other passages refer, in a similar way, to the universal cyclicity of wealth and poverty: 'The world is like a water-wheel [galgala], of which the full [buckets] are emptied and the empty are filled.'[12]

[9] Furthermore, the terms used for 'good' and 'bad' in this saying are zekhut and ḥovah; these terms (as a pair of opposites) are drawn specifically from juridical terminology, where they are commonly used in the sense of innocence/guilt, merit/blame, award/liability, acquittal/conviction (depending on the context, e.g. whether the context is civil or criminal law). The term megalgelin, likewise, has in mishnaic Hebrew a distinctive juridical connotation: it is used to express how a financial liability can be transferred entirely (literally, 'rolled on') to one of two partners (Mishnah BB 1: 3–4) or to some other party (Tosefta Ket. 9: 3, p. 271; Tosefta BM 9: 17, p. 392; Tosefta Arakh. 1: 5, p. 543), or how the obligation of taking an oath in court can lead to the imposition of further oaths (which are 'rolled over') upon the litigant (Mishnah Shevu. 7: 8). The verb gilgel is also used for divine punishment (Sifrei Deuteronomy 2, p. 8 ed. Finkelstein). The entire saying, finally, finds a close parallel in the phrase מגלגלין זכות על ידי זכאי וחובה על ידי חייב ('merit is rolled through the meritorious, and blame through the blameworthy'), of which the context is clearly divine justice, reward, and punishment (Tosefta Yoma 5: 12, p. 191; JT San. 10: 2 (28b); and parallels). The wording of R. Yose's saying suggests therefore that the recurrence of events on designated days is the fulfilment of some form of inherent cosmic or divine justice.

[10] Genesis Rabbah 63: 14 (p. 698 ed. Theodor and Albeck; see ibid. for minor textual variations): ha'olam asui kegalgal. The word galgal generally means 'wheel' (e.g. Mishnah Kel. 11: 3, 14: 5), or refers to round objects such as the eye (Mishnah Par. 2: 2) or the sun (Tosefta Sot. 4: 4, p. 299).

[11] In the parallel source in BT BB 16b, indeed, the text reads instead (according to a well-attested recension): אבילות גלגל שחוזר בעולם, 'mourning is a circle that returns in the world [olam]'. For other recensions (all similar in sense), see Dikdukei soferim ibid. The term olam can certainly not be translated as 'time': see below, and Ch. 6.

[12] Leviticus Rabbah 34: 9 (p. 792 ed. Margaliot; cf. ibid. 34: 3, p. 778); see also BT Shab. 151b, and parallels.

It is clear from sources we have considered above that the calendar has a determining effect on the periodic or even annual recurrence of events; but reference is
only ever made in these sources to the calendar (or dates within the annual calendar), not to the notion of time itself. The calendar is certainly cyclical, but this has
no bearing on a notion of the abstract time-continuum. Indeed, the only reason
why the calendar is cyclical is that it is based on the concrete, astronomical cycles of
the sun and the moon, or on the annual cycle of the seasons. From an early rabbinic
perspective, therefore, the recurrence of historical events on the same days of the
year need not be any different from the annual recurrence of agricultural events;
there is no reason to ascribe it to the cyclicity of the dimension of time as such. The
highly structured relationship between the calendar and history only implies an
intrinsic affinity between astronomical or seasonal phenomena and earthly, historical events. Universal cyclicity is thus purely process- or event-related: it does not
imply a concept of cyclical time, but only a concept of interdependent, cyclical
events.[13]

The only cycle in the Jewish calendar that is not based on natural phenomena is
that of the sabbath or the seven-day week. At first sight, the seven-day week is
completely abstract and arbitrary, and could thus be interpreted as representative
of the cyclicity of time. Indeed, the conception of the week as planetary, attested in
some marginal rabbinic sources,[14] whereby each of the seven days corresponds to
one of the seven planets, is only nominal and does not correspond, in any empirical
way, with real astronomical phenomena. Even if the week originated, as some
believe, as a quarter (or 'phase') of the lunar month, there is no reflection of this in
rabbinic or even biblical literature; in practical terms, the weeks could not coincide
with lunar phases, since the lunar month is twenty-nine or thirty days long, one or
two days in excess of a four-week period.

However, the arbitrary nature of the seven-day cycle does not relate it, *ipso
facto*, to an abstract concept of 'pure time'. The week is primarily a socially (or reli-
giously) sanctioned cycle of human activity, defined by the cyclical recurrence of
the sabbath, a day of (human) rest: its frame of reference, therefore, is completely
process-related. Moreover, it is evident already from Genesis 1 that the observance
of a sequence of seven days culminating with the sabbath represents a cyclical re-
enactment of the creation of the world. Thus the week is not perceived as an
abstract or arbitrary time-measurement: it is rather a fundamental structure of the
concrete, created world. The week and weekly observance of the sabbath do not
imply the cyclicity of 'pure time', but rather the cyclicity, and perhaps the cyclical
recurrence, of the world's creation.

[13] Sorabji, *Time, Creation and the Continuum*, 182–5, similarly argues that when Greek philosophers
refer to time as cyclical, what they actually mean is that events, or the motion of the spheres, are cyclical.
[14] *Pirkei derabi eli'ezer* 6–7, and *Sefer yetsirah* 4: 4–12; see BT *Ber.* 59*b* and BT *Eruv.* 56*a*.

COMPLEX TIME?

Another calendar-derived concept of time was suggested by me in an article published in 1996 under the title 'Fictitious Calendars: Early Rabbinic Notions of Time, Astronomy, and Reality'. I now have strong doubts as to whether the word 'time' should have been included in the title. Indeed, the body of the article hardly made any reference to it. In this article, I showed how the authors of a late eighth-century text (*Baraita deshemuel*, ch. 5) constructed a schematic calendar on the basis of values for the lunar and solar cycles which they knew themselves to be excessively approximate and thus erroneous. The reason why these erroneous values were adopted for their calendar was that an astronomical event in 776 CE— the coincidence of the autumn equinox with a lunar conjunction—had given the *appearance* of confirming, empirically, these values. Thus in a certain sense, these values were known to be erroneous, but in another sense, they were valid because they seemed to have been empirically confirmed. I argued, on this basis, that the authors of the *Baraita deshemuel* entertained a complex or multi-dimensional view of time, which allowed for different calendrical values to be simultaneously true.

This conclusion must now be corrected. The authors of the *Baraita deshemuel* did hold, it would seem, a complex or multi-dimensional view of the *lunar and solar cycles*, based on the conflicting evidence that was generated by the lunisolar coincidence of 776 CE. But the dimension of time itself was never their concern. The complexity of astronomical processes is irrelevant to an abstract concept of time and to the way it might have been perceived. Time and calendar, again, should not be confused. Inasmuch as calendars are fundamentally process-related, being constructed, in this case, on lunar and solar cycles, they cannot be taken to reflect notions about the time-continuum as such.

SACRED TIME?

A further calendar-derived concept of time, which I should again like to retract, arises from the considerable changes that the rabbinic calendar underwent from the third to ninth centuries CE. These changes have been studied in detail in my book on the Jewish calendar;[15] I shall present them here only in brief.

The Mishnah and Tosefta suggest that until the third century CE, the rabbinic calendar was almost entirely empirical. The beginning of the month was determined on the basis of regular sightings of the new moon. The decision whether to intercalate the year (by adding a thirteenth lunar month to the year, so as to keep up with the solar year or with the cycle of agricultural seasons) was taken annually on the basis of purely empirical data (for instance, the state of ripening of the crops).

[15] *Calendar and Community*, ch. 4.

Because of their empirical foundation, calendar dates were largely unpredictable, even from one month to the next; moreover, they depended entirely on the decisions of a rabbinic court that controlled all calendrical decisions.

Between the third and ninth centuries, as talmudic and geonic sources reveal, the calendar evolved into a system that was based entirely on calculation. By the ninth century, a fixed and standard calendar had emerged of which the dates could be calculated by anyone and predicted in advance, in theory *ad infinitum*. This calendar, which has become normative today, no longer depended on the *ad hoc* monthly and yearly decisions of any rabbinic court or authority.[16]

In my book I argued that this calendar change is likely to have led to a radical transformation of the rabbinic concept of time.[17] In the context of the mishnaic system, where the rabbinic court determined the dates of the calendar on a regular basis, the rabbis would have been perceived as exerting control over the passage of time, and hence, over the entire cosmos and even the divine order. Indeed, a number of early rabbinic sources present God and his angelic court as refusing to sit in judgement on Rosh Hashanah, the New Year or Day of Judgement (1 Tishrei), until the rabbinic court below has declared it the first day of the new month and new year.[18] The cosmic implications of rabbinic calendrical decisions would explain perhaps why the determination of new months is referred to in the Mishnah (*Rosh hashanah* 2: 7, 3: 1, etc.) as an act of 'sanctification' (*kidush ha-ḥodesh*). Not only was man—or more specifically, the rabbinic court—empowered over the flow of time, but time itself was consequently perceived as flexible, man-made, and in a certain sense, *sacred*.

After the institution of a calculated calendar, I argued in my book, the rabbinic experience of time would have radically changed. Because the calendar was now governed by fixed, mathematical rules, time came to be experienced as a rigid, objective, and 'desacralized' homogeneous continuum.

This interpretation—which, I should stress, was based on inference rather than on any explicit evidence—must be completely retracted. There is actually no necessity to assume that the rabbinic calendar determined any particular view of

---

[16] Note that these changes were not necessarily restricted to the rabbinic calendar: Jewish calendars in general in the late antique period (at least in the 4th–6th cc. CE) also show signs of a gradual shift from empirical to calculated schemes (*Calendar and Community*, ch. 3).   [17] Ibid. 230–1.

[18] Tosefta *RH* 1: 12 (p. 209); JT *RH* 1: 3 (57*b*); BT *RH* 8*b*; and in more expanded form, *Pesikta derav kahana* 5: 13 (p. 54*a* ed. Buber; pp. 102–2 ed. Mandelbaum; cited in Stern, *Calendar and Community*, 230). The Tosefta (ibid.) adds that during the forty years in the wilderness, the court's decisions regarding the dates of festivals would have determined when the manna fell (just as the manna did not fall on the sabbath (Exod. 16: 21–30), so, it is assumed in this passage, it did not fall on festivals). A passage in the Jerusalem Talmud (JT *Ket.* 1: 2 (25*b*); JT *Ned.* 6: 13 (40*a*); JT *San.* 1: 2 (19*a*)) possibly implies that since the court's calendrical decisions could determine when a girl reached the age of 3 years, this would affect the point in time when loss of her hymen would become *physically* irreversible; on this passage and its interpretation, see *Calendar and Community*, 231.

time. As I have argued above, the rabbinic calendar is only about solar, lunar, and diurnal cycles, and their synchronization; it does not assume or necessitate the existence of an abstract time-dimension. The shift from an empirical system to a fixed, calculated calendar is likely to have had important cultural implications, perhaps even of a cognitive and ideological nature. But what would have been affected by this shift was not the concept of time as such—which is irrelevant to the calendar—but only the perception of astronomical processes and of their articulation, in the form of calendars, in the social context of lived reality.

Let us begin by examining the suggestion that under the mishnaic system, time itself was perceived as 'sacred'. This suggestion is evidently flawed: the 'sanctification' I have referred to above was not one of time, but only of the new moon (*kidush hahodesh* means 'sanctification of the month' or 'sanctification of the new moon'). It was the moon, not time, that in the mishnaic system the rabbinic court controlled.

This finds vivid expression in a story of Rabbi Hiya, who is said to have instructed the moon to hide itself so as not to contradict the decision of the rabbinic court. The story exists in many versions, which need not be surveyed in detail here.[19] Essentially, the *old* moon crescent was seen by Rabbi Hiya on the morning of the twenty-ninth day of the month[20]—a clear indication that the *new* moon crescent would not be visible that same evening.[21] Rabbi Hiya took some pebbles, or earth,

---

[19] The main sources are JT *RH* 2: 4 (58a); for the Leiden MS reading, see E. Goldman, 'Critical Edition', 206); BT *RH* 25a (cited in *Yalkut shimoni* 2: 862, on Ps. 104: 19); and *Midrash tanhuma* (Buber), 'Bo' 8 (p. 24a; cited in *Yalkut shimoni* 1: 191, on Exod. 12: 2). These sources themselves are subject to significant recensional variation (especially BT *RH* 25a, on which see *Dikdukei soferim*, and *Yalkut shimoni* 1: 191, on which see Hyman and Shiloni, *Yalkut shimoni*, 125). The version of the *Tanhuma* could be interpreted as a completely different story, in which the *new* moon had appeared one evening too early (without any reference to the old moon); but in view of the parallels, this interpretation is less likely. The reference to R. Abun in JT *RH* is internally inconsistent and unparalleled in other sources; it may be the result of some textual error (likewise, the references to R. Zeira or R. Levi in various manuscripts of BT *RH* 25a: see *Dikdukei soferim*, n. 4). Although a detailed and comprehensive study of such variations is beyond my scope, reference to some of these will be made below.

[20] A number of versions specify that it was 29 Elul (so in some recensions of BT *RH* 25a: see *Dikdukei soferim*, n. 1), i. e. the eve of the New Year (so in *Tanhuma* ibid.). R. Hiya's intention was to make Elul a 29-day month, as appears to have been most common in this period (which is why, as in this story, the end of Elul sometimes had to be artificially brought forward: see Stern, *Calendar and Community*, 165–6). The next day, starting in the evening, was to be 1 Tishrei.

[21] It is astronomically impossible for the new moon to be visible so early after the last visibility of the old moon (see *Calendar and Community*, 99–101). According to JT *RH* 2: 4 (58a), R. Hiya had walked 4 *mil* under the light of the old moon, which suggests that it had been visible for quite some time (see above Ch. 2 n. 41). However, as Yaakov Loewinger points out to me, if we assume that a 4-*mil* walk is equivalent to approximately 72 minutes (as most medieval commentators assume, on the basis of the amoraic saying that an average day's walk, in 12 hours, is 40 *mil*: see BT *Pes.* 93b, and Tosafot on *Pes.* 11b, s.v. *ehad*), then it would have been astronomically impossible for the new moon crescent to appear not only on that evening (about 12 hours later), but also on the next evening (about 36 hours later): it would only have first appeared on the evening following the next, some 60 hours later. This would

or a clod of earth (according to different versions of the story), and threw them at the moon, saying: 'Tonight we want to sanctify you, and you are still here! Go and hide yourself!' Some sources refrain, prudently, from specifying whether the moon complied. But others (e.g. the Jerusalem Talmud) report that the moon immediately disappeared, because—the *Tanḥuma* adds—it was under Rabbi Hiya's control.[22]

In actual fact, the disappearance of the moon would hardly have been miraculous, because the old moon crescent always ceases to be visible (and thus 'disappears') by the time of sunrise. The Talmud's suggestion that the moon complied with R. Hiya's orders is thus either scientifically naive, or, perhaps, facetious.[23] Still, the point of the Jerusalem Talmud, and even more clearly, of the *Tanḥuma*, is well made: it was the moon—not time—that Rabbi Hiya was in control of.[24] For as

imply that R. Hiya and the rabbinic court had wanted to create a discrepancy of *two* days between the first day of the calendar month and the evening when the new moon was visible; the need for such a discrepancy is inexplicable and rather unlikely. For the new moon to be visible on the next evening (i.e. 36 hours later), hence only a one-day discrepancy, R. Hiya's old moon could not have been visible for much more than half an hour (calculation courtesy of Yaakov Loewinger). Other versions read 3 *mil*, a distance that had been traversed (in these versions) not by R. Hiya but by cattle-drivers (בהמין: *Tanḥuma* (Buber), 'Bo' 8 (p. 24*a*) or sailors (ספנין, presumably at sea: so in the printed editions of *Yalkut shimoni* 1: 191). Whether this brings us closer to half an hour is unclear, but perhaps ultimately not that important.

[22] *Tanḥuma* ibid.: למה? שהוא ברשותו. This conclusion looks like a later gloss.

[23] I am grateful to Jean Ajdler for drawing my attention to this. No suggestion is made, in any of the versions of this story, that on the same evening the new moon became visible for R. Hiya to sanctify it—which would truly have been a miracle! However, the new moon did not need to become visible, since the rabbinic court had the right to sanctify the new month after 29 days even if the new moon had not been seen (at least for the months of Nisan and Tishrei: JT *RH* 3: 1 (58*c*), BT *RH* 20*a–b*). R. Hiya's concern was only to prevent the visibility of the old moon on the same morning, which would have positively *contradicted* the rabbinic court's decision in the evening. By contrast, failure to see the new moon in the evening would not necessarily have contradicted the court's decision, and hence would not have bothered R. Hiya, since it could always have been argued that the new moon was really visible that evening but only happened not to have been sighted.

[24] The notion of rabbinic control is also implicit in the Babylonian Talmud, which concludes this episode with the instruction that Rabbi (R. Yehudah Hanasi) gave R. Hiya: 'Go to En Tav and sanctify the moon, and send me the watchword: "David king of Israel is alive and exists!" ' (BT *RH* 25*a*). En Tav was the place in Judaea where the new moon, at some times, was 'sanctified' (Safrai, 'Localities'). Safrai (ibid. 35 n. 42) is of the view that this passage (Rabbi's instruction to R. Hiya) is not connected to the preceding account (R. Hiya's sighting of the old moon), because R. Hiya could not possibly have travelled from Galilee (where Rabbi lived) to En Tav in only one day (following his sighting of the old moon in the morning). However, the impossibility of travelling from Galilee to En Tav in one day would not necessarily have been appreciated by the talmudic redactor in Babylonia who composed this piece. It seems to me more likely that the two passages were intended to be connected, otherwise the second passage (Rabbi's instruction to R. Hiya) is uncalled for and out of place. The watchword, with its reference to 'David king of Israel', may be a subtle allusion to the Davidic ancestry of Rabbi (Goodblatt, *Monarchic Principle*, 164–5), meaning perhaps that Rabbi's control over the calendar and the moon confirmed his status as a quasi-Davidic king. Traditions that explicitly attribute Davidic ancestry, and hence perhaps Davidic status, to Rabbi are confined to the Babylonian Talmud (BT

Rabbi Hiya's statement (in all versions of the story) makes clear, it was the moon, specifically, that he intended that evening to 'sanctify'.

Rabbinic control of the moon and the calendar, with all its cosmic ramifications, is not to be confused with some alleged control over the flow of time. None of the early rabbinic sources support this interpretation. The notion that God and his angelic court do not sit in judgement on the New Year unless the rabbinic court has sanctified it (see above) simply means that heavenly, divine activity—not 'time'— depends on the decisions of the human, rabbinic court. If we are to seek a broader, more conceptual implication to the notion of 'sanctification of the new moon', it should not be rabbinic mastery over time, but rather, rabbinic mastery over the *sacred*.

MATHEMATICAL TIME?

Similar objections apply to the second part of this argument, i.e. that after the institution of a calculated calendar, time came to be experienced as rigid, objective, and 'desacralized'. In actual fact, the notion of time was as irrelevant to the calculated calendar as it had been beforehand. Just as the empirical calendar, the calculated calendar did not constitute a measurement of the time-dimension, but only of astronomical processes. The months still corresponded to the monthly lunar cycle (or 'lunation'), although no longer based on sightings of the new moon, but instead on the calculation of an astronomical event, the lunar mean conjunction (*molad*).[25] Thus, no matter how abstract or mathematical the rabbinic calendar became, it remained a fundamentally process-related, lunar (or lunisolar) scheme.

Calculation did not necessarily imply a notion of the time-dimension. The sometimes complex calendrical calculations that are already found in the Talmud, for instance in BT *Arakhin* (8*b*–10*a*),[26] never relate to the time-dimension *per se*. The main concern of these sources is to co-ordinate various astronomical cycles— days, lunar months, solar years—in an effective manner, so as to produce a calendar that is reasonably accurate and mathematically simple to reckon.

In this respect, the calculated calendar was an astronomical scheme that functioned, just like the empirical calendar, as a standard reference system for the schedule, measurement, and co-ordination of other processes in human and social

Shab. 56*a*, BT *Ket.* 62*b*), but there are also implicit references in the Jerusalem Talmud. In one passage we find that Rabbi was from the tribe of Benjamin, though perhaps also from the tribe of Judah on his mother's side (JT *Kil.* 9: 4 (32*b*); JT *Ket.* 12: 3 (35*a*)); in this same passage, however, Hillel is mentioned as Rabbi's ancestor, while elsewhere in the Jerusalem Talmud Hillel is attributed Davidic ancestry (JT *Ta'an.* 4: 2 (68*a*); *Genesis Rabbah* 98: 8, p. 1269 ed. Theodor and Albeck).

[25] For an explanation of this concept, see Stern, *Calendar and Community*, 100, 112.

[26] Passages of this kind are particularly prominent in Babylonian sources: for references, discussion, and explanation, see ibid. 258–63.

life. The change from empirical to fixed calendar was no more than the substitution of one standard, astronomical 'yardstick' for another. The new calendar would only have affected, at most, the rabbinic perception of astronomical processes—we might regard the calculation of the conjunction a 'mathematization' or 'desacralization' of the moon and the lunation—but it had nothing to do with how time itself was (if at all) perceived.

Nevertheless, there may be a case to argue that the introduction of a calculated, mathematical calendar was *conducive* to the formation and development of an abstract concept of the time-dimension. Although this new calendar was not a measurement of time, but only of astronomical processes, the relative dissociation of the calculated calendar from observable, empirical phenomena (such as the appearance of the new moon crescent, which had been central to the mishnaic, empirical calendar) may have led to the notion that the calendar was not really a representation of astronomical processes, but rather the arbitrary measurement of an abstract, transcendent entity: the time-dimension. Elias has similarly suggested, with reference to the modern period, that as calendars became increasingly mathematical and divorced from their original astronomical foundations, the relationship between calendars and natural processes was gradually forgotten. The new, artificial calendars came to be seen instead as measurements of an abstract time-dimension, a notion which itself developed partly as the result of these calendrical changes.[27]

This argument may be valid for the modern period, but it is unlikely to apply to Judaism of late antiquity. The fixed rabbinic calendar, indeed, was considerably less divorced from its astronomical foundations than is the modern Gregorian calendar. In the modern calendar, the only astronomical element that has survived is the year, which corresponds, in astronomical terms, to the length of the mean tropical year. This, however, is of limited empirical significance to the ordinary person. Everyone knows in theory that the annual cycle of the sun and the seasons corresponds to the calendar year, but in practice, the ordinary person is not able to verify this. It is certainly not possible, for the ordinary person, to establish what is the date on the basis of observable astronomical phenomena. Equinoxes and solstices are too difficult for the ordinary person to calculate or observe, variations of the length of the day are too difficult to measure, and the succession of seasons is usually too erratic, to establish even approximately what is the date through purely empirical means. This is why the calendar is more readily treated, in prevailing modern culture, as an arbitrary measurement of abstract time than as a measurement of the course of the sun and seasons.

In the fixed rabbinic calendar, by contrast, correspondence with astronomical

---

[27] Elias, *Time*, 16–17, 197–8. A similar argument is put forward by Elias with regard to the introduction of mechanical clocks for the purpose of timing: see above Ch. 2 n. 19.

phenomena remained far more in emphasis. In spite of being based on a standard mathematical calculation, including some non-lunar calendrical rules,[28] its months still corresponded quite closely to the monthly cycle of the moon. This would have been easily verifiable to the ordinary observer. The phases of the moon are sufficiently obvious, especially at night, to be meaningfully related to the dates of the fixed rabbinic calendar month. Indeed, the correlation between certain days of the calendar month and the lunar phases was regularly reasserted even after the institution of the fixed rabbinic calendar, through ritual practices such as the blessing over the waxing moon.[29] Furthermore, as late as the tenth century—long after the establishment of the fixed calendar—the actual new moon was still so important to the calendar users that its occasional visibility one day *before* the beginning of a calendar month could cause considerable embarrassment, and even challenge the legitimacy of the calendar calculation.[30] The rabbinic calendar was thus not completely divorced from its original astronomical context, in the same way as has

[28] The main non-lunar calendrical rule is *lo* אדו *rosh*, i.e. that the New Year (1 Tishrei) cannot occur on a Sunday (א), Wednesday (ד), or Friday (ו), but must be postponed to the next day. On the origins and history of this rule, see Stern, *Calendar and Community*, 166–7, 192–5.

[29] BT *San*. 41*b*–42*a*. The correlation between the actual phases of the moon and specific days of the calendar month (the 7th, the 16th) is explicitly spelt out in this passage. The correlation between the 7th of the calendar month and the moon's first quarter appears in a saying attributed to R. Jacob b. Idi in the name of R. Judah, which suggests (if the attribution is reliable) a 3rd-c. dating, still in the period of the empirical calendar; but the correlation between the 16th of the calendar month and the full moon, in a saying attributed to the *Nehardai*, is likely to date from after the institution of the fixed calendar. Although the period of the *Nehardai* themselves cannot be known, the correlation between the 16th and the full moon suggests a calendar month beginning at the conjunction, which is only compatible with the later, fixed rabbinic calendar; contrast JT *Ber*. 9: 3 (13*d*), which cites a similar saying attributed to the 'rabbis of Caesarea', but referring instead to the 14th and to be considered earlier. In any event, it is clear that this talmudic passage did not become irrelevant after the calendar was fixed. R. Sa'adiah Gaon (early 10th c.), in whose period the fixed calendar had certainly reached its final form, ruled in his *Sidur* that the blessing over the waxing moon should be recited between the 4th and the 14th of the month (Davidson et al., *Sidur rav sa'adiah gaon*, 90–1). Maimonides (late 12th c.), followed by subsequent codifiers, ruled that the latest date for this blessing was the 16th of the month, in accordance with the talmudic ruling (*Mishneh torah*, 'Laws of Blessings', 10: 17). Both were thus reasserting, each in his own way, the correlation between calendar month and the lunar monthly cycle. This correlation only began to weaken towards the end of the 13th c., apparently in the circle of R. Meir (Maharam) of Rothenburg, with the innovative ruling that the latest time for the blessing over the waxing moon should not be defined according to the days of the month, but rather according to a calculation based on the *molad* (i.e. the mean conjunction: R. Shimshon b. Tsadok, *Tashbets*, 87; then R. Jacob b. Asher, *Arba'ah turim*, 'Orah hayim', 426: 1, and R. Alexander Zuslein Hakohen, *Agudah*, *San*. 47).

[30] Early visibility of the new moon appears to have occurred in (or rather just before) Tishrei 922 CE, and to have been used by Ben Meir as an argument against R. Sa'adiah's calendar calculation: see Bornstein, 'About the Last Days', 244–7. Nowadays, however, early visibility of the new moon is non-problematic and almost goes unnoticed (as recently, when the moon was visible in Jerusalem on 30 Aug. 2000 CE in the evening, which corresponded to 30 Av and not 1 Elul). See Stern, *Calendar and Community*, 180–1.

occurred, perhaps, with the modern secular calendar. This reduces the likelihood that the introduction of a rabbinic calculated calendar generated the development of an abstract concept of the time-dimension.

In the next chapter, we shall see that a concept of time *per se* made its first appearance in rabbinic literature in the works of R. Sa'adiah Gaon, in the early tenth century. R. Sa'adiah was himself an expert on the fixed rabbinic calendar, on which he wrote a whole monograph (no longer extant), and which he did much to propagate throughout the Jewish world.[31] But the calendar calculation is unlikely to have been the source of R. Sa'adiah's concept of time. His reflections on time are confined to his philosophical writings; it is to the influence of Muslim and Greek philosophy, as I shall argue in the next chapter, that his innovative concept of time must be attributed.

CHRONOLOGY IN THE *SEDER OLAM*

Let us now turn to chronology or long-range time-reckoning. Early rabbinic interest in chronology, particularly biblical, follows an ancient Jewish tradition that goes back to the book of Jubilees, Qumran literature, and further back, the Bible itself.[32] Interest in chronology has been treated by some as evidence of early Jewish awareness of the time-continuum.[33] But this inference is dependent on a particular interpretation of chronology as 'time' reckoning, which I shall now question. As we shall see, the early rabbinic discourse on chronology relates entirely to historical events and processes, without assuming the concepts of a 'time-line' or the time-continuum.

The importance of biblical chronology in early rabbinic culture is exemplified in a monograph that is dedicated entirely to this theme: the *Seder olam*. This work traces the chronology of the world from the Creation to the Bar-Kokhba revolt (the second century CE), with its main focus on biblical chronology and history. Many of its passages are paralleled, sometimes quite frequently, in other talmudic and midrashic works.[34]

Particularly conspicuous is the absence, in the *Seder olam*, of any general time-scale or era. The era 'from the Creation' which Jews are familiar with today (thus 5764 from the Creation = 2003/4 CE) and which might have given a sense of

---

[31] See Stern, *Calendar*, 264–75.

[32] The literature on this is vast: see e.g. Wacholder, *Jewish Chronology and Chronography*.

[33] e.g. Barr, *Biblical Words*, 28–9.

[34] To cite just a few, arbitrary examples: *Genesis Rabbah* 33: 7 (pp. 312–13 ed. Theodor and Albeck: the Flood chronology); BT *Shab.* 86b–88a (the chronology of the Revelation at Mount Sinai); BT *Meg.* 17a (the chronology of Jacob's life). On the *Seder olam* (sometimes referred to as *Seder olam rabah*) see Milikowsky, 'Seder olam and Jewish Chronography'; Stemberger, *Introduction to the Talmud and Midrash*, 326–7.

continuous time or history does not appear at all in this work. This is evident already in the first chapter of *Seder olam*, which states that there were 1,656 years from Adam (i.e. from his birth/creation) to the Flood, and 380 years from the Flood to the dispersion at the Tower of Babel: no attempt is made to add up these two figures so as to obtain a continuous era from the Creation.[35] In the remaining twenty-nine chapters of *Seder olam*, the periods of time that are given (usually also in years) are considerably shorter;[36] the epoch of Adam is completely ignored and forgotten. Although it should be possible for the reader to add up its figures and obtain a world-era from Adam or the Creation, the *Seder olam* itself does not engage in the construction of such a scheme.

In the absence of any era or absolute time-scale, events in the *Seder olam* (and parallel sources) are not dated according to a system of numbered years, but purely in *relative* terms, usually in relation to the ages of individual characters. For instance, we are told that Abraham was 48 years old when the Tower of Babel was built (ch. 1).[37] This use of relative dating, pervasive in the *Seder olam*, is consistent with rabbinic usage elsewhere. With reference to post-biblical, more recent historical events, we are told for instance in other sources that one rabbi died on the day when another was born,[38] or that a given event occurred so many years before the destruction of the Temple;[39] absolute dates are almost never provided.

[35] Milikowsky, '*Seder olam* and Jewish Chronography', 122; Stemberger, *Introduction to the Talmud and Midrash*, 326. This contrasts with the contemporary (early 3rd c. CE) Christian chronography of Julius Africanus, which establishes an era from Adam.

[36] The end of *Seder olam* (ch. 30) provides somewhat longer periods, namely the lengths of the Persian empire, Hellenistic empire, Hasmonaean kingdom, and Herodian kingdom, as well as the intervals between the Jewish revolts against Rome (parallel in BT *AZ* 9a). However, this section is out of character with the rest of the *Seder olam*, which leads Milikowsky, '*Seder olam* and Jewish Chronography', 117, to suggest that it might have been a later addition. It may also be relevant to note that the progression of *Seder olam* is not always linear: ch. 4, for instance, is a regression back to the Flood chronology.

[37] This contrasts with a similar but considerably later work, the *Seder olam zuta*, in which all events are systematically dated by the era from the Creation. According to Milikowsky, '*Seder olam* and the Tosefta', the *Seder olam* (or *Seder olam rabah*, to distinguish it from the *Seder olam zuta*) was redacted before the Tosefta, thus in the early 3rd c. CE at the latest; Stemberger, *Introduction to the Talmud and Midrash*, 326 considers it to be early amoraic (i.e. 3rd c. CE), but with later additions or revisions. *Seder olam zuta*, by contrast, is a geonic work dating from the 8th c. at the earliest (ibid. 327). There are reasonable grounds to assume that, in the later geonic period, rabbinic perceptions of time were shifting: see discussion below, Ch. 4.

[38] *Genesis Rabbah* 58: 2 (pp. 619–21 ed. Theodor and Albeck), BT *Kid.* 72b. The purpose of these parallel passages is not chronology for its own sake, but rather to demonstrate the historical continuity of Torah teachers.

[39] BT *San.* 41a. The event in question is the exile of the Sanhedrin, forty years before the Destruction of the Temple. Inasmuch as this event *precedes* the destruction, it cannot be interpreted as dated by the era from the Destruction (on which see below). Relative dating is particularly effective in this context, as it is far more significant to relate this event to the destruction of the Temple than to date it according to some abstract, chronological time-scale.

The absence of any overall chronological time-scale or era, with the preference instead for event-based, relative dating, does not mean that the *Seder olam* has no interest in chronology. Chronology, after all, is what this work is all about. The question is, however, whether the chronology of the *Seder olam* implies or necessitates a concept of time-continuum or 'pure time'. It is certainly significant, as Milikowsky has pointed out, that the regnal years of all the kings of Judah and Israel are provided, even where the *Seder olam* has nothing to add to what is already in the Bible.[40] The *Seder olam* clearly attaches importance to these regnal years because of their potential use for dating historical events. This becomes evident, at least, at the end of the book, where the *Seder olam* explicitly states that after the Herodian period and the cessation of Jewish kings, the era from the destruction of the Temple or the Seleucid era should instead be used (ch. 30).[41] But dating events according to regnal years only amounts to the co-ordination of one historical process with another. Just as with calendars (as argued above), regnal years are only standard reference scales or 'yardsticks' in relation to which other historical events or processes can be co-ordinated and measured. This process-related activity, which we can only call 'time-reckoning' in a loose sense, does not imply or require any notion of the time-continuum *per se*.

There is a case to argue, moreover, that chronology is not the ultimate concern of this work. As Milikowsky has shown, the *Seder olam* only dates events where this helps to elucidate the biblical narrative.[42] The purpose of the *Seder olam* may thus be biblical exegesis rather than the construction of a continuous time-line of history. Although it covers a chronological continuum from Adam to the Bar-Kokhba revolt, its focus is not the long-term duration and its reckoning, but rather the relative anteriority, simultaneity, and posteriority of biblical characters and events—for instance, how old Abraham was when the Tower of Babel was built. Its focus is on the narrative of the Bible, rather than on time as an end in itself.

The title of this work, *Seder olam*—attested already in the Babylonian Talmud (BT *Yevamot* 82b and BT *Nidah* 46b)—is itself of interest. I will discuss the meaning of the biblical term *olam* in detail later (see Chapter 6); although it is often translated as 'eternity', I shall argue that it expresses the event-related idea of 'permanence' rather than the temporal idea of an endless time-continuum. In any event, however, the term *olam* is unlikely to mean 'eternity' in this context. In early rabbinic Hebrew (and so in contemporary Aramaic), the term *olam* takes on the additional meaning of 'world', and this new meaning appears to have become the

---

[40] Milikowsky, '*Seder olam* and Jewish Chronography', 123–4.
[41] On the origin of ch. 30, however, see n. 36 above.
[42] Milikowsky, '*Seder olam* and Jewish Chronography', 120.

most frequent.[43] The meaning of the title *Seder olam* is thus more likely to be 'Order of the World', in the sense, perhaps, of 'Order of World History'; this clearly does not imply any concept of time-line or time-continuum.

The *Seder olam* (in its present version) concludes with the following version of a *midrash* on Genesis 5: 1:

God showed Adam every [future] generation and its leaders, every generation and its prophets, every generation and its exegetes, every generation and its sages, every generation and its administrators, every generation and its judges; the sages of every generation, the prophets of every generation, the righteous of every generation; the number of their names, the count of their days, the calculation of their hours, the sum of their footsteps. (ch. 30)

Although 'days' and 'hours' are mentioned, Adam's vision was not primarily temporal. It was not the continuum of time that unfolded before him, but rather the generations and great men that would arise in the future, every day and hour of their lives, including even their 'footsteps'. This was not a vision of future time *per se*, but rather a vision of people and events, i.e. the whole of history.

ERAS AND MILLENARIANISM

As has been noted above, the sense of a continuous and endless time-line can sometimes be generated through the use of large-scale time units such as eras. The era from the Creation—which spans the entire history of the world, assuming there was nothing before Creation—would have been most suitable to convey the notion of time as a whole, continuous entity.

This era is absent, however, from the *Seder olam*; it is rarely attested, furthermore, in other early rabbinic sources and, more generally, in Jewish sources from

---

[43] See Koehler and Baumgartner, *Hebrew and Aramaic Lexicon*, ii. 798–9. A good illustration of this shift of meaning can be found in *Targum Psalms* 89: 3, and *Sifra* 'Kedoshim', 10: 11 (citing the same verse): the word *olam* in Ps. 89: 3 means 'for ever', but it is rendered by the Targum and the *Sifra* as 'world'. See also Abraham ibn Ezra's commentary on Exod. 21: 6 and Eccles. 3: 11. The origins of this usage are very unclear. Wiesenberg, 'The Liturgical Term *melekh ha-'olam*', 3–13, argues that the spatial meaning of *olam* as 'world' can already be found in the Bible (his evidence, however, is weak); Brin, *Concept of Time*, 14, 226, and 289–92, argues that it is first attested in the Dead Sea Scrolls. The dual use of *olam* in early rabbinic Hebrew, meaning both 'long duration' and 'world', may be itself significant, as it may suggest some conceptual blurring of the categories of time and space, or rather perhaps their subsumption under a more general category of process. Wiesenberg's comment on this point is worthy of quote: 'Our present distinction between the spatial and temporal connotations of *'olam* would probably have seemed to the ancient Hebrews, not only in the biblical period but also in the early rabbinic period, as quibbling at what to them were but two aspects, not altogether distinct, of the selfsame thing. They thought in terms of concrete reality. For the abstract notion of infinite duration, they just had no expression at all. Their *'olam* . . . basically meant to them "enduring as long as the physical world endures" ' (ibid. 3).

late antiquity.[44] Rabbinic sources suggest instead that documents would normally be dated according to the sabbatical cycle[45] or regnal years,[46] and in the 'Diaspora', according to the Seleucid era;[47] a passage in the Babylonian Talmud assumes, indeed, that scribes normally use the latter.[48] Documentary and epigraphic Jewish sources from late antiquity confirm the use of sabbatical year datings,[49] regnal years,[50] the Seleucid era,[51] as well as other secular dating systems[52] and—distinc-

---

[44]   The era from the Creation first appears in an inscription of the (5th-c. CE?) Horvat Susiya synagogue (Gutman et al., 'The Synagogue at Horvat Susiya', 127), and then twice in the Babylonian Talmud: BT *San.* 97*b* and BT *AZ* 9*b*. It appears again in the late 8th-c. *Baraita deshemuel*, ch. 5 (see Stern, 'Fictitious Calendars'). However, it only becomes commonly used in the late 9th c., starting with the date of [4]644 (= 883/4 CE) in *Seder tana'im ve'amora'im* (p. 7 ed. Kahan): see Bornstein, 'Jewish Dates', 222–30.

[45]   Tosefta *Mak.* 1: 2 (p. 438); BT *San.* 32*a*. Witnesses in court would also date events according to the sabbatical cycle: Mishnah *San.* 5: 1 (cited above, Ch. 1).

[46]   JT *RH* 1: 1 (56*b*); BT *RH* 2*a* and 8*a*. Divorce bills have only regnal years or provincial eras: Tosefta *Git.* 8: 3 (p. 332) = Tosefta *Edu.* 2: 4 (p. 457), Mishnah *Git.* 8: 5 (implicitly), and BT *Git.* 80*b*; see further Lieberman, *Tosefta kifeshutah*, viii. 890–1. An interesting but obscure *midrash* admonishes the Jews for not using an era from the Creation, the building of the Temple, or the Exodus, but only Roman regnal years: Schechter, *Agadath Shir Hashirim*, 16 (with notes on p. 58), on S. of S. 1: 6; see parallel in *Mekhilta derabi yishma'el*, 'Baḥodesh' 1 (p. 203 ed. Horovitz and Rabin). Note, however, the suggestion (ultimately rejected) in BT *AZ* 10*a* that the Seleucid era is really an era from the Exodus, with the omission of the 1,000 years that happen (according to the chronology of the *Seder olam*) to lie between their epochs.

[47]   *Seder olam* 30 and BT *AZ* 10*a*, where it is referred to as the era or regnal years 'of the Greeks'. 'Diaspora' (*golah*) usually means Babylonia (e.g. JT *RH* 2: 2 (58*a*); BT *RH* 23*b*). The Seleucid era began from 312/11 BCE, and was probably the most commonly used era throughout the late antique Near East: see Meimaris, *Chronological Systems*, 53–9. The Seleucid era was also pervasive in the late geonic period (e.g. in the *Igeret* (Epistle) of R. Sherira Gaon, 987 CE); it was referred to in this period and later as 'the era of documents [*lishetarot*]', e.g. responsum of R. Hai Gaon, cited by R. Abraham b. Hiya in his *Sefer ha'ibur* 3: 7 (p. 97 ed. Filipowski; B. M. Lewin, *Otsar hage'onim*, v (Jerusalem: Hebrew University Press, 1932), *RH*, 17)—a reflection of its widespread use.

[48]   BT *AZ* (9*a*–10*a*). The Seleucid era is not explicitly mentioned in BT *AZ* 9*a*–*b*, but the system attributed to scribes in this passage cannot be interpreted in any other way.

[49]   Sabbatical-year datings are pervasive in the Zoar inscriptions (4th–6th cc.: see Stern, *Calendar and Community*, 87–93), and also attested in the Horvat Susiya inscription (above, n. 44) and the *ketubah* of Antinoopolis (Egypt) dating from 417 CE (Stern, ibid. 137–9).

[50]   P. Murabbaʿât 18, for instance, is dated to the second year of Nero (55/6 CE), and also perhaps according to the sabbatical year (Benoit et al., *Discoveries in the Judaean Desert*, ii. 100–4; Stern, *Calendar and Community*, 92). Aramaic ostracon no. 1 published by Yardeni, 'New Jewish Aramaic Ostraka', is dated to 'year 13', possibly also the regnal year of a Roman emperor (alternatively, the era of Provincia Arabia). The Dura-Europos synagogue is dated to the second year of Emperor Philip (244/5 CE: Levine, 'Synagogue of Dura-Europos', 173). Jewish documents from Ptolemaic Egypt use Ptolemaic regnal years (Tcherikover and Fuks, *Corpus Papyrorum Judaicarum*, e.g. no. 4, i. 126), and those from Nabataea (before 106 CE) use Nabataean regnal years (Yadin, *Documents from the Bar-Kokhba Period*, nos. 1–3, and Starcky, 'Contrat nabatéen').

[51]   e.g. at the Dura-Europos synagogue (Levine, 'Synagogue of Dura-Europos', 173), and at Palmyra (Cantineau, *Inscriptions de Palmyre*, VIII. 61 and VII. 4 = Frey, *Corpus Inscriptionum Judaicarum*, ii, no. 820).

[52]   e.g. civic or provincial eras (e.g. in the Berenike inscription: Stern, *Calendar and Community*, 58–61; and the Babatha archive, where the era of Provincia Arabia is commonly used: Yadin,

tively Jewish—the era of the destruction of the (Second) Temple.[53] None of these systems allowed retrospective dating from before the beginning of the era (or regnal period), like our negative BCE years. Their scope was therefore limited, and there was no mechanism for relating one era (or regnal period) to another that had preceded it. Each of these systems is likely to have carried a range of specific, implicit meanings: sabbatical cycle years would have reminded the Jews of the forthcoming or current sabbatical year, regnal years and the Seleucid era would have reminded them, perhaps, that they were under foreign rule, and the era of the Destruction would have reminded them that the Temple was no more.[54] But in the absence of the era of the Creation, none of these dating systems would have conveyed the notion of a complete time-line or the totality of history.

The only references, in early rabbinic literature, to the whole of historical time are in a few millenarian or eschatological statements that are confined almost exclusively to one section of the Babylonian Talmud, the last chapter of BT *Sanhedrin*.[55] The duration of the world is given there as six thousand years, sub-

Documents from the Bar-Kokhba Period), or consular years (e.g. the Catania inscription: Stern, *Calendar and Community*, 132–3; and the *ketubah* of Antinoopolis, above, n. 49). See above, n. 46.

[53] Pervasive again in the Zoar inscriptions (above, n. 49), and used in the *ketubah* of Antinoopolis (ibid.) and on a lintel of the Kefar Nevuraya synagogue (dated 494 from the Destruction: Naveh, *On Mosaic and Stone*, 31–3, and 'Ancient Synagogue Inscriptions', 137). The era from the Destruction is unique in that it is probably the only distinctively Jewish era to have been consistently used in late antiquity and the early Middle Ages: see further Stern, *Calendar and Community*, 88–9 n. 123. It is mentioned in *Seder olam* 30 (parallel in BT *AZ* 9a), and possibly used in BT *AZ* 9b ('400 years after the Destruction'), although this may just be a relative dating. The statement, in BT *AZ* 9a, that there is a difference of twenty years (ignoring the hundreds) between the Seleucid era and the Destruction era suggests that the latter had 69/70 CE as its year 1 (thus the year 20, in 88/9 CE, was 400 in the Seleucid era). The same epoch was assumed at Zoar for the Destruction era (see Stern, *Calendar and Community*, 91, and as further confirmed by the new inscription in Cotton and Price, 'Bilingual Tombstone').

[54] Irshai, 'Dating the Eschaton', 152, reads into the era of the Destruction a messianic expectation, at least in the context of the Zoar necropolis.

[55] BT *San.* 97a–b and parallels. These passages may reflect Babylonian or Persian influence, as suggested by Boyce, *History of Zoroastrianism*, i. 286 n. 37 and iii. 412; and Gafni, 'Concepts of Periodization', 23–4. The origin of millenarianism is perhaps more likely to be Babylonian than Persian, because of the absence of millenarian schemes in the (Iranian) Avesta (Almut Hinze, pers. comm.); Gignoux, 'Hexaéméron et millénarisme', argues that the millenarianism of later Persian sources is likely to be of Judaeo-Christian origin; but for possible external sources confirming the existence of Persian millenarianism already in the 5th and 4th cc. BCE, see West, *Greek Philosophy and the Orient*, 32. The theory of Babylonian or Persian influence is particularly plausible in the context of early rabbinic literature, because millenarian schemes are rare in Palestinian sources, and largely confined to the Babylonian Talmud. However, for an early and non-rabbinic Palestinian source, see Pseudo-Philo, *Biblical Antiquities* 28: 8 (1st c. CE), referring to the period of 7,000 years (4,000 according to some recensions). For later Jewish sources, drawing perhaps on the Babylonian Talmud passages, see R. Eleazar Hakalir's *Siluk leparashat shekalim* (*Az ra'ita*), cited below; and *Tana devei eliyahu* (pp. 6–7 ed. Ish-Shalom). The concept of 7,000 years also appears in early Christian sources: the *Epistle of Barnabas* 15: 4, and some versions of 2 Enoch (Slavonic Enoch) 33: 1–2 which are likely to be a Christian interpolation (F. A. Andersen in Charlesworth, *Old Testament Pseudepigrapha*, i. 156 n. b).

divided into two thousand years of *tohu*, two thousand years of Torah, and two thousand years of the messianic age. Other sages, in the same passage, give the world a minimum of eighty-five jubilees; others still give 4,291 years from the Creation to the coming of the messianic age. The messianic age itself is given various lengths, including 'the same as from the Creation until now'.[56] These few passages, however, are only concerned with the total duration of world history. There is no reason to infer from this concern a concept of the time-continuum *per se*.

TIME AND MEASUREMENT

A relatively late source, from the liturgical work of R. Eleazar Hakalir, presents a comprehensive list of time-measurement units in such a way as to suggest, at first sight, the notion of time as a measurable entity. This remarkable composition, the *Siluk leparashat shekalim* (*Az ra'ita*), comprises in fact four sections, on the measuring systems of length, volume, time, and weight (or coinage); each section starts from the largest unit or denomination, and finishes with the smallest. Thus, the section on time ranges from the largest unit, the whole of world history, to the smallest fraction of the day. At first sight, this list implies the existence of time as a measurable entity, or a dimension capable of being measured; but on further analysis, as we shall see, the only concern of this passage are the measurements *per se*.

Our section is introduced as follows: 'And just as there is volume to the offspring of the earth, so there is measure [*kets*] to the days of the earth [or world: *ha'arets*].'[57] Then comes the list of the units of measurement:

For the whole world [*olam*][58] is 6,000 (years)

which make 5⅔ cycles[59]

and the number of the cycle [*mahzor*] is 22 jubilees

and the year of the jubilee is [at the end of] 7 weeks of years

and the weeks of years [i.e. sabbatical cycles] are 28 seasons[60]

and the days of a season are 91⅓ days

and the 'times' [*onot*] of the day are 576[61]

---

[56] The latter in BT *San. 99a*; according to another opinion, 'the same as from Noah until now'. The meaning of 'until now' is not clarified: it may mean until the saying was uttered, or until the end of the present (non-messianic) age. This ambiguity is likely to be deliberate. On these passages, see further Irshai, 'Dating the Eschaton'.   [57] וכמו נתן כיל לתולדות הארץ, כן נתן קץ לימי הארץ.

[58] The term *olam* is used here, very effectively, both in its sense of 'world' and in its sense of 'eternity', hence meaning something like 'total duration of the world'; see above, n. 43.

[59] On the meaning of 'cycle' (*mahzor*), see below.

[60] The tropical seasons of spring, summer, autumn, and winter are four in each year and hence twenty-eight in each sabbatical cycle.

[61] $576 = 24^2$. The 'time' (*onah*) is thus $\frac{1}{24}$ of the hour, slightly in excess of two minutes. Note that for some reason (perhaps poetical licence), the division of the day into hours ($\frac{1}{24}$ of the day) is omitted.

and the 'moments' [*rigei*] are to the 'time' [*onah*] as the 'times' [*onot*] are to the whole day[62] and the meticulous divide the 'moment' [*rega*] into further [sub-]'moments' [*rega'im*][63]

The integration of these units of measurement into a single scale is often only approximate. Thus, the division of the 'world' (6,000 years) into 5⅔ 'cycles', which in turn are divided into 22 jubilees, does not exactly square.[64] Although the identity of the 'cycle' (*maḥzor*) is unspecified, it may well represent a great lunisolar cycle of 1,064 years;[65] but this corresponds neither to 6,000 ÷ 5⅔ years, nor to 22 jubilees, but only to something in between.[66] The units of measurement in this list are also very disparate in nature: some are astronomical (e.g. season, day, and, as presently suggested, 'cycle'), some historical (the world's duration of 6,000 years), some religious (jubilees, sabbatical cycles), and some purely arithmetical (the division of the day into fractions and sub-fractions of 576).

It is precisely the disparateness of these units of measurement that suggests, at first sight, an underlying notion of the time-dimension. Indeed, the time-dimension appears to be the only common denominator that would justify the integration of these units, albeit approximate, into a single scale. One cannot argue—as I have argued regarding the calendar—that this scale is really about astronomical processes, because the majority of its terms have nothing to do with astronomy at all.

---

[62] In other words, one 'moment' (*rega*) is ¹⁄₅₇₆ of the 'time' (*onah*), i.e. considerably shorter than a second (roughly a quarter of a second). On the use of fractions of 24 (rather than the sexagesimal system of fractions of 60), and on the theoretical nature of these minute subdivisions of the hour, see above Ch. 2 n. 12.

כי העולם כלו ששת אלפים[63]

עושים חמשה ושתי ידים מחזורות

ומנין המחזור בעשרים ושנים יובלות

ושנת היובל שבע שבתות שנים

ושבתות השנים בעשרים ושמונה תקופות

וימות התקופה תשעים ואחד יום ושליש

ועונות היום חמש מאות ושבעים ושש

ורגעי העונה כעונות כל היום

והמדקדק מחלק הרגע לכמה רגעים

[64] Whether we assume the jubilee cycle to be 49 or 50 years (this is a tannaitic dispute in JT *Kid*. 1: 2 (59*a*), BT *Ned*. 61*a*), 22 jubilees do not amount to 6,000 years divided by 5⅔.

[65] This at least is the only interpretation I can think of (Stern, *Calendar and Community*, 197). The great cycle of 1,064 years corresponds to a multiplication of the 28-year cycle by the 19-year cycle, doubled. The 28-year cycle assumes a year-length of exactly 365¼ days, as according to the Julian calendar (see BT *Ber*. 59*b*, BT *Eruv*. 56*a*); at the end of this cycle, the notional vernal equinox recurs on the same day of the week and at the same time of the day. The 'Metonic' 19-year cycle synchronizes the lunar month with the solar year; at the end of this cycle, the beginning of the first lunar month coincides with that of the solar year. The multiplication of these two cycles yields a great cycle of 532 years, at the end of which the equinox recurs on the same day of the week, at the same time of the day, and on the same day of the lunar month. Double this great cycle is 1,064 years. Why this cycle needs to be doubled would, however, remain completely unclear.

[66] 6,000 years ÷ 5⅔ makes 1,059 years; 22 jubilees of 49 years each (better than of 50 years) makes 1,078 years. The number of 1,064 years lies therefore somewhere in between.

At first sight, therefore, what holds this list together is only that all its terms are measurements of the time-dimension.

If this interpretation is correct, we shall have finally hit on implicit evidence of a notion of time as an entity on its own, and more specifically, as a measurable dimension. It should be stressed, however, that this source is relatively late (seventh century, although this date is somewhat conjectural); there is a strong case to argue that *piyut*, liturgical literature, belongs to the post-talmudic period. The lateness of this source may be significant. In the next chapter, indeed, it will be shown that by contrast with late antiquity, in the medieval period (though not before the period of R. Sa'adiah, in the early tenth century), the abstract notion of time became an integral part of rabbinic Judaism.

The question is, however, whether this passage really does assume the concept of time as common denominator between its terms. The concept of time is certainly not mentioned anywhere explicitly in this passage. The opening sentence which introduces this section (cited above) refers only to the 'measure of the days of the earth', but not to the measure of 'time'. 'Days of the earth' presumably means the total duration of the world (6,000 years) and its subdivisions, and can thus be interpreted purely as a process. Even if the term *kets*, which also appears in this opening sentence, is translated as 'time' (rather than as 'measure', hence: 'so there is *time* to the days of the earth'), this could only be in the sense of 'limited time' or 'measure of time'; it would make little sense, in the context of this sentence, to interpret this word as referring to the entity or dimension of time *per se*.[67] In this context, however, the translation 'measure' is definitely to be preferred.

The emphasis on the concept of measure or measurement (rather than time) is clearer still in the opening sentence of the next section, which deals with weight (or coinage): 'And just as there is calculation [*heshbon*] for everything, so there are weight and balance for everything.'[68] The first clause ('And just as there is . . .') refers to our section (which precedes it);[69] it calls our section not 'time', but merely 'calculation'.

This rather neutral designation is also used near the beginning of the composition, where the four sections are introduced and described thus:

every number, count, calculation, and its numbers,

every weight, balance, wallet,[70] and its fractions,

[67]   Such an interpretation of the word *kets* would also be unattested elsewhere. The term *kets* in the sense of 'time', but always only punctual or of limited duration, is first attested at Qumran and then in the writings of Hakalir (see above Ch. 1 n. 3).

[68]   ‏וכמו נתן חשבון על כל, כן נתן משקל ופלס לכל.‏

[69]   Similarly to the opening sentence of our section (cited above), in which the first clause ('And just as there is volume to the offspring of the earth') refers to the section that precedes it (on volume).

[70]   In which weights are kept (Baer, *Sidur avodat yisra'el*, 653). I should stress that translation of this whole passage is difficult.

every capacity, wet and dry, and its measures,

every line, dimension, measurement, and its quantities[71]

The four sections are listed out of order, but are easy to identify: lines 2–4 refer to the sections on weight, volume, and length, respectively. Line 1, therefore, can only refer to our section; yet no mention is made there of 'time', but only of 'number, count, calculation, and its numbers'.

The definition of our section as one of 'count, calculation, and numbers' suggests that from the perspective of the author of this text, the common denominator between the terms of this scale is not the dimension of time: it is measurement itself. What binds together the disparate set of cycles, jubilees, years, seasons, moments, etc., is not that they measure time, but simply that they are measurements—in his words, 'calculation' and 'numbers'. *What* these measurements measure is not clarified, and not particularly important. We might say they measure 'processes', 'periods', 'intervals', or even possibly (from our modern perspective) 'time', but these are concepts that the author is clearly not considering or conceiving. All that matters to him are the measurements themselves.[72]

In conclusion, all attempts to infer a notion of time from the calendar, chronology, and various other 'time-measurements' have been unsuccessful. In early rabbinic culture, the calendar, chronology, and related measurements are only seen as means of measuring and co-ordinating ritual activity, historical events, and a range of other social and human processes. The importance of measurement and co-ordination, as means of organizing and structuring religious and social life, should not be underrated. It gives rise, in early rabbinic culture, to systems of process—measurement-a better term, perhaps, than 'time-measurement'—which reach a high level of complexity, as can be seen for instance in the last source we have examined. This confirms that sophistication and a sophisticated world-view are possible even without the abstract notion of time as a continuous dimension.

---

[71] כל מנין ומפקד וחשבון ומספריו,
כל משקל ופלס וכיס וגזוריו,
כל כיל לח ויבש ומשוריו,
כל קו וקצב ומדד ושעוריו

[72] This fits into the general theme of this whole composition, which, in accordance with the occasion when it is meant to be recited (the sabbath known as 'Shekalim', just before or at the beginning of the month of Adar, when the commandment of the shekel is commemorated), is all about measurement and measures.

Time and Ethics: From Antiquity to the Middle Ages

THE concept of time plays a dominant role in the structure and management of modern society and its economy; but it also shapes and governs the lives of individuals. The discipline of time[1] has become deeply ingrained into the modern individual's behaviour, character, and *habitus*.[2] For some modern people, the pressure of time can be a motivating factor; for others, time can be a source of profound internal anxiety, perceived as a dominant, dynamic force over which there is no control.[3]

Life is very different in societies where time is not conceived as a distinct category or entity. In such non-modern societies, individuals and/or the social group experience themselves as progressing from one *process* to the next, without the feeling of being subjected to an overriding, homogenous time-continuum. The social, cultural, and experiential implications of this are potentially vast, and likely to vary considerably from one non-modern society to the next. It is clear at least that without the concept of time, social and economic activities run according to very different principles, and individual behaviour and *habitus* are also profoundly affected.

The social and personal implications of a process-based world-view in early rabbinic culture have already been explored (very partially, because the evidence is limited) in previous chapters, mainly with reference to the practices of timing and time-reckoning (Chapters 2–3). In this chapter, I shall address the question by considering the evidence of early rabbinic ethics. Ethical sources should tell us something, at least, about the *expected* behaviour and *habitus* of individuals within a process-based world-view.

Ethics will also provide a convenient way of contrasting early rabbinic culture with that of the later Middle Ages. I shall argue in this chapter that by the later

[1] Phrase drawn from Landes, *Revolution in Time*, 6.

[2] Elias, *Time*, 135–6. *Habitus* is a term used by phenomenologists to refer to a person's way of being, habitual state, and system of dispositions, which function as a matrix that engenders thoughts, perceptions, expressions, and actions (see Bourdieu, *Outline of a Theory of Practice*, 72, 83, 95, and 214 n. 1).

[3] In this respect, time has effectively become—among other things—a modern, secular reformulation of one form of determinism.

Middle Ages, the concept of time as a category in itself had become well assimilated in rabbinic culture. The significance of this remarkable change, and its possible causes, will need to be thoroughly assessed.

Some peculiarities of early rabbinic ethics may be attributed at first sight to the absence of a concept of time, but perhaps not very convincingly. Consider, for example, the modern virtue of punctuality—attending at the right time or appointed time—and correspondingly, the vice of lateness.[4] In the modern Western world, punctuality within a margin of only a few minutes has become an expected norm, obviously facilitated by the advent and universal use of clocks and watches. Such precision would never have been possible in the ancient world, but wider margins might still have been expected. However, although timing is central to early rabbinic halakhah (see Chapter 1), the concept of punctuality as an ethical virtue appears to be absent from early rabbinic culture, and indeed from the whole of ancient Judaism. Halakhic timing dictates that certain activities take place at certain times, but these times are never punctual (i.e. a specific point in time): they invariably consist of periods or 'bands of time', which give considerable freedom as to when the designated activity is actually performed (the requirement to perform certain activities within certain time-bands must be distinguished from punctuality, which would require performance of an activity at a very specific point in time).[5] Although the Talmud condemns whoever misses the time of reciting the *Shema* or the prayers as an example of 'a crooked thing cannot be made straight' (Ecclesiastes 1: 15)[6]—a clear expression of the irreversibility of these time-bands— the virtue of punctuality in its strict (and familiar) sense is unknown in early halakhah and ethics.

However, it is unclear to me why this should be related to the absence of a general concept of time in early rabbinic culture. Punctuality as an ethical virtue should be conceivable even without a time-based world-view: indeed, in a world-view constructed of events and processes in simultaneity and in succession, the virtue of conducting a specific activity in precise conjunction with some other process would have been entirely fitting and appropriate.[7] Inasmuch as the virtue

---

[4] On which see Landes, *Revolution in Time*, 2. Earliness is regarded in modern society, depending on context, as either prudent, unnecessary, inconsiderate, or ridiculous.

[5] For a typical sample of such time-bands, ranging in length from a few hours to the whole night, see Mishnah *Ber.* 1: 1 (cited above, Ch. 2) on the recitation of the *Shema* in the evening. Among the shortest time-bands in rabbinic halakhah are the time of recitation of the *Shema* in the morning, 'from when one can tell the difference between white and blue' till sunrise (according to one opinion in Mishnah *Ber.* 1: 2), and the time for kindling the lights of Hanukah, from sunset till 'when the passer-by has disappeared from the street' (BT *Shab.* 21b).

[6] BT *Ber.* 26a; see also Mishnah *Suk.* 2: 6 (eating in the sukkah on the first day of Sukkot), and Mishnah *Ḥag.* 1: 6 (offering sacrifices on the festivals).

[7] Landes (*Revolution in Time*, 48–62) attributes the development of the modern Western virtue of punctuality, together with the modern Western notion of abstract time, to the rigid, punctual time-

of punctuality is compatible with a process-based world-view, its absence in early rabbinic culture remains to be interpreted and explained.

Other aspects of early rabbinic ethics can be directly related to the absence of a concept of time as such, and I shall now turn to these.

TIME-SAVING AND TIME-WASTING

In modern society, time is conceived and treated as a commodity. It can be utilized in a variety of ways: saved, shared, and spared, or spent, 'burnt', consumed, 'killed', wasted—sometimes even stolen. Time is considered a highly valuable resource (hence the saying, 'time is money'), not least because if lost, it cannot be replaced. Time-saving is therefore considered a virtue, time-wasting a vice.

These assumptions are based on a highly reified concept of time: in order to be treated as a commodity, time must necessarily be regarded a quasi-concrete entity. The absence of such a notion of time in early rabbinic culture will therefore explain why the virtue and vice of time-saving and time-wasting are completely alien to early rabbinic ethics.

The notion of time-wasting is unattested in early rabbinic literature. The rabbinic prohibition of *bitul torah* ('waste of Torah'), which in some circles today has become synonymous with time-wasting, carries a very different meaning in early rabbinic sources: it only means failure to learn Torah. R. Eleazar b. R. Zadok is said never to have wished 'good health'[8] to a person who sneezed, because of *bitul torah*. This does not mean that wishing good health was a waste of time—in fact there is no denial, in this account, of the intrinsic value of wishing someone good health, nor is there any suggestion that it is tantamount to idleness—but rather that it would have deflected R. Eleazar b. R. Zadok from the study of Torah. The issue in this passage is not time-wasting, but rather the correct prioritization of diverse activities.

Closer to the notion of time-wasting is the concept of *batalah* ('waste'), which means straightforward idleness. But idleness is not frowned upon as a waste of *time*, or even as a vice *per se*. The Mishnah (Mishnah *Ketubot* 5: 5) advises against wealthy women's leading a life of total idleness (or 'waste', *batalah*), but only

tables of medieval monasteries. While he may be right on the question of punctuality (although he underestimates, in my view, the impact of the invention of mechanical clocks), I would take issue with him on the question of abstract time. The necessity for collective monastic prayers to be recited at the same times (which incidentally, would also apply to Jewish, early rabbinic communal prayers, *pace* Landes, ibid. 438 n. 17), and hence for these timetables to be developed, bears no relation to the abstract notion of time: collective, simultaneous prayer is nothing really more than a highly regulated process.

[8] מרפא, the equivalent of present-day English 'bless you'. The earliest source of this account is Tosefta *Shab.* 7: 5 (p. 118), which reads: בטל תורה.

because this leads them to either immorality or boredom (the respective views of R. Eliezer and R. Shimon b. Gamliel). Idleness is also condemned elsewhere, but only because it leads—again—to *bitul torah*, i.e. failure to learn Torah (*Avot* 3: 4, as expanded in *Avot derabi natan* (B) 34).

An apparent reference to the virtue of time-saving can be found in Hillel's famous saying, 'If not now, when?' (*Avot* 1: 14). But this statement is not about the value of time or the danger of dissipating it: Hillel only implies that if tasks are delayed, the opportunity to fulfil them may never return. Opportunity is a process-related notion, to which we shall return below.

Another saying from *Avot* has become proverbial, today, for the importance of good time-management: 'the day is short and work is abundant'.[9] But whether the word 'day' is understood in its plain sense, or (as suggested by some commentators) as a metaphor for a person's whole life, this saying does not refer to the shortness of *time*. The term used is 'day' (*yom*), which in this context is most likely to refer to the period of daylight. In ancient society, work was usually completed within the hours of daylight (see Chapter 1). This saying expresses, therefore, the difficulty of fitting one's work into daylight hours (or metaphorically, into one's lifespan), and hence the difficulty of utilizing daylight (one's life) in the most efficient way. It is not about the scarcity of time as such, or the virtue of saving it.[10]

TIME AND OPPORTUNITY

A value that commonly takes the place of 'time' in early rabbinic ethics is the process-related notion of *opportunity*. For example, the common excuse we have today of 'not having time' is never found in early rabbinic sources. Instead, when the ailing R. Eliezer asked his younger colleagues why they had not come to visit him earlier, they answered: 'we did not have the opportunity [*penai*].'[11] It was not time that was lacking, but an appropriate juncture for this visit to be carried out.

In an ethical context, likewise, the term *sha'ah* does not carry its usual, temporal sense of 'hour' or 'short period of time',[12] but more often a process-related sense of

---

[9] *Avot* 2: 15: היום קצר והמלאכה מרובה. Although this saying has acquired today proverbial status, it is not cited elsewhere in early rabbinic literature. It is found in *Midrash Psalms* 119: 10 (p. 247a ed. Buber), but this source is generally assigned to the later Middle Ages (Stemberger, *Introduction to the Talmud and Midrash*, 322–3).

[10] It was only in the 13th c. that this passage was first rephrased, by R. Jonah Gerondi, as '*time* is short' (*hazeman katser: Sha'arei teshuvah* 2: 28).

[11] BT *San.* 68a: *lo hayah lanu penai.* Cf. *Avot* 2: 4: *likheshe'epaneh eshneh* ('when I have the opportunity I shall learn'). The term *penai* is attested in the sense of 'opportunity' or 'availability' without any temporal connotation whatsoever in Mishnah *Ohal.* 7: 4; see also Mishnah *AZ* 5: 6, BT *Shab.* 157a, etc.   [12] On the temporal meanings of this term (*sha'ah*), see above, Ch. 2.

'opportunity'. For instance, Joseph's injunction to his father not to delay (Genesis 45: 9) is expanded in *Genesis Rabbah* with the saying: אל תעמיד את השעה.[13] This rather obscure phrase cannot be literally translated as 'do not stall the hour'— which would be nonsensical, since delaying does not cause time to stall—but rather, 'do not stall the opportunity'. The *midrash* is not suggesting that delay is a waste of time, but rather, that it could be the waste of an opportunity.

The same, process-related interpretation of the term *sha'ah* applies, most probably, to the saying of R. Abin Halevi that 'Whoever forces the hour [*sha'ah*], the hour forces him; and whoever yields before the hour, the hour yields before him' (BT *Berakhot* 64a). To 'force the hour' is unlikely to mean forcing or altering the course of time, because no one is on record, in early rabbinic literature, for ever performing such a seemingly impossible feat. Joshua did make the sun stand still (Joshua 10: 12–14), and similar powers are attributed in rabbinic literature to other biblical and non-biblical characters,[14] but arresting the sun is not the same as arresting time. Furthermore, these powers are certainly beyond the means of the average person whom R. Abin Halevi, in this ethical saying, is presumably addressing.

In the context of this passage, the meaning of *sha'ah* is thus probably 'opportunity', or even possibly 'event' (I have translated it above as 'hour', because 'hour' can also be used in English in these senses). The point of this saying is that if someone tries to force an opportunity (or the occurrence of an event), events eventually get the better of him; but if someone accepts events as they are, events will eventually come his way. As an illustration, indeed, the Talmud goes on to describe in this passage how R. Yosef did well to turn down his appointment as rabbinic leader, and to allow instead his colleague Rabbah to assume the position until his death. This saying is thus not about time-management, but about what we might call 'opportunity management'. It means that opportunities must not be forced or pre-empted: it is wiser to yield before them and use them with restraint.

TIME IN MEDIEVAL SOURCES

Lack of concern for time-management in early rabbinic ethics contrasts with later, medieval rabbinic sources, where time is assumed not only as a category in itself (similarly to the modern notion), but also as a precious commodity. Maimonides often refers to time as a scarce resource. In the introduction to his Code, he writes that the study of Talmud requires much time (*zeman arokh*), and that the purpose

---

[13] *Genesis Rabbah* 93: 6 (p. 1161 ed. Theodor and Albeck). This text has numerous textual variants, but they are not relevant to us here.

[14] JT *Kil.* 9: 4 (32b) (Rabbi's funeral), BT *AZ* 25a (Moses, Nakdimon b. Gurion), and see further references (involving further characters) in Tosafot ibid. s.v. *lemosheh*.

of his Code will be to help people spare it. Elsewhere, he spells out more clearly that the speculative study of Talmud is a 'waste of time'.[15] He says the same, *mutatis mutandis*, of the study of 'external books' such as Ben Sira, physiognomy, chronography, genealogy, poetry, etc.: all discarded by Maimonides as a 'waste of time' (*ibud hazeman*).[16] In his famous letter to Ibn Tibbon, furthermore, Maimonides writes: 'come in peace to see me, but not to get anything out of me, because my time is very scarce'[17]—in contrast with early rabbinic literature, where as we have seen, the excuse of 'not having time' is never found. The phrase *tirdat hazeman* ('the pressure of time') becomes a common excuse, likewise, in the work of later medieval writers; it is mentioned, for instance, in the Code (*Arba'ah turim*) of R. Jacob b. Asher (early fourteenth century).[18]

Later medieval rabbis are also the first to develop the notion of time-saving as an ethical virtue, and of time-wasting as a vice. This idea is raised by R. Menahem Hameiri (late thirteenth century) in his ethical work *Meshiv nefesh*, and developed at length in a homily by R. Isaac Arama (fifteenth century).[19]

But the emergence of time as an entity in itself, in medieval rabbinic culture, goes well beyond the ethical domain. It has an effect, for instance, on late medieval halakhah. The use of sand-clocks or sundials on the sabbath is prohibited by R. Jacob Moellin, known as the Maharil (*c.*1360–1427), even for the purpose of timing one's learning, on the grounds that this constitutes an act of 'measuring time' (measuring is generally prohibited on the sabbath).[20] This ruling is not issued, however, without some reservations. The Maharil concedes that 'the measurement of time is not exactly a measurement'; but still, he concludes, the measurement of time can be 'likened' to other forms of measurement.[21] What he means by 'not exactly [more literally 'not fully'] a measurement' is not explained, but his reservations are clearly due to the abstractness of time. For at the end of his responsum, he adds that sundials are possibly worse than sand-clocks because their user 'literally measures a shadow' (*moded hatsel mamash*)—in other words,

---

[15] Fragment of a letter of Maimonides cited in Twersky, *Introduction to the Code of Maimonides*, 47 (see also Hebrew translation, p. 37).

[16] Commentary on the Mishnah *San.* 10: 1, s.v. *usefarim haḥitsonim* (twice).

[17] Marx, 'Texts', 378 (MS Adler recension): תבא אלינו לשלום לראותנו, לא להועיל ממנו, כי צר זמני מאד.

[18] R. Jacob b. Asher, *Arba'ah turim*, 'Yoreh de'ah' 246: 1: some people cannot learn Torah because of the pressure of time. See also Satz, *Responsa of the Maharil*, 82 (beginning of no. 65): ואני פי מלך שמור להודיע על זאת בקצרה מפני טרדת הזמן ונחיצת הרץ.

[19] Menahem Hameiri, *Ḥibur hateshuvah*, p. 421 (*Meshiv nefesh* 2: 9); R. Isaac Arama, *Akedat yitsḥak*, homily 59, ed. H. Y. Pollack (Pressburg, 1849), iii. 19*a*–21*a*.

[20] Satz, *Responsa of the Maharil*, 317 (no. 200); the prohibition is not only to use but also to handle clocks on the sabbath, because they are defined as *keli shemelakhto le'isur*, a tool designed for forbidden work.

[21] The text in the original reads: ואף על גב דלאו מדידה גמורה היא מדידת הזמן, מ"מ יש לדמות.

this measurement is more concrete.[22] But in spite of these reservations, the Maharil prohibits both sand-clocks and sundials on the sabbath, on the grounds that their use constitutes a measurement of the time-dimension. His ruling was codified in the *Shulḥan arukh* of R. Joseph Karo (sixteenth century);[23] and although halakhists from the beginning of the eighteenth century generally allowed the use on the sabbath of the fast-spreading pocket-size mechanical watches, the assumptions of the Maharil were never questioned or disputed *per se*.[24]

The radical transformation of the rabbinic notion of time in the later Middle Ages is likely to be connected to the rise and influence of Jewish medieval philosophy. Maimonides, whom I have mentioned above, was himself among the first rabbinic philosophers to conceive of time as an entity in itself and structure of reality, and to engage in systematic philosophical discussions about it.[25] But he was

[22] His distinction between sundials and sand-clocks is a bit puzzling. In practice, most medieval sundials do not require any shadow to be measured: it is the *position* of the shadow on the dial that indicates the time of the day. Although the daily rotation of the shadow on the dial is a concrete process, the motion of sand through sand-clocks is no less concrete. See also R. Jacob Castro (Maharikash: late 16th c.), *Ohalei ya'akov* (Leghorn, 1783), 104, arguing, more leniently than the Maharil, that sand-clocks do not require anything to be directly measured; but he does acknowledge that the outcome of the sand-clock being turned over repeatedly is that time is automatically measured (*mimeila nimdad hazeman*).

[23] R. Joseph Karo, *Shulḥan arukh*, 'Oraḥ ḥayim' 308: 51, with R. Moses Isserles' gloss.

[24] The main source for this period is a responsum of R. Meir Eisenstadt in *Panim me'irot* 2: 123. The questioner argues that the Maharil only prohibits devices that require human intervention, such as sand-clocks that need to be turned over, or sundials that need to be positioned in the sun. These interventions are treated by the Maharil as *measuring acts*. Watches, on the other hand, work on their own (once they are wound up), and do not require any intervention or measuring act. The questioner appears to mean that the prohibition is only on *making* measurements, whereas with watches, one only reads *existing, ready-made* measurements. The respondent's argument is far less clear: he states, somewhat obscurely, that watches do not measure time but only 'estimate it' (*mesha'er hazeman*); on the obscurity of this distinction, see R. Samuel Kolin (later 18th c.), *Maḥatsit hashekel*, 308: 78. In support of his lenient ruling, Eisenstadt adduces Mishnah *Yoma* 6: 8 (cited above, Ch. 2), which states that the progress of the scapegoat in the desert had to be ascertained, for those who had remained in the Temple, by 'walking a *mil*, returning a *mil*, and waiting a *mil*': Eisenstadt argues that the latter *mil* must have been estimated on the basis of a shadow (maybe he means the shadow of a *fixed* sundial, which would not have required positioning), which like a watch, would always have been permitted. The invention of small-size mechanical clocks or watches goes back to the 15th c. (Landes, *Revolution in Time*, 89–91), probably too late for the Maharil himself to have considered their halakhic implications. Nevertheless, it would appear that a small-size, movable mechanical clock is what the Maharil's questioner had in mind (Katz, *Halakhah and Kabbalah*, 196 n. 117; I am grateful to Yaakov Loewinger for the reference). Indeed, the Maharil refers to his questioner as asking about *sha'ot shel ḥuliyot* (see the more accurate text of *Beit yosef*, cited by Satz, loc. cit.), which the Maharil interpreted, rather awkwardly, as meaning a sundial (שמראות בצל ע״י חוליות). Although the term *ḥuliyot* can mean 'rings', this is only in the sense of rings of a chain, not of circles drawn on a dial. The general meaning of *ḥuliyah*, indeed, is 'link', 'joint', and/or 'vertebra'. It seems more likely, in this context, to have been used by the Maharil's questioner in the sense of 'interlocking wheel', referring to the mechanism of a clock. Because small-size clocks were a relatively new invention, the Maharil would not have understood the meaning of this question.

[25] Maimonides, *Guide of the Perplexed*, 1: 52, 2: introduction, 2: 13, 2: 30. One of the main issues is

preceded in this by R. Sa'adiah Gaon (early tenth century), traditionally regarded as the earliest rabbinic philosopher, who appears to have been the first to use the term *zeman*, or at least its Judaeo-Arabic equivalent and cognate *al-zamān*, in the sense of 'time' as a general category.[26] This new concept of time became dominant in subsequent medieval Jewish philosophy.[27] It also penetrated other genres of rabbinic literature such as ethics,[28] halakhah,[29] biblical commentary,[30] and poetry.[31]

The advent of this concept of time in R. Sa'adiah's writings was as sudden and innovative as most of the rest of his oeuvre. It was not preceded by any transitional period: as far as one can tell, the early rabbinic process-based world-view persisted unchanged until his period. R. Sa'adiah's novel concept of time was clearly borrowed, together with many other ideas, from the extraneous tradition of Greek and Muslim philosophy.[32]

But to appreciate the role of Greek philosophy in introducing the notion of time to the medieval rabbinic world-view, one must return to its ancient origins. In the next chapter, I shall evaluate the ancient Greek notion of time and whether it had any effect or impact, well before R. Sa'adiah, on the culture of Judaism in late antiquity.

the relationship between time and the Creation: e.g. was time created with the universe, or did it precede it? Maimonides' view about the creation of time was popularized by the 14th-c. Yemenite *Midrash hagadol* (Margaliot, *Midrash hagadol*, i. 30, on Gen. 1: 8).

[26] Sa'adiah Gaon, *Beliefs and Opinions*, 1: 1, 1: 4, 2: 11, pp. 44–5, 85–6, 125–6 trans. Rosenblatt. For a slightly earlier source, see Stroumsa, *Al-Muqammis's Twenty Chapters*, 108–9.

[27] See in general Rudavsky, *Time Matters*, and in particular R. Hasdai Crescas' critique (14th c.) of Aristotle's concept of time, in Wolfson, *Crescas' Critique of Aristotle*, 93–8, 282–91, and nn.

[28] See above in this section, and n. 10.

[29] See the Maharil above, and for another example, Ch. 1 n. 15 (R. Jonah Gerondi).

[30] For examples, see above, Ch. 1 n. 13 (Abraham Ibn Ezra)

[31] See the quasi-personification of time in Moses Ibn Ezra (11th–12th cc.), *Selected Poems*, 53–4, 60, 89.

[32] On R. Sa'adiah's innovativeness and his intellectual background, see Brody, *Geonim of Babylonia*, 284–94.

FIVE

The Greeks and
Jewish Hellenistic Culture

STUDIES on time, as on other abstract concepts, have often drawn distinctions between the 'modern' and the 'primitive'. Norbert Elias, for example, presents the modern, reified concept of time as the product of an advanced stage of social development, or in his words, of the 'civilizing process'; 'primitive' (or more politically correct, 'pre-modern') societies, he argues, have not reached the stage where this social symbol is either useful or necessary. The social evolutionism that underpins this argument, and that served at one time as a fundamental assumption of ethnography, anthropology, and sociology, is clearly problematic and unsatisfactory.[1] At present, however, I wish to take up only one aspect of Elias's evolutionary model: that the notion of time as a reified entity was developed in response to the specific requirements of modern society,[2] and is therefore specific to modern society.

No doubt the concept of time has evolved considerably in Western Europe from antiquity and the Middle Ages until the present day. Elias is right to observe, for example, that before the seventeenth century time-measurement and the concept of time were centred entirely on man and on human events; it is only as clocks began to be used by Galileo and his contemporaries to measure physical, natural sequences, that the concept of time as a law of nature or structure of physical reality gradually took shape.[3] However, it is important to realize that the concept of time as an entity in itself, a continuous flow, and/or a structure of reality, was well established already by the medieval period—even if its relevance was confined, as suggested by Elias, to human and social events. The existence of a general concept of time already in the Middle Ages has become evident, in a Jewish context, in the previous chapter; it is also attested in wider medieval society.[4] This would suggest that the concept of time as a reified entity is by no means specifically 'modern'.

---

[1] Elias, *Time*. He is also rather uninformed, in this work at least, about the nature of time in so-called 'primitive' societies and cultures; but this is not the place to review his otherwise most inspiring essay.

[2] See ibid. 121–2 (cited above in the Introduction).   [3] Ibid. 3 and 104–15.

[4] The history of the concept of time in medieval Europe has been studied extensively: Le Goff, *Time, Word and Culture*; Gourévitch, *Les Catégories de la culture médiévale*; and Landes, *Revolution in Time*.

In this chapter, I shall argue that the present-day concept of time is ancient, and goes as far back as ancient, classical Greece. The origins of this concept cannot be ascribed, as Elias would perhaps argue, to the relative complexity of ancient Greek society: for early rabbinic literature, which did not have this concept, was produced in a social context of similar complexity to that of ancient Greece. The concept of time as an entity in itself was similarly absent from a number of other ancient civilizations of relatively high complexity (see Chapter 6). It is far more plausible, therefore, that the reified concept of time was simply a traditional component of the ancient Greek world-view, which other, contemporary societies happened not to share. This traditional concept was not intrinsically 'modern'; it only evolved, via the Christian Middle Ages, into the modern Western concept of time that is known today.

The ancient Greek view of time has never been comprehensively studied, except for specific studies on time in Greek philosophy.[5] In the first part of this chapter, I shall attempt to fill this gap. My primary purpose will to draw a contrast between the Greek notion of time and its absence in ancient Jewish culture. I shall then assess the possible impact that the Hellenistic world-view may have had on Jewish, and particularly 'Jewish Hellenistic', culture—by which I mean, the culture of the Jews in antiquity whose principal means of linguistic expression was Greek.

My intention is thus to move away from the narrow focus of rabbinic literature, and examine ancient Jewish culture in general. The absence of a concept of time was not unique, indeed, to rabbinic Judaism: it was equally absent in non-rabbinic forms of Judaism, as well as in many non-Jewish cultures of the ancient Near East (this will become evident in Chapter 6). The adoption of the Greek notion of time in some Hellenistic Jewish circles may thus serve as a useful indicator of the extent of their Hellenization or of their resistance to it.

CHRONOS

The concept of time, in its general sense and as an entity in itself, was known to the Greeks from an early age under the designation of *chronos*.[6] It is not yet attested in the works of Homer, where the term *chronos*, only used in the accusative (with or without a preposition) and in an adverbial sense, always means a point in time or a specific duration. The description in the *Iliad* (1. 70) of Calchas the seer knowing 'what is, what will be, and what was before'—i.e. the present, future, and past— does not necessarily imply awareness of a time-continuum.[7]

---

[5] e.g. Sorabji, *Time, Creation and the Continuum*; Callahan, *Four Views of Time in Ancient Philosophy*.

[6] See in general Ariotti, 'Concept of Time', and Lloyd, 'Le Temps dans la pensée grecque'; also Schibli, *Pherekydes of Syros*, 29 n. 39.

[7] As argued above in the Introduction (see also Ch. 1). A similar phrase appears in Hesiod, *Theogony* 38–9.

But the use of *chronos* or 'time' as a general and separate entity is well established, and indeed almost taken for granted, in post-Homeric literature from the sixth century BCE and beyond. The time-continuum is particularly conspicuous in fifth-century Greek tragedy. Aeschylus refers to eternity as 'the whole of time'.[8] Sophocles says of time that it is 'long and without number', i.e. infinite (*Ajax* 646). It is passing or 'flowing', as in Euripides' statement that 'the whole of time [*chronos plērēs*, literally 'full time'] tirelessly moves around in an eternal flow, begetting itself'.[9] Time is also conspicuous in the contemporary historical works of Herodotus and Thucydides, who similarly assume time to be a self-propelling, autonomous entity—much as we popularly assume today—with frequently used expressions such as 'time was progressing' or 'time was going forward'.[10] The expression 'to spend time' (*chronon diatribein*), also frequent in their works, suggests moreover that time is a resource that can be spent or used.[11] In a similar vein, the philosopher Theophrastus (late fourth century BCE) is reported to have frequently said that time is a costly expenditure.[12]

In addition to these widely shared ideas, poets and tragedians of this period attribute *active qualities* to time. Time is said to give wealth and relieve from trouble (Pindar, *Pythian* 1. 46), to exhaust (Sophocles, *Ajax* 605), or alternatively to soothe (Euripides, *Alcestis* 381). Time causes one to forget (Sophocles, *Electra* 179), but it can also reveal, alternatively, what was previously unknown. Thus 'time has revealed, in its motion forward', how Heracles founded the Olympian Games (Pindar, *Olympian* 10. 55);[13] 'ever-ageing' time teaches all things (Aeschylus(?), *Prometheus Bound* 981); time sees, hears, and discloses everything (Sophocles, fr. 301).[14] Time reveals, more specifically, who is righteous and who is wicked (Sophocles, *Oedipus Tyrannus* 614): indeed, it reveals the truth about Oedipus' incestuous marriage, and even passes judgement on it (*Oedipus Tyrannus* 1213).

This last passage suggests that time does not simply reveal, but plays an active part in resolving that which has been revealed. Time has indeed the power of

---

[8] Aeschylus, *Eumenides* 484, 670, 898; cf. *Agamemnon* 554.

[9] Euripides, fr. 597 Nauck: ἀκάμας τε πέριξ χρόνος ἀενάῳ | ῥεύματι πλήρης φοιτᾷ τίκτων | αὐτὸς ἑαυτόν. See in general Romilly, *Time in Greek Tragedy*.

[10] Usually in genitive absolute clauses: χρόνου δὲ ἐπιγενομένου (Herodotus 1. 28), χρόνου πολλοῦ διεξελθόντος (ibid. 2. 52), τοῦ χρόνου προβαίνοντος (ibid. 3. 53), προελθόντος πολλοῦ χρόνου (Thucydides 1. 10. 2), προελθόντος δὲ τοῦ χρόνου (ibid. 1. 24. 3), προϊόντος τοῦ χρόνου (ibid. 5. 25. 2), etc. The phrase χρόνου περιιόντος (Herodotus 2. 121. a. 2, 4. 155. 1) means 'going round' (rather than going forward); Plato refers to time as 'going' (κατ᾽ ἀριθμὸν ἰοῦσαν) but also 'circling round' (κυκλούμενον: *Timaeus* 37 D and 38 A), and see also Euripides (n. 9). On the cyclicity of time among the Greeks, see Vidal-Naquet, 'Temps des dieux'.

[11] The expression χρόνον διατρίβειν, to spend time, first appears in Herodotus 1. 24; note also χρόνον διάγειν, meaning either to spend time (e.g. Xenophon, *Cyropaedia* 5. 2. 1) or to 'drag time out' (Plutarch, *Timoleon* 10).

[12] Diogenes Laertius, *Lives of Eminent Philosophers*, 5. 40: πολυτελὲς ἀνάλωμα εἶναι τὸν χρόνον.

[13] (χρόνος) τὸ δὲ σαφανὲς ἰὼν πόρσω κατέφρασεν etc.   [14] Cf. *Oedipus Tyrannus* 1213.

generating events, as is explicit in Aeschylus' phrase, 'all-accomplishing time' (*Choephoroi* 965), or in Sophocles' statement that 'time *begets* all hidden things and conceals all things revealed' (*Ajax* 646–7, my emphasis). The active nature of time also explains Clytemnestra's remark, in Sophocles' *Electra* (781–2), that time has always protected and guided her.[15] Time is thus presented as an active agent, driving the course of human actions, human events, and more generally, the course of history.[16]

The notion of time as a historical or cosmic agent is not restricted, however, to the genre of tragedy. It is implicit in earlier, pre-Socratic fragments that refer to the 'justice of time' or the 'order of time', and may also be related to the notion, attested in the works of Pherecydes (sixth century BCE), that time is actually a primordial, cosmogonic principle.[17] This notion is developed in full in the Orphic theogonies, where time is personified as a god ('Chronos') or serpent-like monster, who generates the world by producing the primordial egg; he is conflated in some of these sources with the Greek mythological god Kronos.[18] Even if Pherecydes' ideas and the Orphic mysteries were somewhat marginal to ancient Greek society, there is good reason to assume that their underlying assumptions about time were generally shared. The deification of time and its elevation to a cosmogonic principle

---

[15] ὁ προστατῶν | χρόνος διῆγέ μ' αἰεν. The meaning of προστατῶν is unclear, but would appear to be 'ruler', 'guardian', or 'protector'.

[16] The following lines may suggest that time is *itself* the course of human events: οὑπιρρέων γὰρ τιμιώτερος χρόνος | ἔσται πολίταις τοῖσδε ('flowing time will be more glorious for my citizens': Aeschylus, *Eumenides* 853–4).

[17] Kirk and Raven, *The Presocratic Philosophers*, 120 (Solon: ἐν δίκη χρόνου, 'in the justice of time'), 117 (Anaximander: κατὰ τὴν τοῦ χρόνου τάξιν, 'according to the order of time'), and 54–9 (Pherecydes). The main work on Pherecydes is Schibli, *Pherekydes of Syros*, see esp. 14–18, 27–38. See also West, *Early Greek Philosophy*, 9–14 (Pherecydes) and 81–3 (Anaximander); and Guthrie, *Orpheus and Greek Religion*, 248 n. 17. Time as a cosmogonic principle may also be implicit in descriptions of time as a craftsman, in fragments of Diphilus (fr. 84 Kassel and Austin) and Critias (88 B 25. 33 Diels and Kranz), both cited in West, *Early Greek Philosophy*, 54, and in Euripides' obscure reference to time as 'begetting itself' (above, n. 9), inasmuch as a cosmogonic principle cannot be begotten by anything else.

[18] See Guthrie, *Orpheus and Greek Religion*, 79–80 and 85–93, with translated fragments on p. 137 (for the original text of the fragments, see Kern, *Orphicorum Fragmenta*, 112–50); Schibli, *Pherekydes of Syros*, 35–7 (pointing out that some of the Orphic sources go back at least to the 4th c. BCE). The *Orphic Rhapsodies* (cited e.g. by Damascius, *De Principiis* 3. 2. 2, in Westerink and Combès, *Damascius*, 159, 161) depict 'ageless time' as the first cosmogonic principle and as a serpent (δράκων). Time is referred to in various other Orphic fragments as χρόνος ἀγήραος ('ageless time'—contrast with Aeschylus, *Prometheus Bound* 981: ὁ γηράσκων χρόνος, 'ageing time'), ἀφθιτόμητις ('whose counsels never perish'), and μέγας ('great'). On the conflation of Chronos with Kronos, see Schibli, *Pherekydes of Syros*, 27–8, 135–9; Kirk and Raven, *The Presocratic Philosophers*, 56 n. 1; and West, *Early Greek Philosophy*, 10. The term 'ageless time' and its depiction as a serpent-like monster-god appear to be of Iranian origin (from the Iranian notion of *zruuan akarana*, 'endless time', on which see below, Ch. 6). According to Brisson ('La Figure de Chronos'), these Iranian notions penetrated the Graeco-Roman world only in the 1st or 2nd cc. CE, through the intermediary of Mithraism; but Guthrie (*Orpheus and Greek Religion*) believes that they was borrowed from Iran already in the pre-Socratic period, while Kirk and Raven (*The Presocratic Philosophers*, 39) remain open-minded on the question.

is implicit, indeed, in more mainstream sources such as Pindar (fifth century BCE), who refers to time as 'father of all' and 'lord who surpasses all the beatified [gods]',[19] and Sophocles, who explicitly calls time a 'kindly god' (*Electra* 179).

To sum up, time or *chronos* in classical Greek literature is generally presented as an independent, infinite continuum, that flows eternally of its own accord, and that is endowed with active, quasi-divine qualities which determine the course of events and history.

Closely related to the notion of time (*chronos*) is the notion of *aiōn*. This term appears to have meant originally a man's lifetime or his afterlife,[20] but soon became analogous to 'time' in its most general sense (particularly in Plato's work, as we shall presently see). Heraclitus (late sixth–early fifth century) describes *aiōn* as a king or 'Zeus' who plays like a child (i.e., perhaps, with the universe).[21] Euripides describes him as the son of Time, that similarly to Fate, gives birth to many things (*Heraclidae* 898–900).

TIME IN GREEK PHILOSOPHY

Time became the object of systematic philosophical enquiry from the early fourth century BCE.[22] Plato, in the *Timaeus* (37 D–39 E), describes how time was created together with the heavenly bodies, thereby suggesting that its existence depends entirely on the existence (and, presumably, motion) of these bodies.[23] This does not mean, however, that time does not exist as a entity in itself. Plato draws a distinction between *chronos* (time) and *aiōn* (normally translated here as 'eternity'), and posits that eternity is the 'idea' (in the 'world of ideas', i.e. the ideal world) of which time (in the 'world of images', i.e. the created, perceived world) is the 'eternal moving image'.[24] Thus although subordinate to the heavenly bodies,

[19] *Olympian* 2. 17, and fr. 33 Maehler (ἄνακτα τὸν πάντων ὑπερβάλλοντα χρόνον μακάρων), cited by Plutarch, *Platonic Questions* 8. 4, 1007 B, who ascribes to Pythagoras the notion that time is 'the soul of Heaven' (τὴν τοὐρανοῦ ψυχήν).

[20] The term αἰών (*aiōn*) has these meanings e.g. in Pindar, *Olympian* 2. 68, and Euripides, *Hippolytus* 1109. It is a little ambiguous in Aeschylus, *Agamemnon* 554.

[21] Heraclitus, fr. 93 Marcovich and in Clement, *Paedagogus* 1. 22. 1; cited in West, *Early Greek Philosophy*, 158–9.

[22] On the development of time as an abstract notion in early Greek philosophy, see Corish, 'The Emergence of Time'. If the pre-Socratics are considered to be philosophers, then Pherecydes, Heraclitus, and others mentioned in the previous section should belong to this section too.

[23] See especially *Timaeus* 37 D–E and 38 B. Elsewhere, however, Plato appears to be inconsistent on this point: see Rudavsky, *Time Matters*, 11–12.

[24] Plato, *Timaeus* 37 D: εἰκὼ δ᾽ἐπινοεῖ κινητόν τινα αἰῶνος ποιῆσαι, καὶ διακοσμῶν ἅμα οὐρανὸν ποιεῖ μένοντος αἰῶνος ἐν ἑνὶ κατ᾽ ἀριθμὸν ἰοῦσαν αἰώνιον εἰκόνα, τοῦτον ὃν δὴ χρόνον ὠνομάκαμεν ('he [the Demiurge] took thought to make a moving image of eternity, and at the same time that he ordered the heaven, he made, of eternity abiding in unity, an eternal image going forward according to number, to which we have given the name *time*').

and although a mere image of eternity, the eternally moving continuum of time is treated by Plato as an autonomous substance or entity.[25] In this way Plato endorses the view of time that prevailed in contemporary Greek society.

Aristotle, however, does away with Plato's world of ideas, and subjects the notion of time to a much more thorough analysis than his predecessor.[26] This leads him to question the extent to which time should be assumed to be a separate substance or entity. In *Physics* 4. 10–12, he begins with the argument that time is composed of the past and the future, and yet the past no longer is, and the future is yet to be—*ergo*, time does not exist; it cannot exist as an independent substance or essence (*Physics* 217^{b}32–218^{a}3). After rejecting various views about time—that it is the motion of everything, or that it is the sphere (of the universe) itself (*Physics* 218^{a}33–218^{b}1)—Aristotle concludes that 'time is the number of motion according to prior and posterior', which is usually understood to mean the (numerical) measurement of motion in terms of prior and posterior.[27] Time is thus completely predicated on motion: in a motionless world, there would be no time, because time is only the measurement of motion. Moreover, since time is only a number, it cannot exist without someone (a 'soul') to count it.[28] Furthermore, time is depleted of any substance of its own, and demoted to a considerably lesser status: for inasmuch as motion itself is not a substance but only an accident (i.e. a category accidental to substances), time cannot be called an accident of motion. This may explain why Aristotle does not even give time the status of an 'accident', but only calls it an 'attribute' (*pathos*) of movement.[29]

In reaching this conclusion, Aristotle was firmly and radically rejecting the reification of time that prevailed, as we have seen, in contemporary Greek culture.[30] His view of time as only a 'number' (or measurement) was close, in many ways, to the view of time I have presented in the Introduction. However, Aristotle's impact on prevailing culture was limited. He did have an influence on subsequent Greek philosophers, in particular the Stoics, who similarly defined time as 'the extension [or 'dimension'] of the universe's motion'.[31] This definition, generalizing

[25] Plato also says of time that it is 'going forward' (ibid. 37 D, cited in n. 24) and 'circling round according to number' (κατ' ἀριθμὸν κυκλουμένου, ibid. 38 A), suggesting a self-propelling, linear or circular flow, with its own, inherent dynamics (on linear and cyclicity, see above n. 10).

[26] For a general introduction to Aristotle's views on time, see Rudavsky, *Time Matters*, 12–15, and Annas, 'Aristotle, Number and Time', who interprets Aristotle as deliberately rejecting the Platonic view of time. I am grateful to Ursula Coope for her assistance on this topic.

[27] *Physics* 220^{a}24: ὁ χρόνος ἀριθμός ἐστιν κινήσεως κατὰ τὸ πρότερον καὶ ὕστερον. For this interpretation see Annas, 'Aristotle, Number and Time'; but Ursula Coope has reservations about it. *Kinēsis* ('motion') can also be translated, more generally, as 'change'.

[28] *Physics* 223^{a}16–17, 21–9: see Annas, 'Aristotle, Number and Time', 101.

[29] *Physics* 223^{a}18, 251^{b}28, etc.; see Moreau, *L'Espace et le temps selon Aristote*, esp. pp. 106–8.

[30] It should be noted, however, that this rejection is only implicit in Aristotle's discourse.

[31] H. von Arnim, *Stoicorum veterum fragmenta*, 4 vols. (Leipzig, 1903–24), ii. 165–6, no. 520, ap. Diogenes Laertius, *Lives of Eminent Philosophers* 7. 141 (διάστημα τῆς τοῦ κόσμου κινήσεως), who

Aristotle's concept of time into a *universal* category, also appears in the works of Philo.[32]

But Aristotle's influence did not extend much further. The concept of time that had been traditional among the Greeks—i.e. an independent substance and entity—held sway over other contemporary authors. Plutarch (late first–early second century CE), for example, explicitly rejected the Aristotelian and Stoic definitions of time as an attribute of motion or its accident, and, citing instead the authority of Pindar and Pythagoras, wrote that time was 'cause and potency and principle of the symmetry which holds together all things that come to be, and of the order whereby the nature of the universe, being animate, is in motion; or rather, being motion and order itself and symmetry, it is called time'. The relationship between time and motion was thus not denied (Plutarch goes on, in the same passage, to cite Plato's *Timaeus* in support of his opinion), but time was explicitly assigned an essence (*ousia*) in its own right, and treated as the driving force of the entire universe.[33] Elsewhere, Plutarch wrote that 'time is something in motion, appearing together with moving matter, ever flowing, and retaining nothing, a receptacle, as it were, of decay and birth'.[34] The simile of the flowing river is more

adds that time is incorporeal, and that past and future are infinite, whereas present is finite. This definition is also cited in Plutarch, *Platonic Questions* 8. 4. 3, 1007 B, and in other sources. At Iamblichus, fr. 107 Larsen, a fine distinction is drawn between this Stoic definition of time and that of Archytas of Tarentum (early 4th c. BCE), whereby time is the 'extension [or dimension] of the nature of the whole [i.e. of the universe itself]' (διάσταμα τᾶς τοῦ παντὸς φύσιος); see too Larsen's discussion at pp. 295–7.

[32] See especially Philo, *On the Creation* 26, and *On the Eternity of the World* 4, 52–4; but in the last passage the Stoic definition is (not uncharacteristically) conflated with Plato's account of time. See further Lauer, 'Philo's Concept of Time'. Philo's Jewish identity appears to be irrelevant here; Philo must be viewed, in this context, as completely within the Hellenistic philosophical tradition. For other post-Aristotelian philosophers, see Lucretius, *On the Nature of the Universe*, 1. 459–63: 'Time likewise does not exist by itself, but a sense follows from things themselves of what has been done in the past, what is in the present, and what in addition is to follow after. And no one has a sense of time distinct from the movement of things or from their quiet rest' (*tempus item per se non est, sed rebus ab ipsis | consequitur sensus transactum quid sit in aevo, | tum quae res instet, quid porro deinde sequatur; | nec per se quemquam tempus sentire fatendumst | semotum ab rerum motu placidaque quiete*). Lucretius does appear to refer elsewhere to an empty continuum of time and space within which the atomic particles are able to circulate, but this may just be a metaphor (1. 1046–8: 'yet sometimes they must needs rebound, and give the primal atoms space and time for flight to freedom from the union they have created'—*interdum resilire tamen coguntur, et una | principiis rerum spatium tempusque fugai | largiri, ut possint a coetu libera ferri*). See also Sorabji, *Time, Creation and the Continuum*, 81–3, who rejects Sambursky's view ('The Concept of Time in Late Neoplatonism') that Strato, a disciple of Aristotle, regarded time as a quantity flowing independently of motion.

[33] Plutarch, *Platonic Questions* 8. 4, 1007 B: οὐ γὰρ πάθος οὐδὲ συμβεβηκὸς ἧς ἔτυχε κινήσεως ὁ χρόνος ἐστίν, αἰτία δὲ καὶ δύναμις καὶ ἀρχὴ τῆς πάντα συνεχούσης τὰ γιγνόμενα συμμετρίας καὶ τάξεως, ἣν ἡ τοῦ ὅλου φύσις ἔμψυχος οὖσα κινεῖται· μᾶλλον δὲ κίνησις οὖσα καὶ τάξις αὐτὴ καὶ συμμετρία χρόνος καλεῖται.

[34] Plutarch, *The E at Delphi* 19, 392 E: κινητὸν γάρ τι καί κινουμένη συμφανταζόμενον ὕλῃ καὶ ῥέον ἀεὶ καὶ μὴ στέγον ὥσπερ ἀγγεῖον φθορᾶς καὶ γενέσεως ὁ χρόνος.

explicit in Marcus Aurelius' *Meditations* (second century CE), though with reference to *aiōn* ('eternity'): 'a kind of river and violent flow out of what comes to be'.[35] Other philosophers went as far as claiming that time was a body (*sōma*), i.e. that it had a corporeal nature.[36]

In later antiquity, the Neoplatonic philosophers abandoned completely the Aristotelian concept of time, and argued that time existed on its own, independently of motion. Plotinus (third century) defined time as the 'length of the life of the soul' (whatever this exactly means), which could be measured by motion, but which was not generated by it.[37] Iamblichus (early fourth century) and Proclus (mid-fifth century) developed Plotinus' suggestion that time was an essence in itself, Proclus arguing that time was actually prior to the soul.[38] Plotinus and his followers are often regarded as innovators in this area,[39] but to some extent they were only returning to the pre-Aristotelian, traditional Greek concept of time as an independent and dynamic cosmic life-force.

Augustine (end of the fourth century) was alone in resisting this trend: he suggested, most originally, that time only existed as a subjective experience, and that past and future were only constructs of the psychological processes of memory and anticipation (respectively).[40]

THE ROMAN WORLD

Notions of time as an entity in itself, a continuous flow, an active agent, and a resource or commodity, were not confined to ancient Greek culture: they are also attested in classical Latin literature. These notions may have been borrowed from the Greeks, or may have had roots in native Roman culture; but their existence in Roman culture certainly goes back some way.[41]

---

[35] Marcus Aurelius, *Meditations* 4. 43: Ποταμός τις ἐκ τῶν γινομένων καί ῥεῦμα βίαιον ὁ αἰών.

[36] Aenesidemus (1st c. BCE), cited by Sextus Empiricus, *Adversus Mathematicos* 10 = *Against the Physicists* 2. 216–18; trans. R. G. Bury, iii (Loeb Classical Library, 311; Cambridge, Mass., 1936), 316–19. Sextus Empiricus contrasts Aenesidemus' opinion with that of the Stoics who maintain that time is incorporeal although self-existent (καθ' αὑτό τι).

[37] Plotinus, *Enneads* 3. 7. 6–12. Because Plotinus' terminology is completely inconsistent, his definition of time remains, perhaps deliberately, ambiguous. For an interpretation, see Wolfson, *Crescas' Critique of Aristotle*, 93–8 and 633–64; Rudavsky, *Time Matters*, 18–20.

[38] See Sambursky and Pines, *The Concept of Time in Late Neoplatonism*; Sambursky, 'The Concept of Time in Late Neoplatonism'.   [39] Wolfson, *Crescas' Critique of Aristotle*, 96–7 and 654.

[40] Augustine, *Confessions* 11. 11–28. See Callahan, *Four Views of Time in Ancient Philosophy* (on Plato, Aristotle, Plotinus, and Augustine).

[41] Onians (*The Origins of European Thought*, 411–15) writes that for the (sc. early) Romans, 'time was weather, weather time, *tempus*, *tempestas*; and the thought survives in the modern French idiom: *il fait mauvais temps*'. The word *tempestas* can indeed be used, in early Latin, in the sense of 'time'; but whether this means that the concept of time was confused with the weather requires further substantiation.

The historian Livy (first century BCE) commonly uses of the expression *tempus terere* (meaning either 'to spend' or 'to waste' time), similar to the Greek historians' stock phrase, *chronon diatribein* (see above); this phrase implies that time is a usable commodity.[42] Seneca (mid-first century BCE) presents time, in a letter entirely on this topic, as a valuable commodity that we own and that we must save, for otherwise it will irreversibly glide away.[43] The same idea is expressed by Virgil (late first century BCE) in his now proverbial *fugit inreparabile tempus* ('time flies, not recoverable').[44] After citing Sophocles fr. 301 (see above), Aulus Gellius (second century CE) quotes a saying that 'Truth is the daughter of Time' (*Noctes Atticae* 12. 11. 7). The active properties of time are implicit in Ovid (early first century CE), who speaks of love growing with time, in Tacitus (early second century CE), who refers to an illusion dissipating through the effect of 'time itself', and in Ulpian (early third century CE), who gave a legal ruling on goods that will be damaged by the passage of time.[45]

These assumptions about time, common to Greek and Latin literature, must have been common currency throughout the Graeco-Roman world. Certainly by late antiquity, when Neoplatonists like Plotinus were reviving the idea of time as an independent entity, the Greek notion of time had widely spread across the Roman empire, among pagans as well as Christians. Thus at the end of the fourth century, Augustine could write in his *Confessions* that 'in our conversation, no word is more familiarly used or more easily recognized than "time"'. Further, '"Time" and "times" are words forever on our lips . . . We use these words and hear others using them. They understand what we mean and we understand them. No words could be plainer or more commonly used.'[46]

JEWISH HELLENISTIC LITERATURE

Among the Jews, however, the Greek concept of time did not spread in the same way. In Jewish sources written in Hebrew or Aramaic, this concept is totally

[42] Livy 1. 27. 6, 1. 57. 9, *et saepe*. This phrase is attested earlier than Livy (David Levene, pers. comm.): see also Cicero, *Philippicae* 5. 30; Ovid, *Heroides* 7. 142, etc.

[43] Seneca, *Epistles*, 1. 2–3: he writes about setting a value (*pretium*) on time, and states: *omnia aliena sunt, tempus tantum nostrum est* ('nothing belongs to us except time').

[44] Virgil, *Georgics* 3. 284–5; cf. *Aeneid* 10. 467–8.

[45] Ovid, *Metamorphoses* 4. 60: *tempore crevit amor*. Tacitus, *Annals* 2. 40. 1. Ulpian: cited in Justinian's *Digest* 5. 3. 5. pr.: *sed et res tempore perituras permittere debet praetor distrahere*.

[46] Augustine, *Confessions* 11. 22. 28: *Et dicimus tempus et tempus, tempora et tempora . . . Dicimus haec et audimus haec et intellegimur et intellegimus. Manifestissima et usitatissima sunt*, cf. 11. 14. 17: *quid autem familiarius et notius in loquendo conmemoramus quam tempus?*—cited in full above, in the Introduction; cited in English from Pine-Coffin's translation, 270, 263–4. See also Plotinus, *Enneads* 3. 7. 1; Proclus, *Commentary on the Timaeus* 4. 3. 8. 29. Augustine is clearly using the word 'time' in the general sense (not in the sense of 'points in time' or 'limited periods of time'), which is why he has difficulty defining it.

unattested: this applies not only to early rabbinic literature, as we have already seen, but also to non-rabbinic sources, as we shall see below in Chapter 6. But in this chapter I wish to focus attention on Jewish Hellenistic literature, by which I mean Jewish works from the Hellenistic and Roman periods that were originally written in Greek. Here we find that although the Jews were not immune to Hellenistic influence—not surprisingly, as they were writing in Greek—their apparently infrequent use of the Greek concept of time reveals a fundamentally different cultural background that to some extent they were unwilling, or unable, to shed.

In the Septuagint—to begin with what is perhaps the earliest Jewish work in Greek—the term *chronos* is found far less frequently than in contemporary Greek literature.[47] Its meaning in the Septuagint, moreover, is restricted to the sense of 'point in time' or (more commonly) 'period of time'; although this period of time is usually indefinite, it is always of limited duration and does not refer to the time-continuum as a whole.[48] This limited usage of the term *chronos* contrasts, of course, with its much broader use elsewhere in Graeco-Roman literature.

This limited usage of the term *chronos* applies not only to the Septuagint translation of Hebrew biblical books—where the absence of *chronos* in the sense of 'time in general' might arguably reflect its absence in the original Hebrew text (on which see Chapter 6)—but also to books of the Greek Bible that were originally written in Greek. The term *chronos* in its general sense (as a flowing continuum, an active agent, a commodity, etc.) is remarkably absent from the Wisdom of Solomon, a work otherwise known for its Greek philosophical borrowings, as well as the books of Maccabees.[49] For example, instead of the expression 'time having gone by', familiar in Greek historical writings, 1 Maccabees has 'after these things' (5: 37, 7: 33)—identical with the phrase pervasive in the Hebrew Bible and Septuagint (Genesis 15: 1, Esther 2: 1, etc.). Instead of the expression 'he spent time', common in Greek sources, 1 Maccabees 11: 40 has 'he stayed there for many days'. The

---

[47] It is considerably less frequent than the term *kairos* (which normally means the 'right time' or 'critical time' in a purely punctual sense, and functions in the Septuagint as the usual translation of the Hebrew *et* and *mo'ed*), whereas in contemporary Greek literature it is the term *chronos* that is more frequent (Eynikel and Hauspie, 'Καιρός and Χρόνος', 383).

[48] The closest one gets in the Septuagint to the use of *chronos* in the sense of 'time in general' is the phrase εἰς τὸν αἰῶνα χρόνον, which commonly translates the Hebrew עד עולם (*ad olam*) or לעולם (*le'olam*), 'for ever' (e.g. Isa. 34: 10: see Barr, *Biblical Words*, 125–6; Eynikel and Hauspie, 'Καιρός and Χρόνος', 384), and which also appears repeatedly in *Joseph and Asenath*: in this context, the term *chronos* appears to refer to the totality of time. Sometimes the Septuagint translates *le'olam* as εἰς τὸν αἰῶνα (without χρόνον: e.g. Deut. 32: 40), but this usage is equally significant, for as we have seen, the Greek term *aiōn* tends also to be time-related. This specific usage of *chronos* and *aiōn* suggests that in the Hellenistic period, the biblical Hebrew *olam* (on which see below, Ch. 6) *may* have been reinterpreted as meaning the endless flow of time: see Jenni, 'Das Wort 'ōlām'.

[49] On Greek philosophy in the Wisdom of Solomon, see Schürer, *History of the Jewish People*, iii. 568–79. In 2 Macc. 1: 22, χρόνος διῆλθεν may only mean 'the [point in] time came'; see Eynikel and Hauspie, 'Καιρός and Χρόνος', 383–5.

term *dietriben* ('he spent') is found in 2 Maccabees 14: 23 but in the absolute, without the object *chronon* ('time')—significantly, even if this usage is common in Greek. Thus, references to time as a general notion are consistently avoided in the books of Maccabees, sometimes in favour of biblical-sounding phrases. The term *chronos* in its general sense is also absent from 'pseudepigraphic' and other contemporary works, such as *Joseph and Asenath*, the fragments of Ezekiel the Tragedian, and further fragmentary Jewish Hellenistic works.[50]

The Greek concept of time does make an appearance, however, in Philo, Josephus, and some other Jewish Hellenistic works. In each of these cases, the appearance of this concept can be directly related to the influence of Greek tradition. Thus Philo's references to *chronos* in a general, philosophical sense (see above) derive directly from the Greek philosophical tradition which he consciously and explicitly emulates.[51]

Josephus' use of the Greek concept of time is evident in phrases such as 'time was going forward',[52] implying that time is an autonomous, flowing entity, and 'to spend/waste time' (*chronon diatribein*),[53] implying that time is a usable resource; it may be assumed that both phrases are directly borrowed from the classical Greek historians, Herodotus and Thucydides. The Greek concept of time is implicit in Josephus' works in many other ways. Like the Greek tragedians, Josephus suggests that time is endowed with active qualities, capable of either destroying a prophecy (the prophecy not being fulfilled: *War* 1. 79),[54] or, on the contrary, of proving predictions to be have been divine (*War* 4. 625). Time can cause a lesson to be forgotten (*Antiquities* 4. 307) and anger to abate (*Antiquities* 7. 181). Of the four sons of

[50]   It is also absent from the *Testament of the Twelve Patriarchs*, but whether this text represents an originally Greek composition remains completely unclear (see Schürer, *History of the Jewish People*, iv. 767–81). Because of the fragmentary nature of many of these works, the absence of 'time in general' is sometimes difficult to prove. Of Aristobulus of Alexandria (2nd c. BCE), for instance, only a few fragments have survived (see Schürer, *History of the Jewish People*, iii. 579–87); nevertheless, it may be noted that in his apology for the sabbath, Aristobulus claims that 'the whole cosmos of all living beings and growing things revolves in (series of) sevens' (ap. Eusebius, *Praeparatio Evangelica* 13. 12. 13, in Denis, *Fragmenta Pseudepigraphorum*, 225, and Charlesworth, *Old Testament Pseudepigrapha*, ii. 842, fr. 5), whereas a similar statement *could* alternatively have been made, perhaps more appropriately, about the category of time (e.g. that 'time revolves in series of sevens'). However, I would not press this suggestion too far.   [51]   See above, n. 32.

[52]   *Antiquities* 1. 7, 1. 72, 5. 314, 17. 282, 18. 40 χρόνου δε προϊόντος; 18. 179 χρόνου δὲ ἐγγενομένου; 15. 259, 16. 196 χρόνου δὲ διελθόντος. See also *Ant*. 3. 95 (and possibly 2. 308) χρόνου τριβομένου, 'as time dragged on'.

[53]   *War* 7. 96, *Antiquities* 6. 297, 7. 65, 10. 23 ('to spend time'); *Life* 295 ('to waste time'). Note also τριβομένου τοῦ χρόνου in *Ant*. 2. 341, 10. 17, 12. 368 (and possibly also 2. 308; see previous note) meaning 'time was being wasted'.

[54]   This passage appears in a speech attributed to Judas the Essene, which may appear a little odd, if we consider this notion of time to be distinctly Greek. It remains entirely possible, nevertheless, for Judas the Essene to have been a little Hellenized; and even if he was not, Josephus himself—who wrote this speech—might well have been unaware of the incongruity.

Ham, Josephus writes that Chusaios (Kush) alone escaped the 'ravages of time'.[55] But Josephus' most distinctive references to time are in the *Against Apion*, where in one passage he mentions that God is immutable 'within eternal time',[56] and where he concludes his apology with a call upon 'time' or the 'whole of time'[57] to testify to the virtue of Moses and his teachings (*Against Apion* 2. 279–80, 290). This typically Greek personification of time is hardly incongruous, given Josephus' general dependence on Greek literary tradition; but it might be relevant to note that the *Against Apion*, more than any other of his works, is specifically addressed to a Graeco-Roman, non-Jewish readership.

The Greek concept of time can also be found, sporadically, in a few other Jewish Hellenistic works. In the *Letter of Aristeas* (second century BCE), the question is raised of how kings should 'spend most of their time'.[58] It is generally acknowledged that in this passage (*Letter of Aristeas* 187–292), the philosophical questions and answers delivered at the king's banquet are likely to be directly derived from clichés of contemporary Hellenistic philosophy.[59]

According to a fragment of Philo the Epic Poet (third or second century BCE), Joseph was 'revolving the secrets of time with the flood of fate';[60] and the third Sibylline Oracle (second or first century BCE) states in two places that 'time was going round'.[61] Both these works are known for their deliberate emulation of Greek (in the case of the third Sibylline Oracle, Homeric) literary tradition.[62]

To conclude, the absence of a general concept of time in a number of Jewish Hellenistic works suggest that this concept was not fundamentally Jewish. Wherever it is used in Jewish Hellenistic literature, it is clearly directly borrowed from Greek tradition.[63] Its appearance in the works of Philo, Josephus, and a few others (I

---

[55] *Ant.* I. 131: οὐδὲν ἔβλαψεν ὁ χρόνος, literally 'time did not harm him'. The active voice (difficult to render in English translation) suggests very strongly the concept of time as an autonomous agent. See also ibid. 16. 44: 'hallowed by time'.

[56] *Against Apion* 2. 167: πρὸς τὸν ἀίδιον χρόνον ἀναλλοίωτον, which translates perhaps more precisely: 'immutable *in relation to* eternal time' (the meaning of πρός is slightly unclear). Josephus is certainly suggesting that God and time are somehow conterminous.

[57] ὁ πολὺς χρόνος (ibid. 279), which may translate alternatively as 'immense time'. Josephus is clearly referring to the continuum of time as a whole.

[58] *Letter of Aristeas*, 283: τὸν πλείω χρόνον διάγειν.

[59] Schürer, *History of the Jewish People*, iii. 680 and references in n. 280.

[60] H. Lloyd-Jones and P. J. Parsons, *Supplementum Hellenisticum* (Berlin: de Gruyter, 1983), 330, no. 686. 5, ap. Eusebius, *Praeparatio Evangelica* 9. 24. 1, in Denis, *Fragmenta Pseudepigraphorum*, 203–4 and Charlesworth, *Old Testament Pseudepigrapha*, ii. 783–4: δινεύσας λαθραῖα χρόνον πλημμυρίδι μοίρης. The obscurity of this line is not untypical of the author.

[61] Or 'pursuing its cyclical course' (χρόνου περιτελλομένοιο): *Sibylline Oracles* 3. 158 and 289.

[62] On Philo the Epic Poet, see Schürer, *History of the Jewish People*, iii. 559–61. On the *Sibylline Oracles*, book 3, see ibid. 628, and Gruen, 'Jews, Greeks, and Romans in the Third Sibylline Oracle'.

[63] In one text, the concept appears to have been borrowed directly from Persian tradition: Slavonic Enoch (2 Enoch), ch. 65 (Charlesworth, *Old Testament Pseudepigrapha*, i. 190–2). This short passage describes how God established the 'age of creation' before the creation of the world, how this age was

may have left some out) can always be directly related to their emulation of various Greek literary traditions such as philosophy, historiography, and epic poetry.

Avoidance of the Greek concept of time in a number of Jewish Hellenistic works should not necessarily be taken as evidence of Jewish resistance to Hellenistic influence.[64] An author's decision, conscious or unconscious, to leave out the Greek notion of time could often have been just a matter of genre. In the books of Maccabees and the Wisdom of Solomon, for example, omission of the category of time may have reflected a deliberate attempt to emulate the contents, style, and expression of the Bible and related works. It is exactly for the same reason that in the New Testament and early Christian Apocalyptic literature—of which many works were, incidentally, of non-Jewish authorship—the term *chronos* is restricted entirely to punctual or discontinuous meanings, and never means the continuum of time as a whole.[65] Still, adherence to biblical literary traditions would in itself have constituted an important obstacle, in Jewish Greek-speaking literary circles, to the absorption of Greek traditional ideas.

The absence of the Greek concept of time from much of Jewish Hellenistic literature can be related to the absence, in early rabbinic literature, of any notion of time as an entity in itself, a dimension of reality, a flowing continuum, or a useful commodity. This world-view was not specific, indeed, to early rabbinic Judaism: it would appear to have been characteristic of ancient Judaism as a whole. In the context of Jewish Hellenistic culture, it was possible for Greek notions of time to be adopted by some authors, e.g. Philo and Josephus. But in other contexts, the process-related world-view of the Jews would have contrasted quite clearly with the reified notion of time that prevailed in Graeco-Roman culture. This was particularly evident, as we shall now see, in the context of the Hebrew- and Aramaic-speaking Near East.

given to man and divided into times, hours, etc., and how all these time divisions will ultimately to be dissolved again into the 'great age'. 'Age', which could be translated as *aiōn* or simply 'time', is akin in this passage to the Persian notion of 'time of long dominion' (on which see below, Ch. 6): Pines, 'Eschatology and the Concept of Time', 77–82; but see the reservations of Gignoux, 'Hexaéméron et millénarisme', 84 n. 64. The authorship, provenance, and date of Slavonic Enoch are completely unknown: see Schürer, *History of the Jewish People*, iii. 746–50, with a possible dating around the 1st c. CE, and a possible provenance from Egypt; the original language is likely to have been Greek.

[64] On 'Hellenization' and resistance to it in the Jewish Greek-speaking diaspora, see Hengel, *Judaism and Hellenism*; Feldman, *Jew and Gentile*, 19–44; Levine, *Judaism and Hellenism in Antiquity*; Gruen, *Heritage and Hellenism*; and Barclay's review of Collins, *Between Athens and Jerusalem*.

[65] Eynikel and Hauspie ('Καιρός and Χρόνος', 383) have also found that just as in the Septuagint (see above, n. 47), the use of *chronos* in the New Testament is less frequent than *kairos*, whereas in contemporary Greek literature the proportion is closer to the reverse. In Gal. 4: 4, the clause 'when the fullness of time came' (ὅτε δὲ ἦλθεν τὸ πλήρωμα τοῦ χρόνου) refers to the occurrence of a specific point in time, without implying the existence of a general flow of time or of a time continuum. This expression is echoed in Mark 1: 15, 'the time is fulfilled' (πεπλήρωται ὁ καιρός), which means that the messianic age has reached its point of maturation; note that the Greek term *kairos* usually has the restricted meaning of 'point in time', 'right time', or 'critical time' (Eynikel and Hauspie, 'Καιρός and Χρόνος', 376–80, *pace* Barr, *Biblical Words*, 20–5).

SIX

Jewish Culture and the Ancient Near East

NOTIONS of time as an entity in itself, a dimension of reality, a flowing continuum, or a useful commodity—all familiar to ancient Greek culture—are totally absent from ancient Jewish sources written in Hebrew and Aramaic. Besides rabbinic sources that have been studied in previous chapters at length, the absence of these notions characterizes the whole corpus of Qumran, Apocryphal, and Pseudepigraphic post-biblical literature, as well as the Hebrew Bible itself. In this chapter, I shall examine the non-rabbinic sources but also expand my analysis to the ancient Near East as a whole. It will emerge that the concept of time as a separate category or entity, specific to Greek tradition, was alien not only to rabbinic literature but also to Jewish culture in general, and furthermore, to the prevailing culture of the ancient Near East.

QUMRAN, APOCRYPHA, AND PSEUDEPIGRAPHA

The Dead Sea Scrolls from Qumran are probably the largest body extant of post-biblical, non-rabbinic ancient Jewish sources in Hebrew and Aramaic. The concept of time as an entity in itself is nowhere to be found within it. Words for time in Qumran literature include *et*, *mo'ed*, and (specific to Qumran) *kets*, but these terms always refer to appointed times, points in time, or limited periods, and never refer to 'time' in a wider sense.[1] For example, the Community Rule and related sources from Qumran prohibit to advance or delay appointed times (e.g. the times of festivals),[2] but 'times' in these passages are only meant in a punctual sense. Pseudo-Ezekiel talks of an eschatological 'hastening of the days', a theme which has some parallels in ancient Apocalyptic literature (Jewish and Christian).[3] But this only

---

[1] See above, Introduction; Brin, *Concept of Time*; Licht, 'The Doctrine of "Times"'.

[2] 1QS i 13–15 (cf. iii 9–10); 4Q266 2 i 2–3; 4Q268 i 4; all cited in Brin, *Concept of Time*, 241–3.

[3] 4Q 385 iii 2–7, in Strugnell and Dimant, '4Q Second Ezekiel'; cited in Brin, *Concept of Time*, 243–5. Parallel in 2 Baruch 54: 1: 'you [God] hasten the beginnings of the times' (Charlesworth, *Old Testament Pseudepigrapha*, i. 639). See also Ethiopic Enoch (1 Enoch) 80: 2–8, on the shortening of years (Charlesworth, *Old Testament Pseudepigrapha*, i. 58–9); and Matt. 24: 22, Mark 13: 20, on the shortening of the days. *Song of Songs Rabbah* 2: 8 refers similarly to the 'skipping' of years.

refers to the length or number of successive days, a process which does not assume or imply any notion of the flow of time *per se*.[4]

A large number of calendar sources have been discovered at Qumran, suggesting a keen interest in intricate calendrical computations; but as I have argued at length in Chapter 3, calendar is not time, nor is it necessarily conceived as a measurement of the time-dimension. The 364-day calendar and the lunisolar calendars that are represented in detail in Qumran sources constitute attempts to harmonize, often artificially, the heavenly processes of the week, the lunar month, and the solar year. They do not provide a theory or measurement of 'pure' time.[5] In 4Q*Berakhot*[a], reference is made to weeks, months, (new?) years, festivals, and sabbatical years as wondrous mysteries of God, which vividly expresses the religious significance attached to calendars and calendrical periods.[6] But calendrical periods are processes, not segments of abstract time.

The concept of time as an entity in itself is equally absent in Ben Sira, a relatively early work (early second century BCE) that has been preserved, to a large extent, in the original Hebrew. Ben Sira 27: 12, only extant in Greek and Syriac translations, has been interpreted by some as an admonition not to 'waste time' among the fools, which would suggest the notion of time as a commodity or resource.[7] The Greek text, however, uses the word *kairos*, which has only the meaning of 'the right time'. Thus the verse should be translated: 'Among the fools, watch for the right time; but among the wise, persist'. The verse does not explain what this right time is for, but it is best interpreted by analogy with Ben Sira 20: 7: 'the wise person waits silently till the right time, but the fool does not watch for the right time'. Analogously, 27: 12 would mean that among the fools, one should watch for the right time and stay silent; whereas among the wise, one may feel free to speak.[8] Other interpretations of the 'right time' in this verse are also possible (e.g. the right time to leave), but in any event, the concepts of time in general or of time-saving are not implicit. The same applies to Ben Sira 4: 20, which enjoins, without any context: 'watch for the right time' (the Hebrew text, *shemor et*, can also be translated as: 'observe the right time').

---

[4] *Pace* Brin, *Concept of Time*.

[5] For a general introduction to Qumran calendar sources, see Glessmer, 'Calendars in the Qumran Scrolls'; Stern, 'Qumran Calendars: Theory and Practice'; id., *Calendar and Community*, 11–18; VanderKam, *Calendars in the Dead Sea Scrolls*; Talmon et al., *Discoveries in the Judaean Desert*, XXI.

[6] 4Q286, fr.1, 9–12, ed. B. Nitzan in Eshel et al., *Discoveries in the Judaean Desert*, XI. 12–17.

[7] So Charles, *Apocrypha and Pseudepigrapha*, i. 406. On the book of *Ben Sira*, see Schürer, *History of the Jewish People*, iii. 198–212.

[8] The Syriac and Latin versions of 27: 12 lend further support to this interpretation: see Segal, *Book of Ben Sira*, 167–9; Charles, *Apocrypha and Pseudepigrapha*, i. 406. *Ben Sira* 20: 7 is extant in Hebrew, and has the word *et* for 'right time'; the Greek, again, has *kairos*, for which see Ch. 5 nn. 47, 65.

Two other passages in Ben Sira are identified by James Barr as evidence of time as a continuous flow,[9] but these are unconvincing. Hebrew Ben Sira 43: 6 calls the moon *memshelet kets*, 'dominion over time', which Barr takes to mean that the moon controls the continuum of time as a whole. However, this passage could be interpreted as meaning that the moon controls specific *points in time*, namely the succession of months; indeed the term *kets*, which primarily means 'end', is more likely to mean (in its temporal sense) a 'point in time', particularly as this usage is widely attested in Qumran sources.[10] Furthermore, the Greek version of this verse translates the phrase as *anadeixin chronōn*, 'proclamation of *times* [plural]', which suggests punctual times rather than time as a whole.

The other passage is Ben Sira 18: 26, only extant in the Greek version, which states that 'time [*kairos*] moves over [or: changes] from morning to evening'.[11] Again, there is no evidence to suggest that this verse refers to the flow of time. As noted above, the word *kairos* usually just means the 'right time' or a specific time; in this context, indeed, it follows on from the *kairos* mentioned in the preceding verse, which enjoins one to 'remember the time [*kairos*] of hunger at the time [*kairos*] of satiety' (18: 25). The meaning of 18: 26 is simply that good times (satiety) do not always last from morning to evening.

Among Pseudepigraphic works that were originally written in Hebrew or Aramaic, but have only survived in translation, we may first consider 1 Enoch (also called Ethiopic Enoch). Its astronomical and calendrical section (known as the 'Astronomical Book', 1 Enoch 72–82), as attested from Qumran fragments, was originally written in Aramaic as early as the third century BCE.[12] The Ethiopic version of this text, as well as the Aramaic and Greek-translated fragments that are extant, are devoid of any reference to time as an entity in itself. The Astronomical Book describes in detail the courses of the sun and the moon and their calendrical implications, but these are clearly only astronomical processes, not representations of time *per se*. In another section of Ethiopic Enoch (1 Enoch 46: 1–2, and then frequently in chs. 46–71), God or the Divine is called 'the Antecedent of Time' or 'the Before Time'—depending on various English translations[13]—which would imply that God preceded the existence of time, and hence that time is conceived of as an entity in its own right. However, these English translations are misleading. The literal meaning of the Ethiopic is 'Head of Days',[14] and there is no reason to assume that this phrase means anything different. The notion that God presides

---

[9] Barr, *Biblical Words*, 102–7.
[10] On the term *kets*, see Ch. 1 n. 3.
[11] ἀπὸ πρωίθεν ἕως ἑσπέρας μεταβάλλει καιρός.
[12] Milik, *The Books of Enoch*.
[13] See the translations of E. Isaac in Charlesworth, *Old Testament Pseudepigrapha*, i. 34 etc.
[14] As correctly translated by Charles (*Apocrypha and Pseudepigrapha*, ii. 214 etc.) and Knibb, *Ethiopic Book of Enoch*, ii. 131–2 etc. This phrase is reminiscent of the Aramaic *atik yomin* (the 'Ancient of Days') in Daniel 7: 9. Note that Isaac (n. 14) himself is not entirely consistent, as on p. 49 he translates 'Antecedent of days'; see also ibid., p. 34, note a.

over the days, or generated them, or perhaps even preceded them, does not imply or necessitate the notion of an abstract time-continuum.[15]

The division of world history into jubilees, 'weeks', 'hours', 'kingdoms', 'ages', or 'times' (the latter in the sense of limited periods or eras) is an important theme of Apocalyptic and Pseudepigraphic literature, especially in the book of Jubilees (second century BCE), but also in eschatological passages such as 1 Enoch 91: 12–17 and 93, Testament of Levi 16–17, 2 Baruch 26–8, and Apocalypse of Abraham 28–9. However, jubilees and other periods are, by definition, finite. They give structure to the succession of historical events and processes, but without implying or necessitating the existence of a general time-line or continuum of time.[16] For similar reasons, the designation of God as 'king of the ages' in Tobit 13: 7 and 13: 11[17] should not be interpreted as meaning 'king of time', but rather as meaning 'king of history'.

The only source originally written in Hebrew, and indeed of probable Palestinian provenance, where a general concept of time may be identified is Pseudo-Philo (first century CE). In *Biblical Antiquities* 19: 14–15, Moses asks God 'how much quantity of time has passed and how much (of it) is left'; God's answer is obscure, but includes the statement that 'time will accomplish all'.[18] 'Quantity of time' (*quantitas temporis*), in Moses' question, suggests that time is a quantifiable entity or a measurable extension; 'has passed' (*transiit*) suggests that time is a moving flow. 'Time will accomplish all', in God's answer, is reminiscent of the Greek notion that time is a driving force of history.[19]

It may be imprudent, however, to place excessive reliance on this short and cryptic passage. The only extant version of this text is a Latin translation from a Greek version, that would have been itself a translation from the original

[15]   On Slavonic Enoch (2 Enoch) 65, see above Ch. 5 n. 63.

[16]   See my discussion on chronology in Ch. 3.

[17]   The Greek version reads: καὶ ὑψώσατε τον βασιλέα τῶν αἰώνων ('and exalt the King of the ages/*aiōnes*'); however, it is questionable whether the original text had anything equivalent. The Qumran Aramaic version of this passage (4QpapTobitᵃar = 4Q196, fr. 17 ii, l. 3, ed. J. Fitzmyer in Broshi et al., *Discoveries in the Judaean Desert* XIX, 26–8) reads simply [ורו]ממו לה ('and exalt him'); although the text is fragmentary, there is clearly no room on the papyrus for anything else. The Greek phrase is found elsewhere, however, in *Joseph and Asenath* 12: 1, 16: 16, and 21: 21 (of which Greek is the original language).

[18]   Pseudo-Philon, *Les Antiquités bibliques*, i. 164–5: *ostende mihi quanta quantitas temporis transiit et quanta remansit . . . et omnia complevit tempus*. The word *complevit* is plausibly emended by Harrington to *complebit*, hence 'time will accomplish all'.

[19]   This phrase must be distinguished from the notion of time 'being accomplished' (in the passive), which appears in other eschatological passages of Pseudo-Philo's *Biblical Antiquities*. Verse 28: 9, 'time will be accomplished' (*completum fuerit tempus*), probably means in its context an appointed time or period (see also 3: 9). Verse 23: 13, 'until the time of the world is accomplished [or 'fulfilled']' (*quousque compleatur tempus seculi*), refers to the designated time or age of the world, not to an abstract entity called 'time'. Cf. above, Ch. 5 n. 65.

Hebrew.[20] Comparison with other apocryphal sources of which fragments of the original text have been discovered suggests that translations of these sources were not particularly faithful to the exact, original text.[21] The possibility that Graeco-Roman notions of time were introduced, perhaps quite inadvertently, by the Greek or Latin translators of Pseudo-Philo should thus not be discarded.[22]

Similar comments apply to 4 Ezra, a first-century CE Palestinian work which was also composed originally in Hebrew, but only extant (in its oldest version) in a Latin translation from the Greek.[23] In 4 Ezra 4: 45, reference is made to the time that has passed and the time that is left, suggesting that time is a measurable, continuous flow. Again, we cannot know whether this is an accurate translation of the Hebrew original. In 4 Ezra 14: 9–10 we read: '. . . until the times are ended. For the era has lost its youth, and the times begin to grow old' (*usquequo finiantur tempora. Quoniam saeculum perdidit iuuentutem suam, et tempora adpropinquant senescere*). In this passage, the notion of time ('era' and 'times') is clearly confused with the age of the universe; it is a process-related notion and does not represent an independent, abstract entity.[24]

Hebrew or Aramaic Jewish literature from later antiquity that is non-rabbinic or at least marginal to rabbinic literature includes the *Sefer yetsirah* (which has already been dealt with in Chapter 1), *Sefer harazim*, and the multifarious *Heikhalot*. All of these are devoid of any notion of time as an entity in itself.[25]

THE HEBREW BIBLE

The absence of a concept of time *per se* from ancient Jewish literature, which we have now established, can be traced further back to the Bible and ancient Israelite culture. As in Qumran and early rabbinic sources, no word in the Hebrew Bible

---

[20] Pseudo-Philon, *Les Antiquités bibliques*, ii. 66–78; Schürer, *History of the Jewish People*, iii. 325–31.

[21] e.g. the Qumran Aramaic fragment of Tobit, referred to above, n. 17.

[22] It is worth noting that the phrase 'time has accomplished all', or even, as emended, 'time will accomplish all', does not fit the context of Moses' question. It is possible that the original Hebrew read more appropriately 'time will be accomplished' (in the passive), as in other passages of this work (see above, n. 19), but the translator misread the verb, in the unpointed Hebrew text, as being in the active (suggestion of Leofranc Holford-Strevens). The original Hebrew may have read תמלא העת (*nifal*, but misread as *pi'el*), cf. Jer. 25: 12, 29: 10, Dan. 9: 2. For other possibilities cf. 1QpHab vii, lines 2, 13 (courtesy of Shani Berrin), and CD iv. 8–12.

[23] Schürer, *History of the Jewish People*, iii. 294–306.

[24] The reference to the 'son of God' at the beginning of 14: 9 may indicate that this passage is actually a Christian interpolation.

[25] On the *Sefer harazim*, see Schürer, *History of the Jewish People*, iii. 347–50. The *Heikhalot* text known as (Hebrew) 3 Enoch (45: 6), reads 'till the end of time' in P. S. Alexander's English translation (in Charlesworth, *Old Testament Pseudepigrapha*, i. 299). However, the original text (Odeberg, *3 Enoch*, Hebrew section p. 60) only reads *ad sof* ('till the end'), which need not mean more than 'till the end of the *universe*'.

means 'time' in a general sense. The terms *et* and *mo'ed*, most commonly used in the Bible for aspects of time, denote points in time, appointed times, and sometimes periods of time, but never the continuum of time as a whole.[26] Attempts by James Barr to identify such a usage of *et* in late biblical Hebrew are totally unconvincing.[27] Ecclesiastes 9: 11 is usually translated as 'time [*et*] and chance befall them all' (עת ופגע יקרה את כולם); but the idea that time as a whole should 'befall' someone does not make much sense. The meaning of this verse if far more likely to be that points in time, i.e. events or incidents, befall all people.[28]

Barr argues further that even if *et* ('time') in a general sense happened not to be attested in the Bible, this would not mean that the term could not have been used, in ancient Hebrew, in this sense.[29] But although, in strict terms, this argument is correct—indeed, it cannot be *proved* that words for time in a general sense did not exist in the ancient Hebrew language—it remains legitimate to treat the absence of this concept from the entire Hebrew Bible as highly significant.[30]

Attempts to identify this concept in the Bible have never been more than the imposition of modern categories upon the sources. For example, it has often been pointed out to me that the Bible begins with the term *bereshit* ('In the beginning'), which would imply the beginning of the flow of time.[31] However, *bereshit* is only a statement about what came first in the process of the Creation. The appearance of this word at the beginning of Genesis is indicative of the considerable importance attached to *event-sequencing* in the Bible—just as are the genealogies and king-lists

---

[26] As noted already in 1871 by H. C. von Orelli, ap. Barr, *Biblical Words*, 96. See above, Introduction.

[27] Barr, *Biblical Words*, 94–107. For a refutation of Barr's contention that *et* in some passages means 'time' in a general sense, see Eynikel and Hauspie, 'Καιρός and Χρόνος' 379–80.

[28] Eynikel and Hauspie against Barr (see n. 27). Most modern commentators are in broad agreement: see Loader, *Ecclesiastes*, 111–12; Scott, *The Anchor Bible: Proverbs and Ecclesiastes*, 245, who translates: 'when the time comes, bad luck overtakes them all'; and Zer-Kavod, *The Five Scrolls*, 59, who reads עת ופגע as a quasi-construct form, i.e. 'the time of bad luck'. Eynikel and Hauspie ('Καιρός and Χρόνος', 379–80) suggest 'fate and chance' as a translation.

[29] Barr, *Biblical Words*, 102–4.

[30] As I have similarly argued in Ch. 1, with reference to early rabbinic literature. Barr's argument is based, to a large extent, on the tacit conviction that the biblical authors (or 'ancient Hebrews') could not have been unaware of the universal concept of the time-dimension. However, the assumption that time is a universal concept can be refuted through the anthropological study of non-modern cultures, as has been shown in the Introduction. Momigliano ('Time in Ancient Historiography') argues that the absence from the Bible of words for time (in a general sense) may just be due to the fact that biblical books 'do not contain meditations about time such as we find in Greek poets and philosophers' (p. 183). But this argument can be refuted on its own terms: in Greek literature, references to time *per se* are not exclusive to the genres of poetry and philosophy, but also common among the historians and other authors (see Ch. 5 above). As I have argued in Ch. 1, references to time as an entity in itself can often be quite casual (as in the popular saying 'time flies'), and are not restricted to philosophy or poetic 'meditation'. There is no *a priori* reason, therefore, why the genre of the Bible should preclude references to the notion of time *per se*.   [31] As suggested by Néher, 'Vision du temps', 171–2.

throughout the rest of the biblical books. But it is not a programmatic statement about time *per se*.[32]

Another example is Momigliano's observation, to support the existence of the concept of time in the Bible, that the Bible presents the history of a continuous period of which the length, from the Creation to about 400 BCE, is unparalleled in ancient, classical historiography.[33] However, this has nothing to do with the abstract concept of a time-line or time-continuum. History is about events—not about time *per se*.

A further example is Sasson's interpretation of Genesis 1: 5 ('and it was evening and it was morning, one day') as God's 'invention of time'. The second day of Creation is similarly interpreted as the creation of space, and the third day as the Creation of mass.[34] No substantiation, however, is provided for this interpretation; time, space, and mass are modern categories which find no place in ancient biblical culture.[35]

The absence of a category of time in the Hebrew Bible may be reflected, to a certain extent, in the notorious fuzziness of tense in the biblical Hebrew verb.[36] As I have argued in the Introduction, the expression of aspect (and mood) rather than tense in a verbal system is likely to reflect a process-related perception of past, present, and future that does not require a notion of the time-continuum or time *per se*.[37]

OLAM

Because of its apparent associations with the notion of a time-continuum, the biblical term *olam* (*'LM*) deserves special consideration. It is often translated as 'eternity', but its precise meaning is ambiguous and requires clarification.[38] In fact, *olam* has two different meanings in the Bible: perpetuity, and remotest time.[39] I shall examine both meanings separately.

[32] Besides, the force of the word *bereshit* is considerably reduced if one translates Genesis 1: 1, like Sasson ('Time . . . to Begin', 187–8), as: 'When God began to create . . .'.

[33] Momigliano, 'Time in Ancient Historiography', 194.   [34] Sasson, 'Time . . . to Begin', 191–3.

[35] This is not to say that the concept of time cannot be used as a hermeneutic device for the modern reinterpretation of the Bible (see e.g. Ben Zvi, 'About Time'). But to ascribe this concept to the Bible itself is unjustifiable.   [36] On tense in biblical Hebrew, see Introduction, n. 73.

[37] Here again, I am taking issue with James Barr. The conceptual significance of the absence of tense in biblical Hebrew was already suggested by Orelli in 1871 (ap. Barr, *Biblical Words*, 96); Barr objects, however, that it would be absurd to deduce a philosophy of time from language structures (ibid. 136–7). If such a crude deduction is what Orelli meant, then Barr's scathing attack is justified. However, Barr's polemical agenda deflects him from acknowledging the truism that although straight-forward deductions of this kind cannot be made, the verbal system of a language—and indeed, language as a whole—must be of *some* relevance to the general cultural context of its users.

[38] For earlier studies, see Jenni, 'Das Wort ʿōlām'; Wiesenberg, 'The Liturgical Term *melekh ha-'olam*', 3–13; Brin, *Concept of Time*, 278–88.   [39] Barr, *Biblical Words*, 122–3.

The first meaning, perpetuity, is attested in the phrases *hok/hukat olam* ('law in perpetuity'),[40] *berit olam* ('covenant in perpetuity'),[41] *ahuzat olam* ('possession in perpetuity'),[42] *zekher olam* ('memory in perpetuity'),[43] to name some important examples. The point of these phrases is not that the law, covenant, possession, etc. last for ever in time, but rather that they are permanent; thus the term *olam* (in this context) is not temporal, but rather expressive of a state (permanency). For this reason, I would avoid the translation 'eternity', which carries temporal connotations, and prefer terms such as 'permanence', 'stability', 'perpetuity', or 'everlastingness'.[44] This process-related connotation is particularly evident in verses such as Isaiah 55: 13, 'an everlasting sign [*ot olam*] not to be destroyed',[45] and Proverbs 10: 25, 'when the storm has passed the wicked is no more, but the righteous is an everlasting foundation [*yesod olam*]'. The same interpretation applies to the phrase *eved olam*,[46] which cannot literally mean 'slave in eternity', since the life span of a human slave is necessarily limited; all it means is 'slave for life' or 'permanent slave'. The very common *le'olam* (usually translated as 'for ever') almost invariably carries the non-temporal meaning of stability and permanence, for instance in Isaiah 40: 8: 'grass dries up and flowers wither, but the word of our God for ever stands'.[47]

---

[40] Exod. 12: 14, 29: 28, and very frequently in the Pentateuch.

[41] Gen. 9: 16, 17: 7 (regarding circumcision), Exod. 31: 16, etc.

[42] Gen. 17: 8, 48: 4, Lev. 25: 34, etc.   [43] Ps. 112: 6.

[44] *Pace* Brin (*Concept of Time*, 277 and n. 2, 278–80, and 284–8), who takes *olam* to mean 'eternity'. Jenni ('Das Wort 'ōlām', 1–5) concedes the translation of *el olam* (Gen. 21: 33, cf. Isa. 40: 28) as 'God of eternity' or 'eternal God', but rightly cautions that in the context of pre-Hellenistic Near Eastern culture, 'eternity' should only be taken to refer to the concrete permanence or continuity of things, rather than to a self-standing temporal abstraction. Jenni points out, in particular, that the word *olam* is never used on its own in the Bible, but only with a preposition or in a construct form. Note also Brin's interesting suggestion that in some cases, *olam* can be interpreted as a superlative (e.g. 'very strong covenant').

[45] See similarly Isa. 56: 5: 'an everlasting name [*shem olam*] . . . not to be destroyed'.

[46] Exod. 21: 6, Deut. 15: 17, 1 Sam. 27: 12, and Job 40: 28.

[47] Further examples might include Ps. 125: 1, 'like mount Zion which cannot be moved and abides for ever [*le'olam*]' (cf. ibid. 9: 8, 15: 5, 30: 7, 102: 13, 112: 6, Prov. 10: 30); Ps. 111: 8, 'established for ever and ever'; Eccles. 1: 4, 'a generation goes and a generation comes, but the earth stands for ever' (cf Ps. 78: 69); and Ps. 111: 5, 'he will remember his covenant for ever' (cf. ibid. 105: 8). Isa. 34: 10 juxtaposes the term *le'olam* with *lailah veyomam* ('night and day'), *midor ledor* ('from generation to generation'), and *lenetsah netsahim* (a phrase denoting everlasting victory, and translated by the Targum as *le'alam alemaya*), but there is no need to read a temporal connotation into these terms: all they represent is the permanent succession of night and day and human generations (the same applies to Deut. 23: 7, 'all your days for ever'). The phrase *vihi itam le'olam* (Ps. 81: 16) does not mean 'their time will be for ever' in the sense of a continuous time-flow, but rather 'their *appointed* time [either for reward or for punishment, depending on how the verse is interpreted] will last for ever' (i.e. they will be *permanently* rewarded or punished). It is interesting to note that in mishnaic Hebrew, the term *le'olam* comes to mean 'in all cases' (in a legal sense), thus extending the process-related connotation of the biblical Hebrew. See in particular BT *Ḥul.* 17a, where the mishnaic term *le'olam* is interpreted by Rava as meaning (in this particular context) 'at night or in the day, at the top of a roof or of a boat' (thus not only temporal but also spatial).

The second meaning of *olam*, which occurs in an equally large number of cases, is 'very remote period', either in the past or in the future. Here the temporal connotation of *olam* is evident, especially where it is used to qualify a measure of time (days, years, etc.), as is quite common in later biblical books: e.g. *yemei olam* ('the days of *olam*'),[48] *shenat olam* ('the year of *olam*'),[49] etc. In this temporal context, however, *olam* is restricted to the very remote past or future.[50] This is particularly clear in phrases that explicitly connect the term with the notions of remote antiquity[51] or of a distant, eschatological future.[52] Thus the common phrase *me'olam* ('from *olam*') always refers to the distant past,[53] while *ad olam* ('until *olam*') always implies a period in the distant future.[54] The phrase *min olam ve'ad olam* ('from *olam* and to *olam*') is best interpreted as meaning: 'from the distant past to the distant future'.[55]

Because of the temporal connotations of this term, some scholars have summarily concluded that *olam* is proof of a biblical notion of 'time' or of the time-continuum.[56] But this is based on a conflation of the two meanings of *olam*, 'permanence' and 'remote time', into the single concept of 'eternity', which is both inaccurate and misleading. In its meaning of 'permanence', the term *olam* does not imply or require the notion of a time-continuum: permanence is a characteristic of events and processes, and should not be confused with time or abstract temporality. In its second meaning, *olam* does not refer to the whole continuum of time (which would necessarily include the present and the immediate past and future), but only to *distant* periods, in either the past or in the future. It is only in certain contexts that the use of *olam* can imply a notion of the whole of time: for instance, in the phrase *min olam ve'ad olam*, 'from the distant past to the distant future'. But whether this is enough to infer that the Bible conceives of time as an entity in itself or as a

[48] e.g. Isa. 63: 9, 11, Amos 9: 11, Mic. 7: 14, but already attested in Deut. 32: 7.

[49] Jer. 51: 39, 57; cf. Ps. 77: 6.

[50] Jenni ('Das Wort ʿōlām') thus renders *olam* as *fernste Zeit* ('most distant time').

[51] e.g. with the word *kedem*, as in Mic. 5: 1, 'from antiquity, from the days of *olam*' (*mikedem mimei olam*); Mal. 3: 4, 'as the days of *olam* and as ancient years' (*mimei olam ukheshanim kadmoniyot*), and Prov. 8: 23, 'since *olam* . . . from the beginning, since the origins of the earth' (*me'olam . . . merosh mikadmei arets*). Other terms can also be used with *olam* with similar connotations, e.g. *me'az* (Ps. 93: 2).

[52] e.g. Isa. 30: 8, 'to the last day, to *ad*, to *olam*' (*leyom aharon la'ad ad olam*).

[53] Gen. 6: 4, Josh. 24: 2 (referring to the pre-Abrahamic period), etc. The sense of remote past is also implicit in Deut. 32: 7 and Isa. 63: 11 (*vayizkor yemei olam*, 'remember the days of *olam*'), and Prov. 22: 28 (*gevul olam*, 'an ancient boundary'). See also Mic. 5: 1, 'since the days of *olam*' (*mimei olam*); cf. 7: 14. See further Brin, *Concept of Time*, 181–3.

[54] Gen. 13: 15, Exod. 12: 24, Deut. 12: 28, Ps. 18: 51, etc. Note in particular the phrase *me'atah ve'ad olam* ('from now and till *olam*': Mic. 4: 7, Ps. 125: 2, etc.); and *ledor vador ad olam* ('for every generation until *olam*': Ps. 106: 31). See further Brin, *Concept of Time*, 150–1, 280.

[55] Jer. 7: 7, 25: 5, Pss. 41: 14, 90: 2, 103: 17, 106: 48, Neh. 9: 5, 1 Chron. 16: 36, 29: 10. See further Brin, *Concept of Time*, 102–3, 183.

[56] e.g. West, *Early Greek Philosophy*, 29, 35–6; Brin, *Concept of Time*, 277.

continuum is more than doubtful.[57] Certainly the word *olam* does not imply this meaning. How the two meanings of this word (permanence and distant time) are semantically related admittedly remains obscure,[58] but there is certainly no need to conflate them, or to introduce the abstract notion of time-continuum to mediate between them.

In etymological terms, finally, the word *olam* has nothing to relate it to time or any aspect of time. The etymology of *olam* remains unclear,[59] but in its meaning of 'very remote period', it may well be related to the Hebrew root עלם *'LM*, 'to hide': *olam* would thus mean the hidden or unknown (because distant) past and future.[60] Another possibility is that it is derived from the Akkadian *ullānu*, 'to be distant' (hence, distant past or future).[61] But there is certainly no etymological evidence to suggest that *olam* expresses pure time or the time-continuum. These notions, indeed, remain completely unattested in the Hebrew Bible.

THE ANCIENT NEAR EAST

The absence of a concept of time as such was not peculiar to the Bible and ancient Judaism, but characteristic of the culture of the entire Near East. A radical contrast can indeed be drawn between ancient Near Eastern culture as a whole and the culture of ancient Greece, where as we have seen, the concept of time was well ingrained at least by the sixth or fifth centuries BCE.

Words for time as a general category are absent not only in Hebrew and Aramaic, but also in other ancient Near Eastern languages, including Akkadian,

---

[57] On the phrase 'from now and till *olam*' (above, n. 54), Brin writes that it expresses the uninterrupted duration of time, which is the height of abstraction (*Concept of Time*, 8). This interpretation is unwarranted, because it imposes modern concepts of time on a verse which does not necessarily call for them.

[58] The use of *olam* in both senses consecutively in Ps. 125: 1–2 (cited above in nn. 47, 54) suggests a perception that somehow, both senses are closely connected; but it is difficult to know how. Some have suggested that the meaning of 'eternity' was originally derived from the meaning of 'distant past or future' (Brin, *Concept of Time*, 277 n. 1).

[59] See Jenni, 'Das Wort 'ōlām'; Koehler and Baumgartner, *Hebrew and Aramaic Lexicon*, ii. 798–9.

[60] As first suggested by Gesenius, *Hebrew and Chaldee Lexicon*, 612, followed by Orelli (ap. Barr, *Biblical Words*, 95–6), and apparently endorsed by Brown, Driver, and Briggs, *Hebrew and English Lexicon*, 761; but on philological grounds, see the reservations of Jenni, 'Das Wort 'ōlām', 199. The term *ha'olam* is certainly used in the sense of 'concealment' in Eccles. 3: 11, but this is the only example of this usage. It might also be possible to suggest that the phrase *beit olamo* in Eccles. 12: 5, which basically means 'his everlasting home' (i.e. his grave: Koehler and Baumgartner, *Hebrew and Aramaic Lexicon*, ii. 798–9; the term is also frequently used later in Syriac and Palmyrene, see Cooke, *North-Semitic Inscriptions*, 307–8, nos. 142. 1, 143. 1, and Millar, *Roman Near East*, 321), carries a secondary connotation of the home where the dead person is buried or *hidden* away.

[61] Brin, *Concept of Time*, 277 n. 1.

Ugaritic, and Phoenician.[62] Implicit references to such a concept cannot be legitimately inferred in any of the ancient Near Eastern sources, even in passages where it might have been most expected. Ancient Mesopotamian cosmologies, for instance, make no reference to the concept of time, whether created, eternal, or as a cosmological principle.[63] In the *Enuma Elish* (tablet 5), the moon is described as created to 'indicate the days' (i.e. the days of the month)—but not to indicate or measure the dimension of time.[64] Sumerian and other king-lists calculate the succession of regnal years in much detail, but without any reference to a continuous or comprehensive 'time-line' of history.[65]

The same conclusion applies to ancient Egypt (which I shall include in the 'Near East'). A few Egyptian sources referring to 'eternity' have been cited by others as evidence of a notion of the time-continuum: thus a hymn invokes Amon-Re as 'God of eternity, who made everlastingness',[66] and the *Book of the Dead* (85) says of Re again: 'my embodiment is eternity, my form is everlasting; the lord of years, the ruler of eternity'.[67] These phrases certainly suggest that eternity (or 'everlastingness') is an entity in itself, which Re rules over, made, and embodies. However, they could be translated differently as 'Eternal God, who made things everlasting', 'my body is eternal . . . eternal ruler'. Translation is, in fact, a contentious issue with all these sources. The same passage from the *Book of the Dead* has been translated by others as 'my soul and the soul of my body are cobras[!];

[62] See Black *et al.*, *Dictionary of Akkadian*, 323, 373: the Akkadian *simānu* (Assyrian *simunu*, Ugaritic *šimānu*) has the meanings of 'proper time', 'right time', 'time for *x*', 'season', and in Neo-Babylonian astronomical texts, the 'time' of astronomical events. It is thought to derive from the verb *(w)asāmum*, 'to be(come) fitting, seasonable, appropriate' (see also Mankowski, *Akkadian Loanwords*, 54), hence its primary meaning of '*proper* time'. There is no connotation, in this, of 'pure time' or of the time continuum. In Phoenician, the term *'T* (= Hebrew *et*) is also only attested as meaning punctual time, appointed time, season, and period (Tomback, *Comparative Semitic Lexicon*, 259; Krahmalkov, *Phoenician-Punic Dictionary*, 393).

[63] See e.g. sources in Pritchard, *Ancient Near Eastern Texts*, and the general comment of Jenni, 'Das Wort 'ōlām', 4 n. 1. According to Lambert, 'Kosmologie' (see also West, *Early Greek Philosophy*, 35), the three primordial elements of Babylonian cosmology were Earth, Water, and Time. However, for the element of Time very little evidence is supplied by Lambert (on p. 220): it consists entirely of scant references, in a few incantations, to the bisexual pair Dūri Dāri as ancestors of either Enlil or Anu. Besides the fact that genealogical ancestry of gods does not necessarily mean cosmological origins of the world, Dūri Dāri cannot be equated with the notion of 'time': these words are usually translated as 'ever and ever' and express an idea of continuity and permanence (Gelb et al., *Assyrian Dictionary*, vol. D, pp. 107–8, s.v. *dār*), which is clearly not the same as 'time'. Lambert also argues that another pair, (H)almă and (H)al(l)amă, express the notion of time, on the assumption (somewhat conjectural) that these terms are related to the Hebrew *olam*; but as we have seen, this interpretation of *olam* is itself highly unlikely.   [64] Pritchard, *Ancient Near Eastern Texts*, 67–8.

[65] Ibid. 265–6, similarly to biblical and early rabbinic chronology (see above, Ch. 3).

[66] Pap. Boulaq 17, dating from the 18th Dynasty (mid-second millennium BCE), in Pritchard, *Ancient Near Eastern Texts*, 365, section 3: 1.

[67] Papyrus of Ani, dating from *c*.1320 BCE, as cited by West, *Early Greek Philosophy*, 35. West treats these passages as evidence of an abstract notion of time.

perpetuity, lord of years, ruler of eternity, that is [my] image'.[68] The inference of an abstract notion of time or eternity from these passages depends therefore on fine nuances in the translation which are too uncertain to be relied upon. All we can infer with certainty from these passages is that Re was conceived in ancient Egypt as an eternal, everlasting, perpetual god; but there is nothing that demonstrates an abstract, independent notion of 'time' or of eternity.

The absence of a concept of time *per se* is also evident in later Near Eastern sources, dating from the Hellenistic and Roman periods. Expressions of native Near Eastern culture in this period are notoriously rare,[69] but we may refer to Philo of Byblos (early second century CE), who claims, in his *Phoenicica*, to have compiled ancient Phoenician traditions and to have translated them himself into Greek.[70] Although Hellenistic and other borrowings are clearly discernable in this work,[71] Philo's cosmogony is remarkably devoid of any reference to the notion of *chronos* or time, or to its possible role in the process of creation. Given the importance of *chronos* in the contemporary Greek world-view (see Chapter 5), its absence in a Phoenician cosmogony in Greek translation must be regarded as highly significant.

Only a faint allusion to time may be found in Philo's *Phoenicica*: the name of one of the first mortal men is *Aiōn*, which *could* be translated as 'age' or 'eternity', hence possibly 'time'. However, the significance of this name is obscure in this context, and not elucidated by Philo himself.[72] It is generally assumed that this *Aiōn* is a translation of the Phoenician word *'LM*, itself transliterated as *Oulomos* in another Phoenician cosmogony, which we shall presently see.[73] But still, this does not provide evidence of a Phoenician concept of time: for just as in biblical Hebrew, the Phoenician term *'LM*, in all its epigraphic attestations, does not have the meaning of 'time' but only the process-related meaning of 'perpetuity'.[74] Even if Philo

---

[68] Allen, *The Book of the Dead*, 73.

[69] As observed by Millar, *Roman Near East*, who refers to this phenomenon as cultural or historical 'amnesia'.

[70] This work is fragmentarily preserved in Eusebius' *Praeparatio Evangelica* (4th c. CE); see Attridge and Oden, *Philo of Byblos*, and Baumgarten, *Phoenician History*.

[71] Baumgarten, *Phoenician History*, 98–139 (with specific reference to Philo's cosmogony); Millar, *Roman Near East*, 277–9.

[72] Attridge and Oden, *Philo of Byblos*, 40–1; Baumgarten, *Phoenician History*, 13 (text) and 141 (translation); from Eusebius, *Praeparatio Evangelica*, 1: 10: 7. *Aiōn* is said to have discovered food from trees. On the meaning of the Greek term *aiōn*, see above, Ch 6.

[73] Attridge and Oden, *Philo of Byblos*, 80; Baumgarten, *Phoenician History*, 146–8.

[74] In all early Phoenician inscriptions, the term עלם is used in the same sense of 'perpetuity' as in biblical Hebrew: see Cooke, *North-Semitic Inscriptions*, 31, no. 5. 20 (Sidon, early 3rd c. BCE: [לעלם]), 44, no. 9. 8 (Phoenicia, 132 BCE: לעלם), 70, no. 21. 5 (Cyprus, 4th c. BCE: לעלם), 83 (no. 29. 12, Cyprus, 3rd–2nd cc. BCE: עד עלם). Note also שמש עלם ('Eternal Sun') in the Karatepe inscription (9th–8th cc. BCE: West, *Early Greek Philosophy*, 36), similar to the biblical *el olam* (above, n. 44) and to the Palmyrene בעל שמן מרא עלמא ('Ba'al-shamin, eternal lord') in a 2nd-c. CE inscription (Cooke, *North-Semitic Inscriptions*, 296, no. 134. 1).

himself may have assumed that ʿ*LM* was a time-related word, and thus gave it the Greek, time-related translation of *Aiōn*, this would not have been more than an *interpretatio Graeca* of the traditional, Phoenician process-related notion.[75]

Additional sources on Phoenician cosmogony can be found, more briefly, in Damascius' *De Principiis*, 3. 2. 3 (early sixth century CE).[76] Damascius writes that according to Mochus—an obscure Phoenician author whose work, translated into Greek, was available already in the first century BCE[77]—the first cosmological principles were Ether and Air, who subsequently gave birth to *Oulomos*. The latter clearly transliterates the Phoenician ʿ*LM*, but as mentioned above, this term should not be interpreted as meaning 'time'. It is important to note, moreover, that *Oulomos* is interpreted by Mochus himself as either the 'intelligible God' or the 'intelligible intellect'; he appears to have associated the root ʿ*LM* with 'knowledge', as is its meaning in Arabic and may be attested already much earlier in Ugaritic.[78] Time, again, is irrelevant in this context and indeed, completely absent from this cosmogony.

In the same passage, Damascius describes also the cosmogony of the Sidonians, as told by Eudemus of Rhodes (later fourth century BCE, disciple of Aristotle). According to Eudemus, the Sidonians believe that before everything there were Time, Desire, and Mist (*chronos, pothos, omichlē*). At first sight, this clearly indicates that the category of time was known to the Sidonians.[79] However, the status of 'Time' is completely marginal in this cosmogony. Eudemus goes on to say, a little inconsistently, that the first principles were (only) Desire and Mist, out of whose union were born Air and Wind, out of whose union, in turn, was born the primordial Egg. Time is no longer mentioned in the rest of the account; although it pre-existed everything, as mentioned at first, it is immediately forgotten and does not function, in the account, as a cosmological principle. In this respect, Eudemus' cosmogony of the Sidonians (who were themselves, in a sense, 'Phoenicians') resembles the Phoenician cosmogony of Philo of Byblos, where the similar or identical principles of Desire (*pothos*), Air, and possibly Mist are clearly attested as cosmological principles,[80] but where the notion of time, as we have seen above, is completely omitted.

---

[75] Baumgarten (*Phoenician History*, 146-8) prudently refrains from associating *Aiōn* or ʿ*LM* with the notion of time; contrast West, *Early Greek Philosophy*, 29; Boyce, *History of Zoroastrianism*, ii. 150-2; and Kittel ap. Jenni, 'Das Wort ʿōlām', 4.   [76] Westerink and Combès, *Damascius*, 166.

[77] Ibid. 238 n. 4; this work is first cited by Strabo.

[78] Aistleitner, *Wörterbuch der ugaritischen Sprache*, 232. On the semantic relationship between the Hebrew ʿ*LM* 'to hide' and the Arabic ʿ*LM* 'to know', see Kopf, 'Arabische Etymologien', 189-90.

[79] So West, *Early Greek Philosophy*, 28-9.

[80] Attridge and Oden, *Philo of Byblos*, 36-7; Baumgarten, *Phoenician History*, 12 (text) and 96 (translation). The term 'mist' (ὀμίχλη) does not appear in Philo's text, but the notion is implicit in his references to 'dark air' and 'turbid chaos'.

This raises the strong possibility that the reference to 'Time' at the beginning of the Sidonian cosmogony is an extraneous interpolation. The Sidonians themselves may have incorporated this notion, by the fourth century BCE, under Greek or Persian influence. But it seems just as likely that the category of 'Time' was inserted not by the Sidonians, but by Eudemus, and possibly quite inadvertently. Indeed, in Eudemus' account (at least as Damascius presents it), the Sidonian cosmogony follows immediately that of the Magi or Iranians, which (as we shall see below) treated time as the primordial cosmological principle; this may have led Eudemus to include, erroneously, the notion of 'Time' in the Sidonian myth.[81] It is also possible that the insertion of 'Time' and hence a cosmological triad (Time, Desire, and Mist) in the Sidonian myth was made by Damascius himself. Since his entire book, the De Principiis, is devoted to demonstrating the triadic metaphysics of Proclus, Damascius may have the tendency of fabricating cosmological triads which in fact did not exist.[82]

The absence of the category of time in ancient Near Eastern cosmogonies finds further confirmation, finally, in the work of the early Syriac Christian author Bardaisan (early third century CE), whose peculiar cosmological ideas have generally been taken to reflect native Syrian traditions.[83] Bardaisan's cosmology is devoid of any notion of time, although he gives considerable importance, by contrast, to the notion of space.[84]

ANCIENT IRANIAN AND INDO-EUROPEAN CULTURES

Very different world-views existed to the east of Mesopotamia and the Levant. In ancient Iran, an abstract notion of time appears to have been well established very early on, under the name of *Zrvan* (better transliterated *zruuan*).[85] The term *zruuan-* appears in ancient Iranian sources as a common noun for various aspects of

[81] Eudemus may also have been influenced by Pherecydes' cosmology, which he describes earlier on (according to Damascius, just before his account of the Babylonian and Iranian cosmogonies): as is also known from other sources, Pherecydes posited a triad of cosmological principles consisting of Zas (Zeus), Time, and Chthonie (Earth). According to Pherecydes, however, Time produced fire, wind, and water, out of which were produced the gods and the worlds; thus in his cosmology, unlike that of the Sidonians, Time actually functions as a cosmological principle (Damascius, *De Principiis* 3. 2. 2; Westerink and Combès, *Damascius*, 164–5). On time in Pherecydes' thought, see above, Ch. 5.

[82] See the pertinent remarks of Westerink and Combès, *Damascius*, 232 n. 1.

[83] Drijvers, *Bardaisan of Edessa*; Teixidor, *Bardesane d'Edesse*, 74–85.

[84] For a synoptic edition of the different recensions of Bardaisan's cosmology, see Drijvers, *Bardaisan of Edessa*, 96–105 (text), 106–43 (discussion). On the importance of space in his cosmology, see pp. 115, 136.

[85] I am grateful to Almut Hintze for her assistance in this section. A standard work remains Zaehner, *Zurvan*, but his interpretation of the sources is generally tendentious. See also West, *Early Greek Philosophy*, 30–1; Brisson, 'La Figure de Chronos'; Boyce, *History of Zoroastrianism*, ii. 231–42; and Shaked, 'The Myth of Zurvan'.

time: it is well attested in the *Avesta* in the sense of punctual time or limited period of time.[86] But in a more general and abstract sense, the same word can be used to denote the Zoroastrian concept of 'unlimited time' (*zruuan akarana*), a self-standing entity that appears to pre-exist and transcend the creation: this may be suggested, for example, in the statement that the *Ahuna Vairya* prayer was created 'in unlimited time' (*Vīdēvdād* 19: 9).[87] The concept of 'unlimited time' is contrasted elsewhere with the concept of 'time of long dominion' (*Yasna* 72: 10), the latter representing historical time or the duration of the created universe.[88] 'Unlimited time' is invoked (*Vīdēvdād* 19: 13, 19: 16) and worshipped along with 'time of long dominion' (*Niyāyišn* 1: 8), which confirms at least that both types of time are considered as entities *per se*.[89]

Zruuan or Time also appears in some Avestan passages as an active cosmological principle: thus we are told that the wicked and righteous alike proceed along 'the paths created by *Zruuan*' (*Vīdēvdād* 19: 29).[90] But the concept of *Zruuan* as a creator or cosmological principle is attested more explicitly in external sources. Eudemus (fourth century BCE, ap. Damascius) reports that the 'Magians' and 'Aryan people' (i.e. the Iranians) have either Space or Time as first cosmological principle, out of which were created good and evil, light and darkness.[91] Theodore of Mopsuestia (late fourth century CE) describes *Zourouan* as the first cosmological principle of the Iranians, but identifies it with the Greek god *Tyche*

---

[86] An example of the punctual use of *zruuan-* in the *Avesta* is ā rapiθβinəm zruuānəm (*Yasna* 9: 11, *Yašt* 8: 28), 'the time appropriate for the meal' (i.e. noon). For limited periods of time, there is the phrase darəyəmcit̲ aipi zruuānəm (*Yašt* 13: 53, 19: 26), 'for a long time'. The texts in the *Young Avesta* are generally assumed to date from between the beginning of the first millennium BCE and the end of the Persian Achaemenid period (and possibly beyond).

[87] According to Shaked, 'The Myth of Zurvan', 231 n. 28, this passage suggests that *zruuan* was, in a certain sense, the framework of creation. See also the passage from the *Zand* (39–42) in English translation in Boyce, *Textual Sources*, 47: 'from Limitless Time, (Ohrmazd) created Time of long dominion'. [88] See Boyce, *History of Zoroastrianism*, i. 230–2.

[89] Zaehner, *Zurvan*, 275, infers from these passages that *zruuan* is treated as a deity; however in the *Avesta*, objects of worship are never *ipso facto* deities (Almut Hinze, pers. comm.). For a critique of Zaehner, see Shaked, 'The Myth of Zurvan'.

[90] For citations in English translation, see Zaehner, loc. cit. According to some scholars, *Zruuan* is also attested as a progenitor (which of course is not the same as cosmological principle) in a tablet from late 6th-c. BCE Elam (West, *Early Greek Philosophy*, 31 and 242); but see Boyce, *History of Zoroastrianism*, ii. 143. I am restricting myself, in my main text, to sources dating from not later than the 7th c. CE. But the myth of *Zruuan* as primordial creator is elaborated in detail in medieval Zoroastrian sources: see e.g. the passage cited in translation from the second '*Ulema-i Islam* (12th c.?) in Zaehner, *Zurvan*, 409–12, and Boyce, *Textual Sources*, 98–9; and further sources in Zaehner, *Zurvan*, 391–6. Zaehner (pp. 197–8) is of the view that the Iranian concept of *Zruuan* as a cosmological principle was introduced under Greek or Indian influence, whereas West (*Early Greek Philosophy*) argues that the ancient Greek notion of time as a cosmological principle was derived from Iranian or Indian traditions. Zaehner may be justified, at least, with regard to Persian interpretations of *Zruuan* in later sources.

[91] *De Principiis* 3: 2: 3 (Westerink and Combès, *Damascius*, iii. 165); see Zaehner, *Zurvan*, 182, and Shaked, 'The Myth of Zurvan', 230–1.

(Fortune).[92] The Armenian Christian apologist Eznik of Kolb (fifth century CE) cites an elaborate myth attributed to Zoroaster, whereby the 'great god Zurvan' preceded everything and was father of Ormazd and Ahriman.[93] The Syriac Mar Barhad Besabba (late sixth–early seventh century CE) also attributes to Zoroaster the notion that *zruuan* was deified: according to Zoroaster, he writes, the god *Zarvan* begot Hormizd and Ahriman, who in turn created this world.[94]

The notion of time as an almost deified entity was not confined to ancient Iran. Further still to the East, in ancient India, a similar concept is equally well attested under the name of *Kāla*. In the *Atharvaveda* (*c.*1000 BCE) and the later *Upanishads* (*c.*700 BCE), *Kāla* is used not only as an ordinary word for time (mainly for periods of limited duration), but also in a more general sense, as meaning the whole of time or 'time of long duration'. *Kāla* in this sense is conceived of, in these sources, as a formless entity, a cosmological principle, governing force of the universe, and God supreme.[95]

The concept of time as a cosmic power and entity in its own right, which we find to be common to ancient Greece (*chronos*), Iran (*Zruuan*), and India (*Kāla*), may thus be identified as a specifically *Indo-European* tradition, which would stand in contrast with the ancient Semitic cultures of Mesopotamia and the Levant, where this concept appears not to have existed.[96] It appears not to have existed, indeed, in any of the other great civilizations of antiquity: although the ancient Mayas of Central America, for example, had a remarkably abstract, mathematical calendar, the word *kinh*, which some scholars have interpreted as the concept of 'time' *per se*, was actually a concrete, process-related term for 'sun' or 'day', or the succession of days.[97] In ancient and medieval China, the concept of time was—according to

[92] Theodore of Mopsuestia, ap. Photius, *Bibliotheca* 81, 63^{b}384o (i. 187 ed. Henry); text also in Zaehner, *Zurvan*, 447, and translation in Boyce, *History of Zoroastrianism*, iii. 307.

[93] Cited in Zaehner, *Zurvan*, 419–28 (with a parallel from the contemporary Armenian Christian Elishe); and Boyce, *Textual Sources*, 97–8. Eznik also interprets *Zurvan* as meaning 'fate' or 'fortune'.

[94] Cited in Zaehner, *Zurvan*, 439–40; Boyce, *Textual Sources*, 98.

[95] Panikkar, 'Temps et histoire'; West, *Early Greek Philosophy*, 33–4; Brandon, 'Deification of Time', 378–80. The formlessness of *Kāla* is mentioned in the *Maitri Upanishad* 6: 14 (cited in Panikkar, n. 25).

[96] The observation that time is an Indo-European, non-Semitic concept was already made by Orelli in 1871 (ap. Barr, *Biblical Words*, 102). Unfortunately, Orelli's suggestion was completely ignored by Dumézil and his disciples in their monumental work on Indo-European culture, either because of their excessive concentration on Dumézil's theory of the tripartite social ideology (on which see e.g. Dumézil, *Mythes et dieux des Indo-Européens*), or because of a restrictive emphasis on the 'proto-Indo-Europeans' of the second millennium BCE and earlier (evident in Mallory and Adams, *Encyclopedia of Indo-European Culture*).

[97] This is evident from the work of León-Portilla, *Time and Reality in the Thought of the Maya*; see in particular pp.16–34 and 91–112. Although he occasionally lapses into references to time as an abstraction (p. 54), he emphasizes everywhere else that *kinh* did not mean 'time' in the sense of an abstract entity, but rather as the concrete succession of days or cycles of days (*uinal*, 20-day cycle), all of which were deified into a variety of gods (or sun-gods). A similar view of *kinh* or 'sun-day-time' has persisted among the Maya today: see ibid., appendix A (by A. Villa Rojas) and appendix B.

Marcel Granet—an ensemble of eras, seasons, and epochs, but not a pure, homogenous continuum; time was conceived not as neutral or abstract, but only in relation to concrete actions, and undistinguished from the concrete alternation of Yin and Yang events. The main Chinese word for time, *shí*, did not mean time as such, but only punctual times, hours, seasons, or 'the right time'.[98]

The concept of time *per se* was therefore unique, in antiquity, to Indo-European cultures.[99] Although 'Indo-European' is primarily a linguistic category, and therefore not necessarily relevant to other cultural phenomena, in the context of the concept of time this category appears to be entirely appropriate.[100]

Still, some qualifications must be made. Firstly, it is clear that this concept of time did not spread to all Indo-European cultures, in antiquity or in later periods. Gurevitch has shown that early medieval Germanic and Nordic cultures were devoid of any concept of 'pure time' as an abstract extension or entity: their notion of time was completely concrete and undistinguishable from human activity, life, and history.[101] Secondly, my evidence for Greece, Iran, and India does not precede the first millennium BCE; I cannot make any claim, therefore, about the so-called 'proto-Indo-Europeans'. It is quite possible that the concept of time only emerged in India or Iran at the beginning of the first millennium BCE, from where it spread eventually to Greece by the sixth century BCE.[102] By this time, however, this concept could be identified as distinctly Indo-European, at least within these geographical regions.

[98] Granet, *Pensée chinoise*, 86–114; Larre, 'Aperception'. In the last two centuries, however, the term *shí* (or *shíjiān*: Larre, ibid. 47) has taken on Western meanings of 'time' (Tim Barrett, pers. comm.). Granet's theory that Chinese time was concrete and consisted only of discrete units is still widely accepted (see Huang and Zürcher, *Time and Space in Chinese Culture*, 3–14); it has been criticized on the basis of Mohist texts (second half of first millennium BCE) that suggest an abstract notion of duration (*jiǔ*, distinct from the punctual *shí*), but the evidence is extremely sporadic (see Harbsmeier, 'Some Notions of Time'). I am grateful to Tim Barrett for his assistance.

[99] Probably unique in the world: Boyce, *History of Zoroastrianism*, ii. 150–2; West, *Early Greek Philosophy*, 35; Brandon, 'Deification of Time', 375.

[100] The words *chronos* and *zruuan* may, incidentally, share a common etymology: this possibility is mentioned by Chantraine (*Dictionnaire étymologique*, 1278, s.v. χρόνος), at least as more likely than a relationship between *zruuan* and *gerōn* (Greek for 'old man').

[101] Gurevich, 'Space and Time in the *Weltmodell* of the Old Scandinavian Peoples'; Gourévitch, *Catégories de la culture médiévale*, 97–105.

[102] Boyce, *History of Zoroastrianism*, ii. 150–2, argues that the deification of Time was not an ancient and 'native' Indo-European tradition but rather a tradition of Phoenician origin (possibly invented under Egyptian influence), that spread in the mid-first millennium BCE from Phoenicia to Ionia (whence Greece), Iran, and India. West, *Early Greek Philosophy*, 35–6, argues in favour of either Mesopotamian or Egyptian origins. Both arguments are based on the assumption that the concept of time pre-existed in ancient Mesopotamian, Phoenician, and/or Egyptian cultures; but this has been refuted above. It is true that the concept of time does not appear in Greek sources before the 6th c. BCE, which may suggest that it was not native to Greek culture but rather 'imported'. But Indian and Iranian sources are much more ancient, reaching back to the beginning of the first millennium BCE. The origins of concept of Time are thus most likely to be located within some ancient Indo-Iranian tradition.

The deification of Time in India, Iran, and Greece fits into a more general pattern of reification, personification, and deification of abstract notions that is characteristic of their specific cultures and religious traditions. Personification and deification are prominent in Iranian religion, where for instance the concept of *aši* ('reward') was deified as the goddess Aši, or the concept of *mitra* ('contract') as the god Mitra/Mithra; the same is found in ancient Indian sources.[103] In Greek mythology and religion, likewise, the personification and deification of abstract concepts such as Eros (love), Tyche (fortune), Nemesis (wrath), etc. is very well attested. Reification reached a climax in Greek culture with philosophers such as Plato, who considered the world of Ideas to be the only true reality. The tradition of reifying and personifying abstract notions—of which time is only one example— has been perpetuated in the Western world, to some extent, until this very day.[104]

Thus, we may conclude that the reification of the abstract notion of time, and its conception as an entity in its own right, resulted from a cultural tradition that was both specific to, and typical of, these Indo-European religions, without any counterpart in ancient Jewish and ancient Semitic cultures. It is out of this ancient religious tradition that the modern Western concept of time eventually emerged.

THE IRANO-HELLENIZATION OF THE NEAR EAST

By the end of the first millennium BCE, the Semitic Near East had opened its gates to Iranian and especially Hellenistic cultural ideas. This was not merely the result of being geographically positioned between Iran and Greece. For long periods, the Persians (in the sixth–fourth centuries BCE) and then the Greeks (fourth–second centuries BCE) had ruled as imperial powers over the whole region, and the cultural effects of their political dominion were inevitably considerable. Evidence suggests that by the end of this period, the Irano-Greek concept of time had penetrated many areas of the Near East.

A good illustration of this phenomenon, albeit perhaps extreme, can be found in one of the *nomoi* (sacred law) inscriptions of Antiochus I of Commagene, northern Syria (reigned *c*.69–34 BCE), which was erected at his *hierothesion* (temple-tomb) at Nemrud Daği.[105] The inscription (in Greek) claims that the foundation of this *hierothesion* would be 'indestructible by the ravages of time'.[106] The idea that time

---

[103] Almut Hinze, pers. comm. Again, nothing on personification and deification is mentioned in Mallory and Adams, *Encyclopedia of Indo-European Culture* (see above, n. 96).

[104] Elias, *Time*, 42–3.

[105] The standard edition is now in Goell et al., *Nemrud Daği*, 206–24, with text, translation, and concordance. The text is also partially cited in Zaehner, *Zurvan*, 449–50, from Jalabert and Mouterde, *Inscriptions grecques et latines de la Syrie*, i.

[106] On l. 37: ἀπόρθητον χρόνου λύμαις—a prediction which, incidentally, has only been partially fulfilled.

can be destructive, which suggests that time is an active, autonomous entity, is found in various Greek and Roman sources (as we have seen in Chapter 5). But more importantly, the inscription frequently refers to the concepts of 'eternal time' or 'unlimited time', indicating quite clearly the notion of a time-continuum. Antiochus says that he has recorded 'for eternal time' (*eis chronon aiōnion*) the deeds of his clemency (ll. 9–10); his body will rest through 'unlimited time' (*eis ton apeiron aiōna*) in his tomb (ll. 43–4).[107] In one passage, furthermore, this concept of 'unlimited time' appears to be regarded as the cause or driving force of history: Antiochus says that his law is established 'for the generations of all men whom unlimited time will establish in succession in this land, through their special lot in life' (ll. 112–15).[108] The affinity of this concept of 'unlimited time' with the Iranian *zruuan akarana* ('unlimited time') is unmistakable,[109] and indeed, almost explicitly acknowledged in the inscription. For Antiochus prides himself, at the beginning of the inscription, for having blended (in his *hierothesion* and *nomos*) Persian and Hellenistic religious traditions, as a demonstration of his mixed Persian and Hellenistic dynastic ancestry (ll. 24–34).

Antiochus' explicit Persian–Hellenistic syncretism, which is also reflected in the rich iconography of the temple-tomb, may be dismissed at first sight as a peculiar eccentricity of the royal dynasty of Commagene, unrepresentative of the prevailing culture of the contemporary Near East.[110] However, there are reasonable grounds for assuming that this syncretism was not necessarily unique, especially if we consider Fergus Millar's general observation that, by the Roman period, not much of the 'native' culture appears to have survived in the Near East.[111] It is quite plausible that a blend of Persian and Hellenistic traditions, including the notion of time, had largely taken over from earlier, local cultures, not only in Commagene but also in other regions of the late antique Near East.[112]

---

[107] Note also the expression ἐν μακρῶι χρόνωι (ll. 228–30), 'in the long time [to come]'.

[108] The text reads: ἀνθρώπων γενεαῖς ἁπάντων οὓς ἂν χρόνος ἄπειρος εἰς διαδοχὴν χώρας ταύτης ἰδίαι βίου μοίραι καταοστήσῃ, which Goell (*Nemrud Dağı*, 215) translates as: 'who in the immeasurable course of time, through their special lot in life, shall successively be destined to dwell in this land'. This translation, unlike mine, demotes time from being the subject of the verb; but this is to obliterate the active, causative function that is quite evidently attributed to time in the original text.

[109] It has been noted by a number of scholars: Zaehner, *Zurvan*; Boyce, *History of Zoroastrianism*, iii. 332–3; and Shaked, 'The Myth of Zurvan', 223.

[110] On the peculiarities of the royal dynasty of Commagene, see Boyce, *History of Zoroastrianism*, iii. 309–52; Wagner, 'Dynastie und Herrscherkult in Kommagene'.

[111] Millar, *Roman Near East*. Note that when the people of Commagene demanded, in 17 CE, to be ruled by kings in accordance with their 'ancestral custom' (Josephus, *Antiquities* 18. 53: κατὰ τὰ πάτρια), all they could have meant, in fact, was the local Persian-Hellenistic syncretistic dynasty. Terms such as 'ancestral' or 'native' can thus be quite misleading.

[112] Wagner, 'Dynastie und Herrscherkult in Kommagene', shows how much of Antioch's Persian-Hellenistic syncretism goes back to traditions established already by the Seleucid dynasty; these traditions are likely, one would assume, to have affected a wider area than the small territory of Commagene.

The penetration of Iranian or Hellenistic concepts of time in other regions of the Near East is difficult to prove, but there is sporadic evidence. As we have seen above, Eudemus (fourth century BCE) or perhaps Damascius (early sixth century CE) suggest that the Sidonians of Eudemus' period had adopted the principle of 'Time' within their cosmogony, most likely borrowed from the Persians or the Greeks. However, as has been shown above, the reliability of this report is questionable. More reliable is the attestation of the Greek, philosophical concept of time in early Christian, Syriac sources. Part of an argument attributed to Bardaisan (early third century CE) states that 'there is nothing that is not in time [be-zabna], subject to time [taḥit zabna], and performed within time [be-go zabna]'.[113] Ephrem (fourth century), who cites this passage, refutes Bardaisan's argument but does not reject the category of time itself. It is clear from this passage alone that by the late antique period, Greek ideas about time had penetrated the Near East and become well accepted among educated people such as Bardaisan, Ephrem, and presumably other Church Fathers. It must be noted, however, that discussions about time may have been confined to the 'Greek' context of theological, philosophical argument. For the same Bardaisan, as we have seen, omits entirely the notion of time in his cosmogony.

Further evidence, finally, comes from bilingual Palmyrene and Greek inscriptions. The Palmyrene ʿLMʾ or LʾLMʾ, equivalent to the Jewish Aramaic alema or le'alema and biblical Hebrew olam or le'olam (i.e. 'for ever'), are frequently translated in the bilingual inscriptions as eis to panteles or eis to parapan, both meaning something like 'absolutely'. This translation is interesting, as it appears to be a faithful rendering of the original, process-related meaning of the Palmyrene term which would have expressed, as in the biblical Hebrew equivalent, something like 'permanence' or 'perpetuity'.[114] But in some of these inscriptions, time-related translations are used. Thus the phrases eis ton aiōna, which we have already encountered as a translation of the Hebrew le'olam in the Septuagint (Chapter 5), and aiōnion, both of which may imply a notion of temporal eternity, appear as translations of LʾLMʾ or ʿLMʾ or in a number of bilingual Palmyrene and Greek inscriptions.[115] Even more distinctive is the use, in a small number of cases, of the translation eis ton hapanta chronon, which means 'for the whole of time' and clearly suggests not only a temporal interpretation of the term ʿLMʾ, but also the concept of time as an entity in itself and a continuum. One of these inscriptions is dated to the early second century, from the sanctuary of Bel at Palmyra, and erected by an

---

[113] Mitchell, *S. Ephraim's Prose Refutations*, 26 (text) and xi (translation).

[114] As argued above with reference to the biblical *olam*. The phrase εἰς τὸ παντελές can be found e.g. in Cantineau, *Inscriptions de Palmyre*, VII. 13, and εἰς τὸ παράπαν ibid. IV. 7b.

[115] e.g. εἰς τὸν αἰῶνα in Cantineau VII. 5, and αἰώνιον in Cantineau IV. 8. Note also, as mentioned above, that Philo of Byblos *may* have translated the Phoenician ʿLM as *Aiōn*.

ostensibly Palmyrene family; but another, also from Palmyra and dated to the early third century, happens to be Jewish.[116]

This single piece of evidence is sufficient to demonstrate that the Jews of the late antique Near East, like all other people of the region, were not immune from adopting the Hellenistic concept of the time-continuum—especially, it would seem, when they were writing an inscription (or part of it) in Greek.[117] As we have seen in Chapter 5, Jews writing in Greek—even those who were of Judaean origin (such as Josephus)—could easily adopt the Greek notion of *chronos*.

Still, we have also seen that even in Hellenistic Jewish literature, the incidence of the notion of *chronos* is relatively low; while Jews who wrote in Hebrew or Aramaic—e.g. Qumran or early rabbinic literature—refrained from this notion completely. This contrasts with non-Jewish authors such as Bardaisan and Ephrem, who adopted in their Syriac writings the Greek notion of *chronos*, translated into Syriac as *zabna*. Notwithstanding the Greek-Palmyrene inscription mentioned above, the overwhelming evidence of Palestinian and Near Eastern provenance suggests that in the context of the concept of time, the Jews resisted Irano-Hellenization far more than any of their immediate neighbours.

To some extent, this conclusion comes hardly as a surprise. It is generally recognized that the persistence of native Jewish culture was unusual and probably unparalleled in the context of the Roman and late antique Near East.[118] Early rabbinic Judaism did not adopt the genre of Greek philosophical discourse, unlike Syriac Christianity, which easily explains why Bardaisan's philosophical argument about time (quoted above) finds no parallel in early rabbinic literature. But it seems to me, as I shall elaborate in my concluding remarks, that the absence in Jewish literature of even casual, non-philosophical references to the notion of time sheds considerable light on the limits of Irano-Hellenization among the Jews of the late antique Near East.

---

[116] Cantineau VIII. 61, and VII. 4 (= Frey, *Corpus Inscriptionum Judaicarum*, ii. 820) respectively. The term לעלמא is partially illegible in the Palmyrene section of the latter inscription, but there is no reason to doubt the reliability of its reconstitution. The phrase εἰς τὸν ἄπαντα χρόνον is very frequent in ancient sources.

[117] There is no particular reason to suggest that the Jews who commissioned this inscription were not responsible for the text of the Greek section, or did not understand it.

[118] So Millar, *Roman Near East*, 337–86.

Concluding Remarks

IN this study I have shown that the concept of time as an entity *per se* was alien to the ancient Jewish world-view. Reality was conceived only as a series of discrete events and processes. This world-view, however, was by no means unique. Process-based world-views were common in the ancient Near East, and probably in most pre-modern societies. The modern, Western concept of time goes back however to ancient Greece, and may draw its roots from a specifically Indo-European tradition.

Although the Jews of late antiquity lived within a dominantly Graeco-Roman culture, their world-view appears to have been little affected by it. Jewish literature in Hebrew and Aramaic, in particular, suggests that the concept of time as an entity in itself remained unknown to Near Eastern Jews. They maintained, throughout antiquity, a process-related world-view.

The historical implications of this finding are potentially quite considerable. Much has been written on the degree to which ancient Judaism was (or was not) influenced by Hellenistic culture. Although this question remains inherently problematic and impossible to answer, no history of Judaism can be written without giving proper consideration to the complex processes of cultural interaction, influence, and exchange that it would always have been continually exposed to. The question of 'Hellenization'—to give it a more simplistic formulation—has been approached from a variety of angles, with evidence ranging from literary sources to epigraphy and material culture. In the context of early rabbinic literature, the focus of attention in modern scholarship has traditionally been on the possible influence of Hellenistic or Roman disciplines such as law, rhetoric, and philosophy on the development of rabbinic halakhah, aggadah, Midrash, and other aspects of rabbinic intellectual activity.[1] A problem with this argument, however,

---

[1] On Hellenism in rabbinic Judaism, see in particular Lieberman, *Greek in Jewish Palestine*; id., *Hellenism in Jewish Palestine*; id., 'How Much Greek in Jewish Palestine?'; Alon, review of Lieberman, *Greek in Jewish Palestine*; Daube, 'Rabbinic Methods of Interpretation and Hellenistic Rhetoric'; Fischel, *Rabbinic Literature and Greco-Roman Philosophy*; Hengel, *Judaism and Hellenism*; Alexander, 'Quid Athenis et Hierosolymis?'; Feldman, *Jew and Gentile*, 19–44; Ulmer, 'Advancement of Arguments'; Levine, *Judaism and Hellenism in Antiquity*, 110–24, 131–8; Hezser, 'Interfaces'. On Hellenism in non-rabbinic ancient Judaism, see references above in Ch. 6. On Iranian influence on early Judaism, see Hultgård, 'Das Judentum in der hellenistisch-römischen Zeit'; Shaked, 'Iranian

is that social interaction between rabbis and Graeco-Roman lawyers, teachers, and philosophers is known to have been considerably limited. Moreover, explicit awareness of any of these Graeco-Roman disciplines is almost impossible to find in early rabbinic sources. How these disciplines were able to infiltrate and influence early rabbinic Judaism—a process which presumably took place to some extent—remains therefore unclear.

This present study has ignored the highbrow academic disciplines of law, rhetoric, and philosophy, and dealt instead with a more fundamental aspect of human experience. Concepts of time and process, indeed, are not contingent on any particular discipline or educational training; they are common to all people, belonging to what may generally be referred to as 'world-view'. This is not to say, however, that I have studied the world-view of common people. Inasmuch as I have been restricted almost entirely to the evidence of the written word (literary and epigraphic)—simply because it seemed too difficult to infer anything sensible about time and process from art, architecture, and material culture—the world-view I have investigated could only belong to the Jewish literate élite. That other elements of Jewish society shared similar views about time and process is likely, but impossible to prove. However, the point I wish to make is that time and process are such fundamental experiences that they are likely to have been far more impor-tant—even to intellectual élites—than academic disciplines such as law, ethics, and exegesis. Whether ancient Jewish world-views were subject to Hellenistic influ-ence becomes, therefore, a question of paramount importance.

Paradoxical as this may seem, fundamental concepts such as time and process would have been much more vulnerable to foreign influence than any highbrow academic discipline. The reasons for this are multiple. Unlike Roman law and Greek philosophy, which were mastered only by lawyers and philosophers, the Greek notion of time is likely to have been shared by a much larger section of Graeco-Roman society. Although it is difficult to estimate the proportion of the fifth-century BCE Athenian public that fully understood the performances of Sophocles' and Euripides' plays, it is likely that the constant references in these plays to the notion of time as a separate entity and infinite continuum were intended to be understood by more than a small circle of literate intellectuals in the audience. When Augustine wrote, in the late fourth century CE, that 'in our conversation, no word is more familiarly used or more easily recognized than "time" ',[2] he surely

---

Influence on Judaism'; Boyce, *History of Zoroastrianism*, iii. 389–440; these studies are restricted to pre-rabbinic literature, with particular emphasis on the apocalyptic or eschatological themes of the Apocrypha and Pseudepigrapha. See also Gignoux, 'Hexaéméron et millénarisme', who seems to argue that the influence may have gone in the opposite direction. On the limited impact of Iranian cul-ture on rabbinic Judaism, see Neusner, 'How Much Iranian in Jewish Babylonia?'; also my remarks in Ch. 3 n. 55.   [2] Augustine, *Confessions* 11. 14. 17, cited at the beginning of Ch. 1.

meant more than the conversation of the élite. The significance of this is that in their daily lives Palestinian rabbis and other educated Jews would have had a much greater exposure to the Greek notion of time than to the academic disciplines of law, rhetoric, and philosophy. The notion of time would have been mentioned and used in daily conversation by Greek-speaking soldiers, officials, traders, and slaves. The chances of Jews encountering this notion and, perhaps, adopting it, would thus have been considerably higher.

Another reason why the Greek notion of time could easily have infiltrated ancient Jewish, even rabbinic, culture, is that rabbis and other Jews would have had no particular reason to resist it. Although a Greek or Iranian deification of time could have been objectionable to Jews, evidence that time was actually worshipped is non-existent for the Greeks, and debatable for ancient Iran.[3] In the case of the Greeks, deification of time was only a marginal feature of their concept of *chronos*, which consisted primarily of a reification of time as a continuous flow and an entity. This could not have been objectionable to any Jew. Consequently, the absence of time from the ancient Jewish world-view did not constitute an explicit religious dogma or imperative. Indeed, it is questionable whether anyone ever noticed, in the ancient world, that Greeks or other 'Indo-Europeans' believed in the notion of time, whereas Jews and others did not. I have certainly not found any ancient source suggesting such awareness. The notion of time or its absence went largely unnoticed, and was certainly not regarded as a cultural issue. This explains, indeed, why the Greek notion of time crept into later medieval Judaism without anyone objecting or even seemingly noticing (see Chapter 4).

Yet in spite of all this, ancient Judaism—particularly, as we have seen, in the Near East—resisted the adoption of the notion of time and maintained its traditional, process-related world-view. This is unlikely to have been deliberate: as stated, there was no religious or halakhic reason why this notion could not have been adopted and embraced. All this reveals, I would argue, is the profound gulf that separated the early rabbis, and possibly other literate Jews, from the dominant culture of the Graeco-Roman world. It says something important, perhaps not sufficiently appreciated, about the extent of the cultural isolation of ancient Jews.

The study of time and process in ancient Judaism thus has the side-effect of confirming, as many will have noted beforehand, that Near Eastern Judaism did not become Hellenized in the Hellenistic, Hasmonaean, or Roman periods. It was only in the Middle Ages—ironically, long after the Greek-speaking Roman rulers had been expelled from Palestine by the Muslim conquest—that the Hellenization of Judaism began, through the influence of Muslim intellectual society.

[3] See Ch. 6 n. 89.

In antiquity, the world-view of Hebrew- and Aramaic-speaking Jews remained completely process-related. Reality was seen as a succession of objects and events, whereas the notions of time as an entity in itself, a human resource, a continuous flow, or a structure or dimension of the created world, were simply non-existent. On close examination, this time-less, process-based approach to reality turns out to be eminently plausible. The study of ancient Judaism teaches us as much about its history as about our own assumptions and world-views.

Bibliography

For the numerous editions and translations of rabbinic sources, see Stemberger, *Introduction to Talmud and Midrash*.

AISTLEITNER J., *Wörterbuch der ugaritischen Sprache*, 4th edn. (Berlin: Akademie-Verlag, 1974).

ALBANI, M., and U. GLESSMER, 'An Astronomical Measuring Instrument from Qumran', in D. W. Parry and E. Ulrich (eds.), *The Provo International Conference on the Dead Sea Scrolls* (Leiden: Brill, 1999), 407–42.

—— —— 'Un instrument de mesures astronomiques à Qumrân', *Revue biblique*, 104 (1997), 88–115.

—— —— and G. GRASSHOFF, 'An Instrument for Determining the Hours of the Day and the Seasons (Sundial)', in Adolfo Roitman (ed.), *A Day at Qumran* (Jerusalem: Israel Museum, 1997), 20–2.

ALEXANDER, P. S., 'Quid Athenis et Hierosolymis? Rabbinic Midrash and Hermeneutics in the Graeco-Roman World', in P. R. Davies and R. T. White (eds.), *A Tribute to Geza Vermes* (Sheffield: Journal for the Study of the Old Testament Supplement, 1990), 101–24.

ALLEN, T. G., *The Book of the Dead or the Going Forth by Day* (Chicago: University of Chicago Press, 1974).

ALON, G., review of Lieberman, *Greek in Jewish Palestine* (Heb.), in *Kiryat Sefer*, 20 (1943–4), 76–95.

ANNAS, J., 'Aristotle, Number and Time', *Philosophical Quarterly*, 25 (1975), 97–113.

ARIOTTI, P. E., 'The Concept of Time in Western Antiquity', in J. T. Fraser and N. Lawrence (eds.), *The Study of Time*, ii (Berlin: Springer-Verlag, 1975), 69–80.

ATTRIDGE, H. W., and R. A. ODEN, *Philo of Byblos: The Phoenician History*, Catholic Biblical Quarterly Monograph Series 9 (Washington, DC, 1980).

AUGUSTINE, *Confessions*, trans. R. S. Pine-Coffin (Harmondsworth: Penguin, 1961).

AZOR, M., *The Syntax of Mishnaic Hebrew* [Taḥbir leshon hamishnah] (Jerusalem: Academy of the Hebrew Language, 1995).

BACHELARD, G., *L'Intuition de l'instant* (Paris: Gonthier, 1932).

BAER, S., *Sidur avodat yisra'el* (Rödelheim: Lernberger, 1868; repr. [Berlin]: Schocken, 1937).

BARCLAY, J. M. G., review of J. J. Collins, *Between Athens and Jerusalem: Jewish Identity in the Hellenistic Diaspora*, 2nd edn. (Grand Rapids, Mich.: Eerdmans, 1999), *Journal of Jewish Studies*, 52 (2001), 363–7.

BARR, J., *Biblical Words for Time*, 2nd edn. (London: SCM Press, 1969).

BAUMGARTEN, A. I., *The Phoenician History of Philo of Byblos: A Commentary* (Leiden: Brill, 1981).

BEN ZVI, E., 'About Time: Observations about the Construction of Time in the Book of Chronicles', *Horizons in Biblical Theology*, 22 (2000), 17–31.

BENISH, H. P., *Times in Halakha* [Hazemanim bahalakhah], 2 vols. (Benei-Berak: Keter Torah, 1996).

BENOIT, P., J. T. MILIK, and R. DE VAUX, *Discoveries in the Judaean Desert*, II (Oxford: Clarendon Press, 1961).

BLACK, J., A. GEORGE, and N. POSTGATE, *A Concise Dictionary of Akkadian* (Wiesbaden: Harrassowitz, 1999).

BLAU, J. (ed.), *R. Moses b. Maimon: Responsa* [Teshuvot harambam], 3 vols. (Jerusalem: Mekitsei Nirdamim, 1957).

BOHANNAN, P., 'Concepts of Time among the Tiv of Nigeria', in J. Middleton (ed.), *Myth and Cosmos: Readings in Mythology and Symbolism* (Garden City, NY: Natural History Press, 1967), 315–29.

BORNSTEIN, H. Y., 'About the Last Days of Calendar Intercalation' [Divrei yemei ha'ibur ha'aharonim], part 2, *Hatekufah*, 16 (1922), 228–92.

—— 'Jewish Dates' [Ta'arikhei yisra'el], part 2, *Hatekufah*, 9 (1921), 202–64.

BOURDIEU, P., 'The Attitude of the Algerian Peasant toward Time', in J. Pitt-Rivers (ed.), *Mediterranean Countrymen* (Paris: Recherches méditerranéennes, 1, 1963), 55–72.

—— *Outline of a Theory of Practice*, trans. R. Nice (Cambridge: Cambridge University Press, 1977).

BOYARIN, D., *Carnal Israel: Reading Sex in Talmudic Culture* (Berkeley: University of California Press, 1995).

BOYCE, M., *A History of Zoroastrianism*, 3 vols. (Leiden: Brill, 1975–91).

—— *Textual Sources for the Study of Zoroastrianism* (Manchester: Manchester University Press, 1984).

BRANDON, S. G. F., 'The Deification of Time', in J. T. Fraser, F. C. Haber, and G. H. Müller (eds.), *The Study of Time*, i (Berlin: Springer-Verlag, 1972), 370–82.

BREGMAN, M., 'Past and Present in Midrashic Literature', *Hebrew Annual Review*, 2 (1978), 45–59.

BRIN, G., *The Concept of Time in the Bible and the Dead Sea Scrolls* (Leiden: Brill, 2001).

BRISSON, L., 'La Figure de Chronos dans la théogonie orphique et ses antécédents iraniens', in D. Tiffeneau (ed.), *Mythes et représentations du temps* (Paris: CNRS, 1985), 37–55.

BRITTON, J., and C. WALKER, 'Astronomy and Astrology in Mesopotamia', in C. Walker (ed.), *Astronomy Before the Telescope* (London: British Museum Press, 1996), 42–67.

BRODY, R., *The Geonim of Babylonia and the Shaping of Medieval Jewish Culture* (New Haven: Yale University Press, 1997).

BROSHI, M., et al., *Discoveries in the Judaean Desert*, XIX: *Qumran Cave* 4, xiv: *Parabiblical Texts, part 2* (Oxford: Clarendon Press, 1995).

BROWN, F., S. R. DRIVER, and C. A. BRIGGS, *A Hebrew and English Lexicon of the Old Testament* (Oxford: Clarendon Press, 1977).

CALLAHAN, J. F., *Four Views of Time in Ancient Philosophy* (Cambridge, Mass.: Harvard University Press, 1948).

CANTINEAU, J., *Inventaire des inscriptions de Palmyre* (Beirut: Musée National Syrien de Damas, 1930–3).

CARROL, J. B., *Language, Thought, and Reality: Selected Writings of Benjamin Lee Whorf* (Cambridge, Mass.: Massachusetts Institute of Technology Press, 1956).

CHANTRAINE, P., *Dictionnaire étymologique de la langue grecque* (Paris: Klinksieck, 1968).

CHARLES, R. H., *The Apocrypha and Pseudepigrapha*, 2 vols. (Oxford: Clarendon Press, 1913).

CHARLESWORTH, J. H. (ed.), *The Old Testament Pseudepigrapha*, 2 vols. (New York: Doubleday, 1983–5).

CHILTON, B. D., *The Aramaic Bible*, xi: *The Isaiah Targum* (Edinburgh: T. & T. Clark, 1987).

CHRISTENSEN, F., 'The Theory of Space-like Time', in J. T. Fraser, N. Lawrence, and D. Park (eds.), *The Study of Time*, iii (Berlin: Springer-Verlag, 1978), 167–84.

CLARKE, C. J. S., 'Process as a Primitive Physical Category', in J. T. Fraser and L. Rowell (eds.), *The Study of Time*, vii (Madison, Conn.: International University Press, 1993), 53–69.

COHEN, D., *Dictionnaire des racines sémitiques ou attestées dans les langues sémitiques*, fasc. 8 (Leuven: Peeters, 1999).

COMRIE, B., *Tense* (Cambridge: Cambridge University Press, 1985).

COOKE, G. A., *A Text-Book of North-Semitic Inscriptions* (Oxford: Clarendon Press, 1903).

CORISH, D., 'The Emergence of Time: A Study in the Origins of Western Thought', in J. T. Fraser, N. Lawrence, and F. C. Haber (eds.), *The Study of Time*, v (Amherst, Mass.: University of Massachusetts Press, 1986), 69–78.

COTTON, H., and J. PRICE, 'A Bilingual Tombstone from Zo'ar (Arabia)', *Zeitschrift für Papyrologie und Epigraphik*, 134 (2001), 277–83.

DAN, J., *The 'Unique Cherub' Circle* (Tübingen: Mohr-Siebeck, 1999).

DANBY, H., *The Mishnah* (Oxford: Oxford University Press, 1933).

DAUBE, D., 'Rabbinic Methods of Interpretation and Hellenistic Rhetoric', *Hebrew Union College Annual*, 22 (1949), 239–62.

DAVIDSON, I., S. ASSAF, and B. I. JOEL, *Sidur rav sa'adiah gaon*, 2nd edn. (Jerusalem: Mekitsei Nirdamim, 1963).

DAVIES, P. C. W., *Space and Time in the Modern Universe* (Cambridge: Cambridge University Press, 1977).

DENIS, A.-M., *Fragmenta Pseudepigraphorum quae supersunt Graeca* (Leiden: Brill, 1970).

DRIJVERS, H. J. W., *Bardaisan of Edessa* (Assen: Van Gorcum, 1966).

DUMÉZIL, G., *Mythes et dieux des Indo-Européens*, ed. H. Coutau-Bégarie (Paris: Flammarion, 1992).

EILBERG-SCHWARTZ, H., *The Savage in Judaism: An Anthropology of Israelite Religion and Ancient Judaism* (Bloomington: Indiana University Press, 1990).

——(ed.), *People of the Body: Jews and Judaism from an Embodied Perspective* (Albany: State University of New York Press, 1992).

EISENSTEIN, J. D., *Otsar midrashim* [The Treasure of the Midrashim] (New York: Grossman, 1956; orig. pub. 1915).

ELIAS, N., *Time: An Essay* (Oxford: Blackwell, 1992).

ESHEL, E., et al., *Discoveries in the Judaean Desert*, XI (Oxford: Clarendon Press, 1998).

EVANS, J., *The History and Practice of Ancient Astronomy* (Oxford: Oxford University Press, 1998).

——'The Material Culture of Greek Astronomy', *Journal for the History of Astronomy*, 30 (1999), 237–307.

EVANS-PRITCHARD, E., *The Nuer* (Oxford: Clarendon Press, 1940).

EYNIKEL, E., and K. HAUSPIE, 'Καιρός and Χρόνος in the Septuagint', *Ephemerides Theologicae Lovanienses*, 73 (1997), 369–85.

FABIAN, J., *Time and the Other: How Anthropology Makes its Object* (New York: Columbia University Press, 1983).

FELDMAN, L. H., *Jew and Gentile in the Ancient World* (Princeton: Princeton University Press, 1993).

FEYNMAN, R. P., R. B. LEIGHTON, and M. SANDS, *The Feynman Lectures on Physics*, i (Reading, Mass.: Addison-Wesley, 1963).

FIELD, J. V., 'European Astronomy in the First Millennium: The Archaeological Record', in C. Walker (ed.), *Astronomy Before the Telescope* (London: British Museum Press, 1996), 110–22.

FISCHEL, H. A., *Rabbinic Literature and Greco-Roman Philosophy: A Study of Epicurea and Rhetorica in Early Midrashic Writings* (Leiden: Brill, 1973).

FREY, J.-B., *Corpus Inscriptionum Judaicarum*, 2 vols. (Rome, 1938–52).

FRIEDMAN, S. Y., 'The *Baraitot* of the Babylonian Talmud and their Relationship to Parallels in the Tosefta' [Habaraitot batalmud habavli veyaḥasan lemakbiloteihen shebatosefta], in D. Boyarin et al., *Atara l'Haim: Studies in the Talmud and Medieval Rabbinic Literature in Honor of Professor Haim Zalman Dimitrovsky* [Atarah leḥayim: meḥkarim besifrut hatalmudit veharabanit likhevod profesor ḥayim zalman dimitrovski] (Jerusalem: Magnes Press, 2000), 163–201.

GAFNI, I., 'Concepts of Periodization and Causality in Talmudic Literature', *Jewish History*, 10 (1996), 21–38.

GELB, I. J., et al., *The Assyrian Dictionary* (Chicago: Oriental Institute, 1956–).

GELL, A., *The Anthropology of Time: Cultural Constructions of Temporal Maps and Images* (Oxford: Berg, 1992).

GESENIUS, W., *Hebrew and Chaldee Lexicon to the Old Testament Scriptures*, trans. S. P. Tregelles (London: Bagster, 1846).

GIBBS, S., *Greek and Roman Sundials* (London and New Haven: Yale University Press, 1976).

GIBSON, J. J., 'Events are Perceivable but Time is Not', in J. T. Fraser and N. Lawrence (eds.), *The Study of Time*, ii (Berlin: Springer-Verlag, 1975), 295–301.

GIGNOUX, P., 'Hexaéméron et millénarisme: Quelques motifs de comparaison entre mazdéisme et judaïsme', *Irano-Judaica*, 2 (1990), 72–84.

GINZBERG, L., *A Commentary on the Jerusalem Talmud* [Perushim veḥidushim bayerushalmi], 3 vols. (New York: Jewish Theological Seminary, 1941).

GLESSMER, U., 'Calendars in the Qumran Scrolls', in P. W. Flint and J. C. VanderKam (eds.), *The Dead Sea Scrolls after Fifty Years: A Comprehensive Assessment* (Leiden: Brill, 1999), ii. 213–78.

GOELL, T. B., et al., *Nemrud Daǧı: The Hierothesion of Antiochus I of Commagene*, i (text), ed. D. H. Sanders (Winona Lake, Ind.: Eisenbrauns, 1996).

GOLDBERG, H. E. (ed.), *Judaism Viewed from Within and from Without* (New York: State University of New York Press, 1987).

GOLDBERG, S.-A., *La Clepsydre: Essai sur la pluralité des temps dans le judaïsme* (Paris: Albin Michel, 2000).

GOLDMAN, E., 'A Critical Edition of Palestinian Talmud Tractate Rosh Hashana, Chapter Two', *Hebrew Union College Annual*, 47 (1976), 191–216.

GOLDMAN, S. C., 'On the Beginnings and Endings of Time in Medieval Judaism and Islam', in J. T. Fraser, N. Lawrence, and D. Park (eds.), *The Study of Time*, iv (Berlin: Springer-Verlag, 1981), 59–72.

GOODBLATT, D., *The Monarchic Principle* (Tübingen: Mohr-Siebeck, 1994).

GOURÉVITCH, A. J., *Les Catégories de la culture médiévale*, trans. H. Courtin and N. Godneff (Paris: Gallimard, 1983).

GRANET, M., *La Pensée chinoise* (Paris: Renaissance du livre, 1934).

GRUEN, E. S., *Heritage and Hellenism: The Reinvention of Jewish Tradition* (Berkeley: University of California Press, 1998).

—— 'Jews, Greeks, and Romans in the Third Sibylline Oracle', in M. D. Goodman (ed.), *Jews in a Graeco-Roman World* (Oxford: Oxford University Press, 1998), 15–36.

GRUENWALD, I., 'Some Critical Notes on the First Part of *Sefer Yezira*', *Revue des études juives*, 132 (1973), 475–512.

GUREVICH, A. Y., 'Space and Time in the *Weltmodell* of the Old Scandinavian Peoples', *Medieval Scandinavia*, 2 (1969), 42–53.

GUTHRIE, W. K. C., *Orpheus and Greek Religion* (London: Methuen, 1935).

GUTMAN, S., Z. YEIVIN, and E. NETZER, 'Excavations in the Synagogue at Horvat Susiya', in L. I. Levine (ed.), *Ancient Synagogues Revealed* (Jerusalem: Israel Exploration Society, 1981), 123–8.

HALL, E. T., *The Silent Language* (Garden City, NY: Doubleday, 1959).

HALLPIKE, C., *The Foundations of Primitive Thought* (Oxford: Clarendon Press, 1979).

HARBSMEIER, C., 'Some Notions of Time and of History in China and in the West', in Chun-Chieh Huang and E. Zürcher, *Time and Space in Chinese Culture* (Leiden: Brill, 1995), 49–71.

HATAV, G., *Semantics of Aspect and Modality: Evidence from English and Biblical Hebrew* (Amsterdam and Philadelphia: John Benjamins, 1997).

HAWKING, S. W., *A Brief History of Time: From the Big Bang to Black Holes* (London: Bantam Press, 1988).

HEINEMANN, I., *The Ways of Aggadah* [Darkhei ha'agadah] (Givatayim: Magnes Press, 1970).

HENGEL, M., *Judaism and Hellenism*, trans. J. Bowden, 2 vols. (Philadelphia: Fortress Press, 1974).

HERR, M. D., 'The Conception of History among the Sages' [Tefisat hahistoria etsel ḥazal], *Proceedings of the Sixth World Congress of Jewish Studies* (Jerusalem: World Union of Jewish Studies, 1977), iii. 129–42.

HERSHLER, M. (ed.), *Sidur rabenu shlomo mivarmaiza vesidur ḥasidei ashkenaz* [The Prayer-book of R. Solomon of Worms and the Prayer-book of the Ḥasidei Ashkenaz] (Jerusalem: privately published, 1971).

HEZSER, C., 'Interfaces between Rabbinic Literature and Graeco-Roman Philosophy', in P. Schäfer and C. Hezser (eds.), *The Talmud Yerushalmi and Graeco-Roman Culture*, ii (Tübingen: Mohr-Siebeck, 2000), 161–87.

HORST, P. W. VAN DER, *Ancient Jewish Epitaphs* (Kampen: Kok Pharos, 1991).

HOSKINS, J., *The Play of Time: Kodi Perspectives on Calendars, History, and Exchange* (Berkeley: University of California Press, 1993).

HOUTMAN, A., 'Targum Isaiah according to Felix Pratensis', *Journal for the Aramaic Bible*, 1/2 (1999), 191–202.

HUANG, CHUN-CHIEH, and E. ZÜRCHER (eds.), *Time and Space in Chinese Culture* (Leiden: Brill, 1995).

HULTGÅRD, A., 'Das Judentum in der hellenistisch-römischen Zeit und die iranische Religion—ein religionsgeschichtliches Problem', in W. Haase and H. Temporini (eds.), *Aufstieg und Niedergang der römischen Welt*, II 19.1 (Berlin and New York: Walter de Gruyter, 1979), 512–90.

HURWITZ, S. (ed.), *Maḥzor vitry* (Nuremberg: Mekitsei Nirdamim, 1923).

HYMAN, D., and Y. SHILONI, *Yalkut shimoni al hatorah* (Jerusalem: Mosad Harav Kuk, 1977).

IRSHAI, O., 'Dating the Eschaton: Jewish and Christian Apocalyptic Calculations in Late Antiquity', in A. I. Baumgarten (ed.), *Apocalyptic Time* (Leiden: Brill, 2000), 113–53.

JACKSON, M., *Paths toward a Clearing: Radical Empiricism and Ethnographic Inquiry* (Bloomington and Indianapolis: Indiana University Press, 1989).

JALABERT, L., and R. MOUTERDE, *Inscriptions grecques et latines de la Syrie*, i: *Commagène et Cyrrhestique* (Paris: P. Geuthner, 1929).

JARITZ, G., and G. MORENO-RIAÑO (eds.), *Time and Eternity: The Medieval Discourse* (Turnhout: Brepols, 2003).

JENNI, E., 'Das Wort ʿōlām im Alten Testament', *Zeitschrift für der Alttestamentliche Wissenschaft*, 64 (1952), 197–248; 65 (1953), 1–35.

JONAH GERONDI (R.), *Sha'arei teshuvah* [The Gates of Repentance] (Benei-Berak: Siftei ḥakhamim, 1990).

JONES, A., *Astronomical Papyri from Oxyrhynchus*, 2 vols., Memoirs of the American Philosophical Society, 233 (Philadelphia, 1999).

KADUSHIN, M., *The Rabbinic Mind* (New York: Jewish Theological Seminary, 1952).

KAGAME, A., 'Aperception empirique du temps et conception de l'histoire dans la pensée bantu', in P. Ricœur (ed.), *Les Cultures et le temps* (Paris: Payot, 1975), 103–33.

KANT, I., *Critique of Pure Reason*, trans. N. Kemp Smith (London: Macmillan, 1933).

KASHER, M. M., 'The Concept of Time in Rabbinic Literature' [Musag hazeman], *Talpiyot*, 25 (1952), 799–827.

—— *Torah shelemah*, v (Jerusalem: privately published, 1935).

KATZ, J., *Halakhah and Kabbalah* [Halakhah vekabalah] (Jerusalem: Magnes Press, 1984).

KAUFMAN, S. A., and M. SOKOLOFF, *A Key-Word-in-Context Concordance to Targum Neofiti* (Baltimore: Johns Hopkins University Press, 1993).

KERN, O., *Orphicorum Fragmenta* (Berlin: Weidmann, 1922).

KIRK, G. S., and J. E. RAVEN, *The Presocratic Philosophers* (Cambridge: Cambridge University Press, 1957).

KNIBB, M., *The Ethiopic Book of Enoch*, 2 vols. (Oxford: Oxford University Press, 1978).

KOEHLER, L., and W. BAUMGARTNER, *The Hebrew and Aramaic Lexicon of the Old Testament*, 5 vols. (Leiden: Brill, 1994–2000).

KOPF, L., 'Arabische Etymologien und Parallelen zum Bibelwörterbuch', *Vetus Testamentum*, 8 (1958), 161–215.

KRAHMALKOV, C. R., *Phoenician-Punic Dictionary* (Leuven: Peeters, 2000).

KUTSCHER, E. Y., *A History of the Hebrew Language* (Jerusalem: Magnes Press and Leiden: Brill, 1982).

LAMBERT, W. G., 'Kosmologie', in *Reallexikon der Assyriologie*, vi (Berlin: De Gruyter, 1980–3), 218–22.

LANDAU, L., and E. LIFSHITZ, *The Classical Theory of Fields*, trans. M. Hamermesh (London: Pergamon Press, 1951).

LANDES, D. S., *Revolution in Time: Clocks and the Making of the Modern World*, 2nd edn. (Cambridge, Mass.: Harvard University Press, 2000).

LARRE, C., 'Aperception empirique du temps et conception de l'histoire dans la pensée chinoise', in P. Ricœur (ed.), *Les Cultures et le temps* (Paris: Payot, 1975), 43–71.

LARSEN, B. D., *Jamblique de Chalcis: exégète et philosophe* (Aarhus: Universitets-forlaget, 1972).

LAUER, S., 'Philo's Concept of Time', *Journal of Jewish Studies*, 9 (1958), 39–46.

LE GOFF, J., *Time, Word and Culture in the Middle Ages*, trans. A. Goldhammer (Chicago: University of Chicago Press, 1980).

LEE, P., *The Whorf Theory Complex: A Critical Reconstruction* (Amsterdam and Philadelphia: John Benjamins, 1996).

LEÓN-PORTILLA, M., *Time and Reality in the Thought of the Maya*, 2nd edn. (Norman, Okla., and London: University of Oklahoma Press, 1989).

LEVINE, L. I., *Judaism and Hellenism in Antiquity: Conflict or Congruence?* (Seattle: University of Washington Press, 1998).

——'The Synagogue of Dura-Europos', in id. (ed.), *Ancient Synagogues Revealed* (Jerusalem: Israel Exploration Society, 1981), 172–7.

LICHT, J., 'The Doctrine of "Times" according to the Sect of Qumran and other "Computers of Seasons"' [Torat ha'itim shel kat midbar yehudah veshel meḥashvei kitsin aḥerim], *Erets yisra'el*, 8 (1967), 63–70.

LIEBERMAN, S., *Greek in Jewish Palestine* (New York: Jewish Theological Seminary, 1942; 2nd edn., 1965).

——*Hellenism in Jewish Palestine* (New York: Jewish Theological Seminary, 1950; 2nd edn., 1962).

——'How Much Greek in Jewish Palestine?', in A. Altmann (ed.), *Biblical and Other Studies* (Cambridge, Mass: Harvard University Press, 1963), 123–41.

——*Tosefta kifeshutah*, 10 vols. (New York: Jewish Theological Seminary, 1955–88).

LIEBES, Y., *Ars Poetica in* Sefer yetsirah [Torat hayetsirah shel sefer yetsirah] (Jerusalem and Tel Aviv: Schocken, 2000).

LLOYD, G. E. R., 'Le Temps dans la pensée grecque', in P. Ricœur (ed.), *Les Cultures et le temps* (Paris: Payot, 1975), 135–70.

LOADER, J. A., *Ecclesiastes: A Practical Commentary* (Grand Rapids, Mich.: Eerdmans, 1986).

LUCRETIUS, *On the Nature of the Universe*, trans. R. Melville (Oxford: Clarendon Press, 1997).

LUCY, J. A., *Language Diversity and Thought: A Reformulation of the Linguistic Relativity Hypothesis* (Cambridge: Cambridge University Press, 1992).

MCFALL, L., *The Enigma of the Hebrew Verbal System* (Sheffield: Orchard Press, 1982).

MALLORY, J. P., and D. Q. ADAMS (eds.), *Encyclopedia of Indo-European Culture* (London and Chicago: Fitzroy Dearborn, 1997).

MANDELBAUM, B., *Pesiqta derav kahana*, 2nd edn. (New York: Jewish Theological Seminary, 1987).

MANKOWSKI, P. V., *Akkadian Loanwords in Biblical Hebrew* (Winona Lake, Ind.: Eisenbrauns, 2000).

MARGALIOT, M., *Midrash hagadol* (Jerusalem: Mosad Harav Kuk, 1956).

MARX, A., 'Texts by and about Maimonides', *Jewish Quarterly Review*, 25 (1925), 371–428.

MEIMARIS, Y. E., with K. KRITIKAKOU and P. BOUGIA, *Chronological Systems in Roman-Byzantine Palestine and Arabia: The Evidence of Dated Greek Inscriptions*, Meletemata, 17 (Athens: Kentron Ellinikis kai Romaïkis Archaiotitos, Ethnikon Idhrima Erevnon, 1992).

MEIRI, *see* MENAHEM HAMEIRI.

MELLOR, D. H., *Real Time* (Cambridge: Cambridge University Press, 1981).

MENAHEM HAMEIRI, *Ḥibur hateshuvah* [A Treatise on Repentance], ed. A. Sofer (Jerusalem: Kedem, 1950).

MERLEAU-PONTY, M., *Phénoménologie de la perception* (Paris: Gallimard, 1945).

MILIK, J. T., *The Books of Enoch: Aramaic Fragments of Qumran Cave* 4 (Oxford: Oxford University Press, 1976).

MILIKOWSKY, C. J., '*Seder Olam* and Jewish Chronography in the Hellenistic and Roman Periods', *Proceedings of the American Academy for Jewish Research*, 52 (1985), 115–39.

—— '*Seder Olam* and the Tosefta' [Seder olam vehatosefta], *Tarbiz*, 49 (1980), 246–63.

MILLAR, F. G. B., *The Roman Near East 31 BC–AD 337* (Cambridge: Harvard University Press, 1993).

MIMICA, J., *Intimations of Infinity: The Mythopoeia of the Iqwaye Counting System and Number* (Oxford: Berg, 1988).

MITCHELL, C. W., *S. Ephraim's Prose Refutations*, ii (London and Oxford: Williams and Norgate, 1921).

MOMIGLIANO, A., 'Time in Ancient Historiography', in id., *Essays in Ancient and Modern Historiography* (Oxford: Blackwell, 1977), 179–204.

MOREAU, J., *L'Espace et le temps selon Aristote* (Padua: Antenore, 1965).

MOSES IBN EZRA, *Selected Poems*, ed. S. Solis-Cohen and H. Brody (Philadelphia: Jewish Publication Society, 1945).

MUNN, N., 'The Cultural Anthropology of Time: A Critical Essay', *Annual Review of Anthropology*, 21 (1992), 93–123.

NAVEH, J., 'Ancient Synagogue Inscriptions', in L. I. Levine (ed.), *Ancient Synagogues Revealed* (Jerusalem: Israel Exploration Society, 1981), 133–9.

—— *On Mosaic and Stone* [Al pesifas va'even] (Tel Aviv: Israel Exploration Society, 1978).

NÉHER, A., 'Vision du temps et de l'histoire dans la culture juive', in P. Ricœur (ed.), *Les Cultures et le temps* (Paris: Payot, 1975), 171–92.

NEUSNER, J., 'How Much Iranian in Jewish Babylonia?', in id., *Talmudic Judaism in Sassanian Babylonia* (Leiden: Brill, 1976), 139–49.

ODEBERG, H., *3 Enoch or the Hebrew Book of Enoch* (Cambridge: Cambridge University Press, 1928).

ONIANS, R. B., *The Origins of European Thought* (Cambridge: Cambridge University Press, 1951).

PANIKKAR, R., 'Temps et histoire dans la tradition de l'Inde', in P. Ricœur (ed.), *Les Cultures et le temps* (Paris: Payot, 1975), 74–101.

PÉREZ FERNÁNDEZ, M., *An Introductory Grammar of Rabbinic Hebrew* (Leiden: Brill, 1997).

PINES, S., 'Eschatology and the Concept of Time in the Slavonic book of Enoch', in R. J. Z. Werblowsky and C. J. Bleeker (eds.), *Types of Redemption* (Leiden: Brill, 1970), 72–87.

PRINCE, J. R., *Science Concepts in a Pacific Culture* (Sydney: Angus and Robertson, 1969).

PRITCHARD, J. B., *Ancient Near Eastern Texts Relating to the Old Testament* (Princeton: Princeton University Press, 1950).

PRUDOVSKY, G., 'Can We Ascribe to Past Thinkers Concepts they had No Linguistic Means to Express?', *History and Theory*, 36 (1997), 15–31.

PSEUDO-PHILON, *Les Antiquités bibliques*, i (text) ed. D. J. Harrington and trans. J. Cazeaux; ii (commentary) C. Perrot and P.-M. Bogaert; Sources Chrétiennes, 229 (Paris: Cerf, 1976).

RICŒUR, P. (ed.), *Les Cultures et le temps* (Paris: Payot, 1975).

ROCHBERG-HALTON, F., 'Babylonian Seasonal Hours', *Centaurus*, 32 (1989), 146–70.

ROMILLY, J. DE, *Time in Greek Tragedy* (Ithaca, NY: Cornell University Press, 1968).

ROVNER, J., 'Rhetorical Strategy and Dialectical Necessity in the Babylonian Talmud: The Case of Kiddushin 34a–35a', *Hebrew Union College Annual*, 65 (1994), 177–231.

RUDAVSKY, T. M., *Time Matters: Time, Creation, and Cosmology in Medieval Jewish Philosophy* (Albany, NY: State University of New York Press, 2000).

SAADIA GAON, *The Book of Beliefs and Opinions*, trans. S. Rosenblatt (New Haven: Yale University Press, 1948).

SACKS, N. (ed.), *Mishnah Zera'im with Variant Readings* [Mishnah zera'im im shinuyei nusha'ot], i (Jerusalem: Yad Harav Hertsog, 1972).

SÁENZ-BADILLO, A., *A History of the Hebrew Language* (Cambridge: Cambridge University Press, 1993).

SAFRAI, S., 'The Localities of the Sanctification of Lunar Months and the Intercalations of Years in Palestine after 70 CE' [Hamekomot lekidush ḥodashim ule'ibur hashanah ba'arets le'aḥar haḥurban], *Tarbiz*, 35 (1965), 27–38.

SAMBURSKY, S., 'The Concept of Time in Late Neoplatonism', *Proceedings of the Israel Academy of Sciences and Humanities*, 2 (1968), 153–67.

——and S. PINES, *The Concept of Time in Late Neoplatonism* (Jerusalem: Israel Academy of Sciences and Humanities, 1971).

SASSON, J. M., 'Time . . . to Begin', in M. Fishbane and E. Tov (eds.), *Sha'arei Talmon: Studies in the Bible, Qumran, and the Ancient Near East Presented to Shemaryahu Talmon* (Winona Lake, Ind.: Eisenbrauns, 1992), 183–94.

SATZ, Y. (ed.), *Responsa of the Maharil* [She'elot uteshuvot maharil] (Jerusalem: Makhon Yerushalayim, 1979).

SCHÄFER, P., *Synopse zur Hekhalot-Literatur* (Tübingen: Mohr-Siebeck, 1981).

SCHECHTER, S., *Agadath Shir Hashirim* (Cambridge: Deighton Bell, 1896).

SCHIBLI, H. S., *Pherekydes of Syros* (Oxford: Oxford University Press, 1990).

SCHÜRER, E., *The History of the Jewish People in the Age of Jesus Christ (175 BC–AD 135)*, revised and edited by G. Vermes and F. G. B. Millar with M. Black (vols. i–ii) and M. Goodman (vol. iii: 1–2), 4 vols. (Edinburgh: T. & T. Clark, 1973–87).

SCOTT, R. B. Y., *The Anchor Bible: Proverbs and Ecclesiastes* (New York: Doubleday, 1965).

SEGAL, M. H., *The Book of Ben Sira* [Sefer ben sira hashalem], 2nd edn. (Jerusalem: Bialik Foundation, 1958).

——*A Grammar of Mishnaic Hebrew* (Oxford: Clarendon Press, 1927).

SHAKED, S., 'Iranian Influence on Judaism: First Century BCE to Second Century CE', in W. D. Davies and L. Finkelstein (eds.), *Cambridge History of Judaism*, i: *Introduction; The Persian Period* (Cambridge: Cambridge University Press, 1984), 308–23.

——'The Myth of Zurvan: Cosmogony and Eschatology', in I. Gruenwald, S. Shaked, and G. G. Stroumsa (eds.), *Messiah and Christos: Studies in the Jewish Origins of Christianity Presented to David Flusser* (Tübingen: Mohr, 1992), 219–40.

SHARVIT, S., 'Tenses in Mishnaic Hebrew' [Ma'arekhet hazemanim bileshon hamishnah], in G. B.-A. Sarfatti et al. (eds.), *Studies in Hebrew and Semitic Languages (in Memory of E. Y. Kutscher)* [Meḥkarim be'ivrit uvileshonot shemiyot] (Ramat Gan: Bar-Ilan University Press, 1980), 110–25.

SORABJI, R., *Time, Creation and the Continuum* (Ithaca, NY: Cornell University Press, 1983).

SPERBER, A., *The Bible in Aramaic*, iii: *The Latter Prophets* (Leiden: Brill, 1962).

STARCKY, J., 'Un contrat nabatéen sur papyrus', *Revue biblique*, 61 (1954), 161–81.

STEMBERGER, G., *Introduction to the Talmud and Midrash*, trans. M. Bockmuehl, 2nd edn. (Edinburgh: T. & T. Clark, 1996).

STENNING, J. F., *The Targum of Isaiah* (Oxford: Clarendon Press, 1949).

STERN, S., *Calendar and Community: A History of the Jewish Calendar, 2nd century BCE–10th century CE* (Oxford: Oxford University Press, 2001).

—— 'Fictitious Calendars: Early Rabbinic Notions of Time, Astronomy, and Reality', *Jewish Quarterly Review*, 87 (1996), 103–29.

—— 'Qumran Calendars: Theory and Practice', in T. Lim (ed.), *The Dead Sea Scrolls in their Historical Context* (Edinburgh: T. & T. Clark, 2000), 179–86.

STROUMSA, S., *Dawud ibn Marwan Al-Muqammis's Twenty Chapters (Ishrun Maqala), Edited, Translated and Annotated* (Leiden: Brill, 1989).

STRUGNELL, J., and D. DIMANT, '4Q Second Ezekiel', *Revue de Qumran*, 13 (1988), 45–58.

TALMON, S., '*Qets*', in *Theologisches Wörterbuch zum Alten Testament*, vii (Stuttgart: Kohlhammer, 1990), 84–92.

—— J. BEN-DOV, and U. GLESSMER, *Discoveries in the Judaean Desert*, XXI (Oxford: Clarendon Press, 2001).

TCHERIKOVER, V. A., and A. FUKS, *Corpus Papyrorum Judaicarum*, 3 vols. (Jerusalem: Magnes Press and Cambridge, Mass.: Harvard University Press, 1957–64).

TEIXIDOR, J., *Bardesane d'Édesse, le premier philosophe syriaque* (Paris: Cerf, 1992).

TOMBACK, R. S., *A Comparative Semitic Lexicon of the Phoenician and Punic Languages* (Missoula, Mont.: Scholars Press, 1978).

TOOMER, G. J., *Ptolemy's Almagest* (London: Duckworth, 1984).

TWERSKY, I., *Introduction to the Code of Maimonides (Mishneh Torah)* (New Haven: Yale University Press, 1980); Hebrew trans. by M. B. Lerner, *Mavo lemishneh torah larambam* (Jerusalem: Magnes Press, 1991).

ULMER, R., 'The Advancement of Arguments in Exegetical Midrash Compared to that of the Greek ΔIATPIBH', *Journal for the Study of Judaism*, 28 (1997), 48–91.

URBACH, E. E., *The Sages: Their Concepts and Beliefs*, trans. I. Abrahams (Cambridge, Mass: Harvard University Press, 1975).

VANDERKAM, J. C., *Calendars in the Dead Sea Scrolls* (London: Routledge, 1998).

VIDAL-NAQUET, P., 'Temps des dieux et temps des hommes', in id., *Le Chasseur noir: Formes de pensée et formes de société dans le monde grec* (Paris: Maspero, 1981), 69–94.

WACHOLDER, B., *Essays in Jewish Chronology and Chronography* (New York: Ktav, 1976).

WAGNER, J., 'Dynastie und Herrscherkult in Kommagene: Forschungsgeschichte und neuere Funde', *Istanbuler Mitteilungen*, 33 (1983), 177–224.

WALKER, C. (ed.), *Astronomy Before the Telescope* (London: British Museum Press, 1996).

WASSERSTROM, S. M., 'Sefer Yeṣira and Early Islam: A Reappraisal', *Journal of Jewish Thought and Philosophy*, 3 (1993), 1–30.

WEST, M. L., *Early Greek Philosophy and the Orient* (Oxford: Clarendon Press, 1971).

WESTERINK, L. G. (ed.), and J. COMBÈS (trans.), *Damascius: Traités des premiers principes*, iii (Paris: Budé, 1991).

WIEDER, N., 'The Term קץ in the Dead Sea Scrolls and in Hebrew Liturgical Poetry', *Journal of Jewish Studies*, 5 (1954), 22–31.

WIESENBERG, E. J., 'The Liturgical Term *melekh ha-'olam*', *Journal of Jewish Studies*, 15 (1964), 1–56.

WOLFSON, H. A., *Crescas' Critique of Aristotle: Problems in Aristotle's Physics in Jewish and Arabic Philosophy* (Cambridge, Mass.: Harvard University Press, 1929).

YADIN, Y., *The Documents from the Bar-Kokhba Period in the Cave of Letters: Greek Papyri* (ed. N. Lewis) (Jerusalem: Israel Exploration Society, 1989).

YARDENI, A., 'New Jewish Aramaic Ostraka', *Israel Exploration Journal*, 40 (1990), 130–52.

YERUSHALMI, Y. H., *Zakhor: Jewish History and Jewish Memory* (Seattle: University of Washington Press, 1982).

ZAEHNER, R. C., *Zurvan: A Zoroastrian Dilemma* (Oxford: Clarendon Press, 1955).

ZER-KAVOD, M., *The Five Scrolls* [Ḥamesh megilot] (Da'at Mikra; Jerusalem: Mosad Harav Kuk, 1993).

ZULAY, M., *The Poems of Yannai* [Piyutei yanai] (Berlin: Schocken, 1938).

Index

Printed and bound by CPI Group (UK) Ltd, Croydon, CR0 4YY

13/04/2025

14656579-0005